Comfort

Ottolenghi
COMFORT

YOTAM OTTOLENGHI   HELEN GOH
VERENA LOCHMULLER   TARA WIGLEY

Photography by
Jonathan Lovekin

TEN SPEED PRESS
California | New York

Contents

Introduction   7

Eggs, crêpes, pancakes   20

Soups, dips, spreads   50

Fritters and other fried things   66

Comfort veg   84

Roasted chicken and other
sheet pan dishes   118

Dals, stews, curries   154

Noodles, rice, tofu   182

Pasta, polenta, potatoes   198

Pies, pastry, bread   236

Sweet things   270

Index   312

Acknowledgments   318

Introduction

When it comes to cooking and eating, what does "comfort" mean? At first glance, we might think of it as the food we make and eat at home, after a tough day. It's the food we make without thinking too much. It might also be the recipes we grew up on, which remind us of being a kid and being cared for. Or the food we eat too much of, unable to resist its ability to hit the spot.

Nurture, convenience, nostalgia, indulgence: agreeing on the notion of comfort food is fairly straightforward. What's harder to pin down, though, are the actual dishes that hit these proverbial spots. One person's idea of comfort food might be the next person's idea of challenging. It's so personal, so tied up with home, with family, with memory, even with the random idiosyncrasies of human taste.

It's culturally specific, as well. One kid's grilled cheese sandwich dream is the next kid's nightmare. Ditto the adult who then makes that same sandwich, years down the line, to remind them of the kid they once were. Mac 'n' cheese, chicken ramen, schnitzel, sausages and mash, pizza, chicken noodle soup, lentils and rice, dal, dumplings—the definitive comfort food for many, certainly, but there is no one-comfort-food-fits-all. Trying to pin down a specific set of comfort food recipes is as slippery as a bowl of noodles.

And yet those noodles, however novel they might be, will always feel somehow nostalgic. It's this—the ability of a dish to be nostalgic and novel at once—that's at the heart of our interpretation of comfort. In this book we offer dishes that are both comfortable and creative, familiar and fresh, reassuring and revelatory.

It is also very much about the personal journeys we've been on, and all the stories these journeys contain. In *Comfort*, rather than trying to take in a whole sweep of comfort food, we're staying on firmer ground, that which we've trodden ourselves. Among the four of us—Yotam, Helen, Verena, and Tara—it's a fair bit of global ground. Yotam's takes in Italy and Germany (from his parents), Jerusalem to Amsterdam (where he lived and ate his body weight in croquettes), to London. Helen's stretches from China (from her grandparents) to Malaysia to Melbourne (where she was raised) to west London. Verena's trodden ground takes in Germany and Scotland, to New York (where she trained), to now London. Tara's more London through and through, but the amount of tahini, eggplants, lemons, feta, and olive oil she's cooked with over the past twenty years means she's pretty good on the subject of Levantine food.

Looking at the ground the four of us had trodden showed us the link between comfort food and movement, between comfort food and immigration. When we move somewhere new, we do two things. We take on (and take in) the culture and cuisine of the place we have moved to and we keep hold of and preserve the culture and cuisine of the place we have left.

Practicalities also play a part. We can't lug around our childhood bedroom, or sofa, or favorite spot we used to go to for a family picnic. If we are missing the chicken soup, the lentils and rice, or the pasta bake our mother or father used to make for us when we needed a hug as a kid, though, we can try to re-create these dishes. They're edible transitional objects, and nothing will fast-track us back to that hug years down the line more than making that soup, or those lentils, or that pasta bake.

We don't cook or eat in a vacuum, so once this dish is made, it's usually shared with someone else: with our new family or friend or neighbor. That's when the ripple effects are felt. What started off as a metaphorical hug becomes a recipe that someone then asks for, makes for themselves, and goes on to share with a whole new group.

This process is happening the world over. It's why a single curious cook can eat their way around the world from their own kitchen table. It's why Italian food is so tied up with American food. It's why we can all buy sushi and seaweed, pizza and pasta, chana dal and curry leaves from the same supermarket.

When done with awareness, acknowledgment, relish, and respect, this is, for us, cultural appreciation, not appropriation. That's what comfort food means to us. It's about our journeys and all the stories contained in them. This book is a celebration of that: of movement, of immigration, of family, of home—of people.

Other ways to define comfort, none mutually exclusive, can also be about a certain type of food, for example: the face-planting comfort of carbs, maybe, or the inherently soothing nature of soup. It might also be about the situation in which food is eaten: the comfort of sitting around with friends, perhaps, or the very opposite—the comfort of quietly eating alone, with the world shut out. Very often, it's about the combination of right food and right time and right place. That explains why an ice cream eaten on a hot day on a park bench can be as comforting as a glass of red wine and a plate of roasted chicken inside on a cold day, when the kitchen windows are blocked out with steam.

What makes food comforting can be about where and how we eat, why we eat, and who we eat with as much as what we're eating in the first place. Something to think about, if you like, as you choose the recipes to try out and make your own. We hope they bring you comfort, in whatever form that comfort may come.

ONE: WHO WE EAT WITH

Behind a comforting dish often lies a *relationship*: a unique attachment. Chicken noodle soup will have a deeper impact on those who have a *memory* of it being made by someone who has cared for them. From **meatloaf** to **mapo tofu**, **matza ball soup** to **mulligatawny**, **meringue** to **marble cake**—for each of us there's a *feeling* we're remembering about them. Perhaps it should be called memory food, then, or community food?

One of the joys of community is that it's so often dynamic and porous: ideas flow and change, move from one person to the next. It happened time and time again to us. This book is the work of four hungries—Yotam, Helen, Verena, and Tara—and we each brought our own memories, childhoods, and travels with us to the (thankfully) large table. But what started off as coming from—belonging to— one of us soon belonged to the next person. Tara and Verena make Helen's **silky zucchini and salmon salad** so often that their own friends now ask for "Tara's" or "Verena's" silky zucchini. Funny and touching!

When things share a pot, they each keep their own identity and, at the same time, take on some of the flavor of the things they're sharing the pot with. It's an exchange that happens as much outside the kitchen as it does inside. Outside the kitchen, it's called the melting pot. Inside the kitchen it's called a stew, a soup, a sheet pan dish. Think of the lentils taking on the smoky flavor of the Polish sausages in our **sausage and lentils**, for example, or the chunks of tofu absorbing the savory **soy-braised pork belly** they share a pot with.

It's an exchange that can also seem to happen between two apparently distinct dishes. We realized how often there are shared connections between recipes we each think of as our own. Helen's Auntie Pauline's **roasted chicken** or her **Bolognese** might not be the exact roasted chicken or Bolognese that Yotam grew up eating, but that first bite of each dish sparked a *familiarity* that resonated with his own versions: a kind of universal notion of comfort.

This sharing of dishes on a much larger scale through immigration is the beating heart of *Comfort*. Think of curry, for example. What comes to mind? It's a big question! Are you thinking of a rich and easy butter chicken or is it a spicy Goan pork vindaloo? Or is it a Thai massaman or Indonesian rendang, a Kashmiri rogan josh or the British creation that is chicken tikka masala?

If there's no such thing as one type of comfort food, then there's *really* no such thing as one curry. It's a single short word that encompasses so many different sorts of dishes—all themselves a reflection of hundreds of years of history, of politics, of travel and movement, and colonialism. There's so much to be read and chewed on here: for our part we'll provide some very delicious curries of our own—**turmeric and peppercorn with shrimp and asparagus**, for instance; **lemongrass and galangal tuna**; **chicken and lime leaf with noodles**—to enjoy as you read.

TWO: WHY WE EAT

Why do we seek comfort in cooking and eating?

For the most part, we live in a batshit-crazy world. Beyond the familiar challenges of the daily kind—work, family, and just keeping one's head above water—there's often no institution, no clear set of traditions to ground us. Food itself is often overly processed and overly packaged: you don't recognize the ingredients in your supermarket sandwich; you can't smell the strawberries in the pint basket; you will never meet the cow responsible for the milk in your flat white. Traditions of cooking and dining, as well, have been set aside in favor of "solutions" and "on the go" meals.

Cooking—real cooking using real ingredients—offers a natural way to reconnect with the environment, with our fellow human beings, and with ourselves. This is why so many of us have more cookbooks than we'll ever need, or plan our supper while eating lunch, or cook when we're happy, or eat when we're sad, or cook to show others we care.

At the end of the day, it often boils down to something simpler: the ability to close the door and impose some sense and structure on our world, not to mention—oh joy!—putting a meal on the table. In these particular instances, what we want is not new or novel, but something totally familiar. It's what Laurie Colwin (in her collection of essays, *Home Cooking*) celebrates as *"the same old thing." "When life is hard and the day has been long, the ideal dinner is not four perfect courses [. . .] but something comforting and savory, easy on the digestion. Something that makes one feel, if only for a minute, that one is safe."*

We all have our go-tos to create this sense of safety. For Helen, as it was for her mother, it's savory **steamed eggs**. For Tara—the batch-cooker—it's reaching for a pre-made Tupperware of **roasted eggplant, red pepper, and tomato soup**. Yotam might be cooking up his **chicken meatballs** while Verena's probably making **leek, tomato, and turmeric frittata**. We made sure *Comfort* is full of recipes that create this feeling, this ease and familiarity.

And if it's not a full dish, it can also be a sauce or condiment. Whether it's **zhoug**, **nuoc cham**, **green tahini**, **chile ginger sauce**, or **aïoli**, it's often just a spoonful of one of these, alongside whatever else is being eaten, that is enough to create a feeling of familiarity. When Helen confessed, on Instagram, to always traveling with a jar of crispy chili oil, the shared confessions of her fellow sauce and condiment travelers flooded in. Marmite was a favorite, as was Tabasco. Colman's mustard got a lot of air miles, along with Branston Pickle.

To provide structure, to soothe, to feel grounded and safe: these are some of the reasons why we cook and eat. For many, food is also simply a way to show we care. This happens daily—every time we cook supper for someone—but it's also often at the heart of special occasions, when a special meal is prepared on Valentine's Day, for example, or a cake is baked for a birthday, or for solace or a show of support. For us, there's possibly nothing more comforting and consoling than **matza ball soup**, handed to you in a great big bowl by someone who cares that you're sad.

Most of the time food isn't about addressing hunger. *"When I write of hunger,"* says M. F. K. Fisher in *The Art of Eating, "I am really writing about love and the hunger for it, and warmth and the love of it [. . .] and it is all one."*

THREE: WHAT WE EAT

In looking at the who, why, and how, perhaps we're overthinking it? The large crossover between different people's comfort food suggests that it could, simply, be all about the what. Chicken noodle soup, pasta bake, fried chicken, macaroni and cheese, any form of chocolate, or cake, or ice cream. No two comfort food lists are ever going to be identical, but clear themes emerge. Theme one: carbs. Theme two: fat. Theme three: sugar.

For all the ways in which comfort food can be defined, the definition we have the least time for is that comfort food is somehow naughty, a guilty pleasure, the thing we eat when no one is looking. Of course, we all have days when we could indulge less, but the labeling of certain types of food as good/virtuous and others as bad/comforting plays very little role in our idea of comfort food. We may feel as comforted by potatoes, pancakes, pasta, and pastries as we do by salads, soups, and stews. Truthfully, there's no difference—in our conscious mind, at least— between a plate of **linguine with miso butter** and our **green tea noodles with avocado and radish**.

Still, it's interesting to look at what is going on in our brain—our unconscious mind—when we eat, say, something high in sugar or carbohydrates. Why are certain food groups so often reached for when we need a comfort quick fix?

In the case of sugar, for example, it's useful to position comfort as the opposite of stress. When we're stressed, why do we often eat certain types of food to excess? When our brain perceives stress, the hypothalamus is activated. The hypothalamus is not only responsible for controlling hunger, it also determines whether we should fight, flight, or feed. The last thing we should be doing, in the process of being stressed, is stop to overeat. In other words, when being chased by a lion, actual or otherwise, hiding under the duvet cover to eat a chocolate bar is not a winning survival strategy.

Once we have escaped danger, though—the lion has gone and we are no longer stressed—we experience a rush of cortisol that craves, in particular, sugar. It makes sense, really, to replenish as fast as possible the energy that has been used to fight or flee from that lion. Moreover, our senses are particularly heightened at this time, so the chocolate bar (or Verena's **malty figgy pudding**) tastes *even* sweeter, *even* better than it would have were we not stressed in the first place.

Sugar not only inhibits stress-induced cortisol, it also stimulates opioid release, one of the body's feel-good chemicals. Dopamine is another of the body's chemicals that the eating of comfort foods increases. As with the irresistible pull of the ping on our phone, consuming these comfort foods (or returning to check our devices) is often hard to resist. Putting the half-eaten **chocolate mousse** back in the fridge for tomorrow might be the rational move, but it's not the way our brain is hardwired.

Perhaps, though, we're still overthinking it. Perhaps it is as simple as being about a single ingredient: about a potato, for example, hitting the spot every time, whichever way it comes, whether as **crispy roasted potatoes with rosemary and za'atar**, **Indonesian "home fries,"** or **garlicky aligot potato**. Can it all boil down to just a single ingredient? If not a potato, then maybe it's eggs? Or pasta? Or rice? Or pastry?

If not a single ingredient, maybe comfort food is all about smell? Can anything beat the smell of a chicken roasting or a batch of **brownie cookies** baking and ready to come out of the oven? Or is it more about texture? About the smooth, forgiving nature of **mulligatawny**, for instance? Or is it textural contrast: the delight of fried things—**mung bean and kimchi "falafel"** or **shrimp spoon fritters**—being not only fried but with a soft center. The slipperiness of **green tea noodles**, the silkiness of **steamed eggplant**, the tenderness of **white-poached chicken**, the comforting softness of **baked custard**. Is it, after all, all just the edible equivalent of that hot bath or duck-down duvet?

Perhaps it's all these things. What it should never be, though, is something we feel bad about. There are a lot of lions out there: don't let what you choose to eat be one of them.

FOUR: HOW WE EAT

Sitting on the sofa with a pint of ice cream, eating a wrap with your hands in a busy street market, perched solo on a bench lifting noodles with chopsticks: is comfort food as much about how we eat as anything else? The number of comforting dishes served in a bowl suggests there might be something to it. It could be the ergonomic shape of a bowl, which our hands cup around so perfectly, that taps into our idea of comfort, regardless of whether it's full of **quick ramen noodles** or **cinnamon baked oatmeal**. Doesn't a bowl and spoon, more so than a plate and knife, just feel a bit more cozy?

If not a bowl, what about eating with our hands? Doing this—especially when we're with others—can be a sign of being at ease, of being comfortable. How many communal meals start with the breaking and sharing of bread, passing it around by hand? There are so many ways in which different foods, the world over, are wrapped up in flatbread that there seems to be something universal going on. And if not flatbread, then it might be food wrapped in lettuce cups, grape leaves, banana leaves, and so on. Or could it be some **cauliflower and butternut pakoras** we're eating by hand? If not pakoras, then pies: **potato, cheese, and chermoula**, for example, or **leek, cheese, and za'atar rugelach**.

Whether we're standing at a food stall, sitting on the floor or around a table, what we're eating is also, often, the sort of food we associate with a crowd. It's something we make for a party, for everyone to help themselves. Sharing food, sharing plates: recipes that make most sense at a get-together will always (or should always!) have comfort built into them. There's something so welcoming about a table full of dishes that people can help themselves to. This also plays really well within a family, especially with kids, when certain dishes are made of different components that you can take or leave, as is the case with our **breakfast boureka**, with all its condiments, or the **meatballs with nuoc cham**. *How* these dishes are eaten feels like a big part of what makes them so comfortable, so comforting.

One-pot or sheet pan dishes have a similar, relaxed appeal. Their preparation is stress-free, as is taking them to the table and letting everyone help themselves, handing over control. A spoonful of extra beans or a wedge of fennel in the **braised fennel and cod**, maybe; a few more green beans or more olive sauce in the **puttanesca-style sheet pan salmon**: there's enough for everyone to help themselves as they like.

There are times when we don't really want to eat with a crowd. Sometimes what we want is a delightfully empty kitchen—one where the only noise comes from a pan of something lovely, serving one, puttering away on the stove. *"Dinner alone is one of life's pleasures,"* writes Laurie Colwin in her book *Home Cooking.* *"Certainly cooking for oneself reveals man at his weirdest. People lie when you ask them what they eat when they are alone. A salad, they tell you. But when you persist, they confess to peanut butter and bacon sandwiches deep fried and eaten with hot sauce, or spaghetti with butter and grape jam."*

Yet even when we are alone in the kitchen or on the sofa, we're never, we don't think, really alone. We share the space we make and eat food in with so many who've come before us. Some of them we know—these are the journeys we're on and the people we carry with us—and some of them we know through the words they write, or the recipes they share, which we take and make our own. Food and words have the incredible power to connect people. It's all about connection. Our hope is that these recipes become for you what they are for us: reassuring on the one hand but revitalizing on the other; nostalgic and novel at the same time; creative and comforting.

Eggs, crêpes, pancakes

Dutch baby with oven-roasted tomatoes

1⅓ cups/160g all-purpose flour
3 tbsp finely grated parmesan
1½ tbsp thyme leaves, roughly chopped
2 tsp English mustard powder
4 eggs
1¾ cups/420ml milk
10 slices of bacon
1–1½ tbsp olive oil
1½ oz/40g cheddar, grated (6 tbsp)
salt and black pepper

Oven-roasted tomatoes
14 oz/380g cherry tomatoes
6 thyme sprigs
1 large garlic clove, smashed
2 tbsp olive oil
1½ tbsp balsamic vinegar
1 tbsp light brown sugar
⅛ tsp dried chile flakes
½ cup/10g basil leaves, roughly torn

If a pancake and a crêpe had a love child, it would be a Dutch baby! This pan-sized, puffed-up, baked eggy delight has something of the soufflé about it, too. The name stems, apparently, from early 1900s Seattle where the German (or *Deutsch*) pancakes were being made by the owner of a family-owned restaurant. The child eating it couldn't pronounce the word *Deutsch* so Dutch they became. This is great for brunch or an easy supper. Kids love it too.

Serves 4

Preheat the oven to 425°F.

Combine all the ingredients for the oven-roasted tomatoes, except the basil, in a 9 x 13-inch/23 x 33cm roasting pan, along with ¾ teaspoon of salt and a good grind of pepper. Mix well and then roast for 30 minutes, stirring a couple of times, until the sauce has become a little syrupy and the tomatoes have softened but not collapsed. Remove from the oven and set aside. Once cool, stir in the basil leaves.

Keep the oven at 425°F.

Meanwhile, in a large bowl, whisk together the flour, parmesan, thyme, mustard powder, ½ teaspoon of salt, and some pepper.

In a separate bowl, whisk together the eggs and milk, then pour over the dry ingredients. Whisk to combine and set aside.

Place the bacon in a large ovenproof frying pan: it needs to be about 11 inches/28cm wide and 2 inches/5cm deep. Cook slowly over medium heat—about 1 minute each side: you don't want it to cook completely. Transfer the bacon to a plate, leaving about 2 tablespoons of fat behind in the pan. Add the olive oil and heat for 1 minute, swirling the pan so that the bottom is slicked with oil. Quickly but carefully pour the batter all at once into the pan. Turn the heat off, drape the bacon on top, and sprinkle with the cheddar. Transfer immediately to the oven and bake for 25 minutes, until the sides of the Dutch baby are golden and puffed up and the middle is soft and custardy. Resist the urge to open the oven door for the first 15 minutes to see what is going on—this will cause the baby to deflate!

Remove the Dutch baby from the oven and slide it onto a large plate. If you need to, slide a spatula underneath to help release it. Cut into quarters and serve with the roasted tomatoes on the side.

Egg and watercress

8 eggs, at room temperature

Aïoli
1 egg yolk
1 garlic clove, crushed to a paste
2 tsp Dijon mustard
2 tsp lemon juice
1 tsp maple syrup
3 tbsp olive oil, plus extra
    for drizzling
3 tbsp vegetable oil
3 tbsp buttermilk (or kefir)
salt and black pepper

Pesto
1 large jalapeño (1 oz/30g)
2½ tbsp pistachios, toasted
1¾ oz/50g watercress
1 garlic clove, roughly chopped
¼ oz/5g chives, roughly chopped
⅓ cup/80ml olive oil
1 tsp lemon juice

To serve
1 packaged bunch of watercress
toasted sliced sourdough (optional)
flaked sea salt

"What's your dream sandwich filling?" Verena goes for egg and cress every time—a real British staple. This is her tribute to the classic. Salad cress is widely available in the UK, but don't worry if you can't find any: some bunched watercress, as an alternative, also works really well.

Getting ahead: The aïoli can be made up to 3 days ahead and kept in the fridge. The pesto—renamed "cresto" by our test kitchen colleague Clodagh—is best made on the day of eating.

Serves 4

Bring a small pot of water to a boil on high heat. Carefully lower in the eggs and cook for 7 minutes. Using a slotted spoon, lift out the eggs and rinse them under plenty of cold running water. Once cool, peel and set aside.

Put the first five ingredients for the aïoli into the small bowl of a food processor, along with ½ teaspoon of salt and a good grind of pepper. Blitz briefly, just to combine. Mix together both oils in a liquid measuring cup and, with the motor running, slowly stream in the oil and process until smooth and glossy. Transfer to a small bowl, stir in the buttermilk, and keep in the fridge. Clean the food processor bowl.

Next, make the pesto. Place a small dry frying pan on medium heat. Once hot, add the jalapeño and char all over for 3–4 minutes, until blackened in places. Set aside and, once cool enough to handle, seed (if you like) and roughly chop. Transfer to the small bowl of the food processor, along with the remaining pesto ingredients and ¼ teaspoon of salt. Blitz until finely chopped—a few larger pieces are totally fine! Transfer to a small bowl and set aside.

To serve, spread the aïoli on a serving platter and arrange the eggs on top, breaking them in half as you do so. Sprinkle the eggs with a small pinch of flaked sea salt and a little pepper, then spoon the pesto on and around the eggs. Using kitchen scissors, snip off the top two-thirds of the watercress and scatter over the eggs. Finish with an extra drizzle of olive oil and serve, with the toasted sourdough alongside, if you like.

Egg sambal "shakshuka"

1½ tsp fennel seeds
2 whole cloves
seeds from 2 cardamom pods
½ tsp ground cinnamon
1½ tbsp medium curry powder
¼ cup/60ml olive oil
½ tsp black mustard seeds
20 curry leaves
1 medium red onion, halved and
  thinly sliced (1¼ cups/160g)
⅓ oz/10g ginger, peeled and
  finely grated
5 garlic cloves, crushed to a paste
⅓ oz/10g cilantro, stalks finely
  chopped and leaves to serve
5¼ oz/150g datterini (or cherry)
  tomatoes
2 tsp sambal oelek
1 x 14-oz/400g can of diced
  tomatoes
7 tbsp/100ml tamarind concentrate
1¼ cups/300ml water
1 tbsp palm (or light brown) sugar
5 eggs
salt and black pepper

Growing up in Malaysia, nasi lemak was something Helen ate a lot of. Wrapped in banana leaves and day-old newspaper, the little packs of coconut rice, spicy sambal, egg, and cucumber are sold on nearly every street corner. While this recipe is very much *not nasi lemak*, it is nevertheless inspired *by* it. The egg and tomato sauce mingling in the pan reminds us, at the same time, of the shakshuka that Yotam grew up eating. Serve with rice, flatbread, or any bread you like.

Getting ahead: This can be made in advance, up to the point just before the eggs are cracked into the sambal. The sambal lasts well in the fridge for up to 3 days.

Serves 4

Put the fennel seeds, cloves, and cardamom seeds into a small dry frying pan and place on medium-low heat. Toast lightly for about 2 minutes, until fragrant, then grind to a powder in a spice grinder or a mortar and pestle. Add the cinnamon and curry powder and set aside.

Put 3 tablespoons of the oil into a large sauté pan (for which you have a lid)—about 10¼ inches/26cm wide—and place on medium heat. Add the mustard seeds and 10 curry leaves and cook for 1 minute, until the seeds begin to pop. Add the onion and cook for about 7 minutes, stirring frequently, until they are starting to color. Add the ginger, garlic, cilantro stalks, and fresh tomatoes, cook for 5 minutes, then add the fennel spice mix. Cook for 2 minutes, until fragrant, then add the sambal oelek, canned tomatoes, tamarind, water, sugar, and 1¼ teaspoons of salt. Stir well and bring to a simmer. Decrease the heat to medium-low and cook for 20–25 minutes, uncovered, until thickened.

Crack the eggs into the sambal and sprinkle a little salt and pepper over each egg. Cover the pan and cook for 7–8 minutes, until the egg whites are fully cooked and the yolks are soft.

Meanwhile, put the remaining 1 tablespoon of oil into a small pan and place on medium heat. Add the rest of the curry leaves, cook for about 1 minute, until very fragrant, then remove from the heat. When the eggs are ready, drizzle the oil and fried curry leaves over the eggs, scatter the cilantro leaves, and serve.

Leek, tomato, and turmeric frittata

¼ cup/60ml olive oil
2 large leeks, white parts, sliced
    ½ inch/1cm thick (3 cups/300g)
2 garlic cloves, crushed to a paste
¾ oz/25g ginger, peeled and
    finely chopped
2 green chiles, seeded and
    finely chopped
1½ tsp cumin seeds, toasted and
    lightly crushed
1 tsp ground turmeric
3 small Roma tomatoes, seeded,
    then roughly chopped
    (scant 1 cup/160g)
6 eggs
1 tbsp all-purpose flour
1 tsp baking powder
salt and black pepper

Zhoug (optional, but recommended)
1 tsp cumin seeds
seeds from 8 cardamom pods
5 whole cloves
2½ oz/70g cilantro, roughly
    chopped, plus extra leaves
    to serve
¾ oz/20g parsley, roughly chopped
4 green chiles, roughly chopped
¼ tsp granulated sugar
½ tsp salt
2 garlic cloves, crushed to a paste
¼ cup/60ml olive oil
¼ cup/60ml water
2 tbsp apple cider vinegar

This is inspired by a dish that our friend Shehnaz Suterwalla whisked up at the end of a New Year's Eve party to get the late-night/early-morning stayers to stay on! Shehnaz's version was scrambled, based on the eggs her mother used to make for her in Mumbai. Ours is cooked as a frittata, which has the advantage of being able to be eaten either warm or at room temperature (at midday or midnight). Serve as it is, or sandwiched inside some flatbread.

Zhoug: Batch-make this Yemeni spice paste if you can. It keeps for about 2 weeks in the fridge and is wonderful spooned over so many things: roasted vegetables, all sorts of eggs, grilled meat, or fish.

Serves 4

If making the zhoug, place the cumin seeds, cardamom seeds, and cloves in a small dry frying pan on medium heat and toast for 2–3 minutes, until fragrant. Transfer to a spice grinder or a mortar and pestle, and roughly blitz/crush. Transfer to the small bowl of a food processor, add all the remaining zhoug ingredients and pulse a few times to create a coarse paste. Keep in the fridge.

Preheat the oven to 450°F.

Put 3 tablespoons of the oil into an ovenproof sauté pan (about 9 inches/23cm wide) and place on medium-high heat. Add the leeks and 1 teaspoon of salt and cook for about 6 minutes, stirring often, until they begin to soften. Add the garlic, ginger, chiles, cumin, and turmeric and cook for 1–2 minutes, stirring often. Remove from the heat, stir in the tomatoes, then tip the mix into a large mixing bowl. Wipe clean the sauté pan (no need to wash) and return it to very low heat.

Put the eggs, flour, and baking powder into a separate bowl, along with a good grind of pepper. Whisk to combine, then pour into the bowl of leek mixture and stir.

When the pan is hot, add the remaining 1 tablespoon of oil and increase the heat to medium. Pour the egg mixture into the pan and cook for about 5 minutes, until the bottom is set, then transfer the pan to the oven. Bake for 5–7 minutes, until the egg is set throughout and lightly golden brown on top. Remove from the oven and set aside for about 15 minutes, if serving warm, or for longer if serving at room temperature. Spoon the zhoug (if using) on top and scatter with cilantro leaves before cutting into quarters.

Tortang talong (eggplant omelet)

4 **eggplants**, pricked a few times
   with a fork
3 **tbsp/45ml olive oil**
1 **large shallot**, finely diced
   (½ cup/70g)
2 **large garlic cloves**, crushed
   to a paste
1 **tsp ground cumin**
¼ **tsp ground allspice**
¼ **tsp ground cinnamon**
7 **oz/200g ground lamb
   (or beef or pork)**, 20% fat
2 **tbsp rose harissa**
2 **green onions**, finely sliced
   (¼ cup/20g)
¾ **cup/15g cilantro leaves**,
   roughly chopped
¾ **cup/15g mint leaves**,
   roughly chopped
4 **eggs**
salt and black pepper

Tahini sauce
½ **cup/125g plain yogurt**
3 **tbsp tahini**
1 **garlic clove**, crushed to a paste
2 **tsp lemon juice**

This is our take on a Filipino dish introduced to Helen by her friend Cora Barba. The main components are traditional—the charring of the eggplant, the omelet—but the spices and tahini sauce are very much our own. It's a fun dish to cook, and made easy by the fact that the main elements can be prepared up to a day in advance, ready to be put together and quickly cooked. *Also pictured on pages 32–33.*

Serves 4

First you need to burn your eggplants. If you have a gas stovetop, switch on four flames and place one eggplant directly over each flame. Char for about 15 minutes, turning with tongs a few times, so that all sides are blackened and collapsing. If you have an electric stovetop, heat a griddle pan until very hot. Rub each eggplant with ½ teaspoon of the olive oil, then place on the griddle. Grill on high heat for about 30 minutes, turning throughout, so that all sides are charred and collapsing. Either way, transfer to a parchment-lined sheet pan or large plate and, once cool enough to handle, carefully remove the skin, leaving the stalk attached.

Spread the eggplants out and, using a fork, press each eggplant lightly all over to flatten it. Don't press too hard, as the flesh will tear. Set aside for 30 minutes or so for the liquid to exude, then pat them dry. Season both sides of the eggplants with a pinch of salt and some pepper.

Meanwhile, mix together all the ingredients for the tahini sauce in a bowl, along with 2 tablespoons of water, ½ teaspoon of salt, and some black pepper.

Put 1 tablespoon of oil into a 9-inch/23cm frying pan and place on medium heat. Add the shallot, garlic, cumin, allspice, and cinnamon and cook for about 5 minutes, stirring a few times, to soften. Increase the heat to medium-high and add the lamb, harissa, and ¼ teaspoon of salt. Cook for 7 minutes more, until the lamb is starting to color. Transfer to a medium bowl and set aside to cool. Once cool, add most of the green onions, cilantro, and mint—keep some to serve— and set aside.

Wipe the pan clean, then add 1 teaspoon of oil and return it to medium heat.

Prepare the omelets one at a time. Crack one egg into a medium shallow bowl—you want the bowl to be large enough to contain the flattened eggplant but not so large that the egg gets spread too thin. Add a pinch of salt and whisk. Dip one of the eggplants into the egg, turning it over so that both sides are covered. Return the eggplant to the large plate or sheet and add a quarter of the cooked lamb mixture to the egg left in the bowl. Mix to combine, then pour into the hot pan. Straight away, place the egg-dipped eggplant on top and cook for about 3 minutes, until the meat is golden brown.

Flip it over and cook for 2–3 minutes, or until golden, then slide the omelet onto a large serving plate, eggplant side up. Keep warm in a low oven, loosely covered with foil, while you cook the rest of the omelets in the same way.

Serve with the tahini sauce drizzled over the top, and scattered with the remaining herbs and green onions.

Steamed eggs with shrimp and chives

Equipment
**Either a rack that fits inside a large
    sauté pan (with a lid) or two sets
    of wooden chopsticks**

Custard
3–4 eggs, lightly beaten (165–170g)
**¾ cup/180ml lukewarm dashi
    (or chicken stock)**
**½ cup plus 2 tbsp/150ml
    lukewarm water**
salt and ground white pepper

Shrimp
2 tsp sunflower oil
**3½ oz/100g cooked tiny brown
    rock shrimp (or 5¼ oz/150g raw
    shrimp, roughly chopped)**
⅓ oz/10g ginger, peeled and
    julienned
2 tsp Shaoxing wine
⅓ oz/10g chives, finely chopped

Sauce
1 tbsp sesame oil
3 tbsp light soy sauce
**1 tbsp Chinkiang black (or other)
    vinegar**

To serve
cooked rice

Helen's mother used to make this for her as a kid. It was shorthand for "I'm tired and don't have the bandwidth for much else." The custard is smooth, silky, and as comforting as can be. We love the taste and look of the tiny brown rock shrimp, but chopped-up regular shrimp work just as well. *Also pictured on page 37.*

Equipment note: Traditionally, a steamer or a wok with a conical lid is used to steam the eggs. Here, we give instructions for how to convert a large sauté pan into a DIY steamer. It's a simple and effective alternative.

Serves 2

Put the eggs, dashi, and water into a bowl with ¼ teaspoon of salt and a dash of white pepper. Beat lightly and set aside.

To steam the eggs, you need a large sauté pan—about 11 inches/28cm wide—for which you have a lid. You also need a wide, shallow, heatproof bowl—about 9 inches/23cm wide and 1½ inches/4cm deep. Place a small rack, or two sets of wooden chopsticks in a hashtag pattern, in the bottom of the pan to create a stable platform. Place the steaming bowl on top, then pour water into the pan—you want it to be very close to the bottom of the bowl without actually touching it. Bring the water to a gentle simmer on medium heat.

Meanwhile, wrap the lid of the sauté pan in a large tea towel (to prevent the condensation from dropping into the custard), securing the ends at the top with a rubber band (or by tying them together).

Give the eggs another gentle whisk, then pour them through a fine-mesh sieve directly into the steaming dish. Decrease the heat to medium-low, and bring the water to a lively boil. Steam, covered, for 15–20 minutes—resisting the urge to lift the lid—until the custard is set around the edges and the middle barely wobbles. Turn off the heat, then remove the lid but leave the custard in the pan.

Put the oil for the shrimp into a medium frying pan and, when hot, add the shrimp and ginger. Sauté for 1 minute on high heat (or for 2–3 minutes, if starting with fresh shrimp), then add the Shaoxing wine. Cook for about 10 seconds, then remove from the heat and stir in the chives.

Remove the egg custard from the pan, mix together the sesame oil, soy sauce, and vinegar and dribble three-quarters of it evenly over the top. Spoon the shrimp on top and serve with the rice and the remaining sauce alongside.

Crêpes 3 ways: breakfast, lunch, and dessert

1 cup/125g all-purpose flour
2 eggs
1¼ cups/300ml milk
1½ tbsp unsalted butter, melted
(plus ¼ cup/50g extra for
cooking the crêpes)
⅛ tsp salt

Crêpes are the savior of many an impromptu meal. If you're organized when it comes to crêpes—like Yotam and Helen!—you'll keep a stash pre-made in the freezer. To store them, place a sheet of parchment paper between each crêpe, and seal the whole stack with reusable plastic wrap. If you're not as well organized—like the rest of us!—you'll welcome a batter that is quickly made and ready to cook straight away.

The base recipe for crêpes is given here, followed by three ideas for serving them, for breakfast, lunch, and dessert. Which order you eat them in is entirely up to you. You'll make eight crêpes and might notice that the recipes for the cheesy crêpes and the lemon, mascarpone, and thyme only account for six. The two spare? One is the practice one, if needed. And the second? Cook's perk, obviously.

Makes 8 crêpes

Place all the ingredients for the crêpes in a blender (or food processor). Blend on high speed just until smooth and combined. Pour into a liquid measuring cup and set aside. The crêpes can also be made by hand, whisking the eggs into the flour and salt before gradually adding the milk and then the melted butter.

When ready to cook, place a 9½-inch/24cm nonstick crêpe or frying pan on medium heat. When hot, add about ¼ teaspoon of butter and swipe around the pan with paper towels. Pour ¼ cup/60ml of the batter into the center of the pan and swirl it around to form a thin, even layer. Cook for about 2 minutes, flipping halfway through, until lightly golden brown. Transfer to a plate and set aside while you continue to cook the remaining crêpes in the same way, adding a swipe of butter before cooking each one.

Sesame and hazelnut chocolate praline spread

8 crêpes (see page 39), kept warm

Praline spread
½ cup/75g sesame seeds
½ cup/75g blanched hazelnuts
**½ cup plus 2 tbsp/120g granulated
    sugar**
scraped seeds of 1 vanilla pod
2 tbsp sunflower oil
5¼ oz/150g milk chocolate
    (about 37% cocoa content),
    roughly chopped
2 tbsp unsweetened cocoa powder

To serve (any or all of the following)
hazelnuts, toasted and roughly
    chopped
powdered sugar, for dusting
lightly whipped cream
sliced banana

Storing notes: This recipe makes one jar of praline spread (about 1⅓ cups/400g). Once made, it will keep for up to 1 week at room temperature or for longer (up to 1 month) in the fridge.

Serves 8

Preheat the oven to 350°F.

Spread the sesame seeds and hazelnuts on a parchment-lined baking sheet and toast in the oven for 15 minutes, shaking the sheet halfway through. Turn off the oven but leave the sheet in there to keep warm.

When the seeds and nuts have been in the oven for about 5 minutes, start the caramel. Put the sugar into a small saucepan, along with 2 tablespoons of water, and place on low heat. Stir to dissolve, then increase the heat to medium-high and bring to a boil. Simmer for 4–5 minutes—resisting the urge to stir from now on, but swirling the pan gently a few times—until it's a honey-colored caramel. Take off the heat and, using the parchment to lift them up, tip the seeds and nuts into the caramel. Stir to coat, replace the parchment on the sheet, then scrape the praline onto the lined sheet. Using a spatula, spread the praline out to form a thin layer. Set aside for 30 minutes, to harden.

Once hardened, use a rolling pin to bash the praline into rough pieces. Transfer to a food processor and blitz for 5–10 minutes (timings will vary depending on the power of the machine), stopping the machine a few times to scrape down the sides of the bowl, until the praline starts to form a rough paste. Add the vanilla seeds and oil and blitz until smooth and runny. Stop the machine but leave the mix in the bowl.

Place the chocolate in a small bowl and set the bowl over a small pot of just-simmering water, making sure the bottom of the bowl and the water do not touch. Stir occasionally to evenly melt, then scrape it into the food processor with the praline paste. Add the cocoa powder and process for a couple of minutes. Once smooth and combined, transfer into a clean jar with a lid.

Smear about 1 tablespoon of the praline spread—or more, if you like—over one side of each crêpe. Fold it in half, to form a semicircle, and then in half again, to form a triangle, or just simply roll it up. Either eat as is, or sprinkle with chopped toasted hazelnuts, dust with powdered sugar, or add whipped cream or slices of banana, or all of the above.

Cheesy curry crêpes

6 crêpes (see page 39)
8½ oz/240g leftover roasted chicken or ham, chopped, or big, soft butter (lima) beans
5 green onions, finely sliced (mounded ½ cup/50g)
½ tbsp olive oil
mango chutney, to serve
salt and black pepper

Béchamel
7 tbsp/100ml milk
3 tbsp Greek yogurt
1 tbsp unsalted butter
2 tbsp all-purpose flour
¾ tsp mild curry powder
¼ tsp ground turmeric
4½ oz/130g cheddar and/or Gruyère, grated (1¼ cups)

Serves 6

Place all the ingredients for the béchamel, except for the cheese, in a small saucepan on medium heat and bring to a simmer. Cook for 2–3 minutes, whisking constantly, until thickened and smooth. Take off the heat and add ½ cup/50g of the grated cheese, along with ¼ teaspoon of salt and a good grind of pepper. Whisk until smooth and set aside.

Preheat the oven to 450°F.

Place the crêpes on a flat surface and spread each one with a heaped large spoonful of béchamel. Scatter about 1½ oz/40g of chicken (or ham or butter beans) over the bottom quarter of each crêpe, followed by half a large spoonful or so each of green onions and grated cheese. Fold the top half of each crêpe over the bottom half to cover the filling. Fold the left side over to cover the right so that you have little open-ended triangular parcels. Place them on a parchment-lined baking sheet, scatter the remaining cheese over the top, and drizzle with the olive oil. Bake for 15–18 minutes, until golden. Scatter the remaining green onions and serve hot, with some mango chutney alongside.

Lemon, mascarpone, and thyme

1 large lemon
6 tbsp/75g granulated sugar
3–4 thyme sprigs, plus 1 tsp leaves
1½ tsp vanilla bean paste
½ cup/100g mascarpone
3 tbsp heavy cream
scant ½ cup/130g lemon curd
6 crêpes (see page 39)
1 tbsp unsalted butter, melted
½ tsp powdered sugar
1 tbsp toasted hazelnuts,
    roughly chopped
salt

Serves 6

Using a small sharp knife, trim the top and bottom off the lemon. Cut along its curved sides, removing the peel and white pith to expose the flesh. Place a sieve over a small bowl. Working over the bowl, slice in between each membrane to release the lemon segments into the sieve. Squeeze whatever is left of the lemon into the same bowl to get 1 tablespoon of juice. Cut each segment into 3–4 pieces and set aside.

Place the granulated sugar in a small saucepan on medium-high heat. Cook, swirling the pan gently, until the sugar has melted and turned to an amber caramel, about 3 minutes. Take off the heat and carefully add the lemon juice (it will splutter!), along with 1 tablespoon of water, a pinch of salt, and the thyme sprigs, whisking until smooth and melted. Add ½ teaspoon of the vanilla bean paste and pour over the prepared lemon segments. Set aside.

Preheat the broiler to its highest setting. Combine the remaining 1 teaspoon of vanilla bean paste with the mascarpone, cream, and 3 tbsp/50g of the lemon curd in a medium bowl and stir together until smooth. Spread out in a 9½-inch/24cm shallow baking dish and set aside.

Assemble the crêpes by spreading a scant 1 tablespoon of the remaining lemon curd on one of the crêpes. Fold the crêpe in half and then in half again, to form a triangle. Repeat with the rest of the crêpes and arrange them on top of the mascarpone cream. Brush with the melted butter and sift the powdered sugar over the top. Place under the broiler for 5–6 minutes, until the crêpes are golden and starting to catch around the edges.

Drizzle some of the lemon thyme syrup over the top and scatter the hazelnuts. Serve hot, with the rest of the syrup alongside.

Polenta pancakes with spiced corn salad

Pancakes

¼ cup/50g unsalted butter,
  roughly cubed
¾ cup plus 3 tbsp/220ml water
⅓ cup/60g instant/quick-cook
  polenta
1 cup/130g all-purpose flour
½ tsp baking powder
¼ tsp baking soda
2 eggs
¾ cup/200g sour cream,
  plus extra to serve
⅓ cup/80ml milk
2 tbsp maple syrup
5 green onions, thinly sliced
  (mounded ½ cup/50g)
salt

Corn salad

2 tbsp peanut (or sunflower) oil,
  plus extra for frying the pancakes
1 tbsp black mustard seeds
1 tsp cumin seeds
1 cinnamon stick
5 whole cloves
20 curry leaves
2 cups/330g corn kernels
  (scraped from 3 fresh cobs,
  or frozen kernels)
2 tbsp lemon juice
½ cup/80g roasted salted peanuts
1 small hot red chile, finely chopped
½ cup/10g cilantro leaves,
  roughly chopped

The corn salad was introduced to us by Anita Kerai, who makes it pretty much weekly for her family to snack on. Canned corn can be used, but we prefer fresh corn, or frozen kernels (cooked from frozen rather than defrosted). Serve these pancakes—our old favorite, from *The Silver Palate Cookbook*—with a few slices of ripe avocado alongside.

Makes 14 pancakes, serves 4

To make the pancake batter, put the butter and water into a medium saucepan with ¾ teaspoon of salt. Bring to a simmer on medium heat, then pour in the polenta in a fine stream. Cook for about 3 minutes, stirring continuously, until thickened. Remove from the heat and set aside to cool for 20 minutes, stirring from time to time.

In the meantime, sift together the flour, baking powder, and baking soda.

In a separate medium bowl, whisk together the eggs and sour cream. Add the milk and maple syrup, whisk to combine, then pour about a quarter of this mixture into the polenta. Whisk to loosen, then gradually add the rest of the egg mixture, whisking until fully incorporated. Add the sifted flour mix, followed by the green onions, fold to combine, then keep in the fridge, covered.

For the corn salad, put the oil into a large nonstick frying pan and place on medium-high heat. Add the spices and curry leaves and cook for 30 seconds to 1 minute, until the mustard seeds begin to pop and the curry leaves start to curl up (careful, as they will splutter in the hot oil!). Add the corn and cook for about 10 minutes, stirring from time to time, until the corn has released its moisture and started to caramelize in places. Take off the heat and add the lemon juice, peanuts, chile, and ½ teaspoon of salt. Transfer to a bowl and set aside to cool, then stir in the cilantro. Before serving, pick out and discard the whole cloves and cinnamon stick.

When ready to cook, wipe clean the frying pan and place it on medium heat. Add a small spoonful of oil and swirl to coat the pan. Spoon about 2 oz/55g of the batter into the pan: it should form a roughly 5-inch/12cm-wide pancake. You should be able to fit 3–4 pancakes at a time into the pan. Cook them for 4 minutes, flipping halfway through, then transfer to a plate and keep warm while you repeat with the remaining batter.

To serve, divide the pancakes among four plates and dollop each with a heaped spoonful of sour cream. Top with a large spoonful of the corn salad and serve.

"Thousand" hole pancakes

1 tbsp unsalted butter, melted
1 tbsp vegetable oil

Pancakes
1½ cups/240g fine semolina
½ cup/60g white bread flour
1 tbsp granulated sugar
¾ tsp fast-acting dried yeast
2⅓ cups/550ml hot tap water
salt

Salted honey butter with pecans
7 tbsp/100g unsalted butter,
   at room temperature
2 tbsp honey
½ tsp flaked sea salt
2 tsp orange blossom water (leave
   out if you don't have any)
½ cup/50g pecans, toasted and
   roughly chopped

These are inspired by Moroccan *beghrir*, the tender, spongy semolina pancakes that Yotam used to start his day with when filming his TV series *Mediterranean Feast*. After a thorough sampling of the freshly baked wares of pretty much every souk in the medina, it was these—reminiscent of a crumpet, but much simpler to make—that kept luring Yotam back for more. With thanks to Mandy Lee for the precise instructions for obtaining the "thousand" holes.

Getting ahead: The batter can be made a day ahead: keep it in the fridge overnight to rise, and decrease the yeast to ¼ teaspoon. The honey butter keeps in the fridge for up to 1 week.

Makes 12 pancakes

Place all the ingredients for the pancakes in a blender (or a tall liquid measuring cup if using an immersion blender), along with ½ teaspoon of salt. Blend for about 30 seconds, until smooth, then pour into a large liquid measuring cup. Set aside at room temperature, covered, for about 1 hour, until foamy.

To make the honey butter, place the butter in a small bowl and beat with a wooden spoon until smooth and creamy. Add the honey, flaked sea salt, and orange blossom water (if using) and beat again until smooth. Fold in the pecans and scrape into a small serving bowl.

When ready to cook, gently stir the batter—it will deflate a little—then set aside for 5 minutes while heating the pan. Place a nonstick pan—7 inches/18cm across the bottom, ideally—on medium-high heat and, when hot, lower the heat to medium. Combine the melted butter and oil in a small bowl, then dip a scrunched-up piece of paper towel into it and swipe the hot pan to grease lightly. Pour about ⅓ cup/80ml of the batter onto the center of the pan and swirl at once, to spread out a bit, roughly 5 inches/12cm wide. Cook for 2–3 minutes—the pancake will start to develop its characteristic holes almost straight away—until the batter is set on top and no longer looks wet. Slide the pancake onto a plate without turning it over—it is only cooked on one side—and repeat with the remaining batter. Set aside to cool before serving, and spread generously with the honey butter. Fold or roll up the pancakes to encase the filling before eating.

Soups, dips, spreads

Roasted eggplant, red bell pepper, and tomato soup

2 eggplants, pricked a few times with a fork (1 lb 9 oz/700g)
¼ cup/60ml olive oil
6 large tomatoes (1 lb 10 oz/725g)
2 red bell peppers (1 lb 1 oz/490g)
2 onions, roughly chopped (12¼ oz/350g)
6 garlic cloves, roughly chopped
1 tbsp thyme leaves
2 tsp ground cumin
1 tsp paprika
⅛ tsp cayenne pepper
¼ tsp saffron threads
1 tbsp tomato paste
2¾ cups/650ml vegetable stock (or water)
salt

Fried almond topping
¼ cup/60ml olive oil
scant ⅔ cup/70g sliced almonds
2 tsp thyme leaves
⅛ tsp saffron threads
⅛ tsp cayenne pepper
⅛ tsp paprika
⅛ tsp ground cumin
¼ tsp flaked sea salt
¼ oz/5g parsley, roughly chopped
1 tbsp sherry (or red wine) vinegar

Our starting point for this, believe it or not, was a can of Heinz cream of tomato soup! The classic British tomato soup, smooth and sweet. For anyone who's ever been brought a bowl when unwell and tucked up in bed, the link between the can and comfort is strong! Realizing that if someone wants a can of Heinz tomato soup they will simply get one, our departure from the original went quite a long way. With its smoky roasted vegetables and sherry vinegar finish, this soup is more reminiscent of the Catalonian dish *escalivada* than anything that comes in a can.

Serves 4–6

Preheat the oven to 450°F.

Place the eggplants on a parchment-lined baking sheet and drizzle with 1 tablespoon of the oil. Roast for 30 minutes, turning once or twice. Add the tomatoes and bell peppers to the sheet, drizzle with another 1 tablespoon of oil and turn the vegetables so that they are all coated. Roast for another 30 minutes, until the vegetables have colored and the skins have wrinkled. Remove from the oven and, when cool enough to handle, peel the skins off all the vegetables: don't worry if some stubborn patches remain. Discard the seeds and stems of the peppers and the stems of the eggplants.

Meanwhile, put the remaining 2 tablespoons of oil into a large saucepan, for which you have a lid, and place on medium-high heat. Add the onions and cook for 10 minutes, until soft and lightly colored. Add the garlic and thyme, then decrease the heat to medium-low and cook for 5 minutes, stirring a few times. Add the spices and tomato paste, cook for 2 minutes, then add all the peeled vegetables, along with their juices, breaking them up with a wooden spoon. Add the stock, along with 2 teaspoons of salt. Bring to a boil, then decrease the heat to medium and simmer gently, with the pan partially covered, for 10 minutes. Remove from the heat and, using an immersion blender or countertop blender, blitz until completely smooth.

While the soup is cooking, make the fried almond topping. Put the oil into a small pan and place on medium heat. Add the almonds and cook for 3–4 minutes, stirring often, until they are lightly golden. In the last few seconds of cooking, add the thyme leaves, spices, and flaked sea salt, then remove from the heat. Once cool, stir in the chopped parsley and vinegar.

Divide the soup among individual bowls and spoon the fried almonds and oil over the top.

Mulligatawny

2½ lb/1.2kg **chicken thighs**, bone in, skin on
¾ cup/150g **wild rice**
¼ cup/50g **unsalted butter**
1 large **onion**, roughly chopped (1⅓ cups/200g)
2 **carrots**, peeled and roughly chopped (1 cup/140g)
2 **celery stalks**, roughly chopped (1 cup/100g)
1 green **bell pepper**, seeded and roughly chopped (1¼ cups/165g)
3 **garlic cloves**, roughly chopped
⅓ oz/10g **ginger**, peeled and roughly chopped
1 tbsp **medium curry powder**
1 tbsp **garam masala**
2 tbsp **chickpea (or all-purpose) flour** (this is fine to leave out if you want a thinner soup)
2 **tomatoes**, finely diced (mounded 1 cup/200g)
1 tbsp **tomato paste**
½ cup/100g **red split lentils (masoor dal)**, rinsed and drained
7 tbsp/100ml **coconut cream**
1 tsp **lime juice**
salt and black pepper

Tadka
1½ tbsp **olive oil**
1½ tbsp **unsalted butter**
2½ tsp **cumin seeds**
2 tsp **black mustard seeds**
1 small **hot green chile**, thinly sliced
25 **curry leaves**

To serve
¼ cup/5g **cilantro leaves**
2 **limes**, cut into wedges

Comfort food is often the food we cook when we are away from home. This happens on all sorts of scales (individual, communal) and in every direction (immigration, emigration). Mulligatawny has its origins in Brits abroad, namely the British Raj. The colonial Brits, missing the soup they normally had at the start of every meal, were keen to have it re-created. The Indian cooks, unfamiliar with the tradition of a standalone soup as a starter, created a thin, spicy Madrasi broth known as molo tunny or "pepper water." Bulked out with meat and vegetables to suit the extravagant tastes of the British, mulligatawny was born. *Pictured on page 56.*

Getting ahead: The chicken and stock base can be made up to 2 days ahead and kept in the fridge. If making in advance, add the chicken before heating through.

Serves 6

Put the chicken thighs into a large saucepan, for which you have a lid, and pour in 8½ cups/2 liters of water. Bring to a simmer, skim off any scum, then simmer on medium-low heat for about 1½ hours, partially covered. Remove the chicken from the stock (reserving the liquid—you should have about 6⅓ cups/1.5 liters) and set aside to cool. Once cool enough to handle, flake off the chicken meat. Discard the bones and skin.

While the chicken is cooking, cook the rice according to the package instructions. Drain well and set aside.

Put the butter into a large sauté pan, for which you have a lid, and place on medium-high heat. Add the onion, carrots, celery, green bell pepper, garlic, and ginger and cook for 18–20 minutes, until softened and starting to brown. Add the curry powder, garam masala, and flour (if using). Cook for about 1 minute, stirring to prevent the spices from sticking to the bottom of the pan, then add the tomatoes and tomato paste. Cook for another 1 minute, then add the lentils, reserved stock, 2½ teaspoons of salt, and some pepper. Stir and bring to a boil. Decrease the heat to low, cover with the lid, and simmer for 30 minutes until the vegetables and lentils are soft. Using an immersion blender (or in batches in a countertop blender), blend to form a smooth soup. Add the coconut cream, lime juice, and chicken and heat through gently.

When ready to serve, make the tadka. Put the oil and butter into a small frying pan and place on medium heat. Add the cumin and mustard seeds and cook for a few seconds, until the seeds begin to pop. Add the chile and curry leaves, standing back to avoid splutter. Stir for 1 minute.

Divide the rice among 6 bowls, followed by a ladle or two of soup. Spoon the tadka over the top, garnish with the cilantro leaves, and serve, with a wedge of lime alongside.

Pea and ham soup

¼ cup/60ml olive oil

2 small onions, roughly chopped (2¼ cups/340g)

2 carrots, peeled and roughly chopped (1¼ cups/160g)

2 celery stalks, roughly chopped (1⅓ cups/130g)

4 garlic cloves, roughly chopped

2 bay leaves

1 tbsp cumin seeds, toasted and roughly crushed

2 tsp coriander seeds, toasted and roughly crushed

2¾ cups/500g green split peas, rinsed and drained

1 x 14-oz/400g can of diced tomatoes

2 lb 2 oz/1kg smoked ham hock

7¼ cups/1.75 liters chicken stock (or water)

salt and black pepper

Pea and mint sauce
¾ cup/180ml olive oil
½ cup/60g pumpkin seeds
¾ cup/15g mint leaves
(½ cup/10g whole and ¼ cup/5g roughly chopped)
2 tsp dried mint
1⅔ cups/250g frozen petis pois (or peas), defrosted
1 tbsp lime juice

The unmistakable sweet scent of smoked ham cooking—in this case with split peas, tomatoes, and spices—is, for Yotam, a new kind of comfort. It's what Christmas smells like in the Ottolenghi–Allen household, where Karl, true to his Irish roots, first boils the smoked ham and then coats it with brown sugar and studs it with cloves—the kids' favorite job—ready to be roasted. The smoky-fatty-sweetness of the ham is just what the peas need in this textbook, timeless old-school comfort dish, seen through the Ottolenghi (and Allen!) lens. *Pictured on page 56.*

Getting ahead: The soup will keep for 4 days in the fridge or longer in the freezer. The sauce is best eaten the day it's made. The lime juice will make it discolor with time.

Serves 8

Put the oil into a large pot, about 11 inches/28cm wide, for which you have a lid, and place on medium heat. Add the onions, carrots, celery, garlic, and bay leaves and cook for 15 minutes, stirring a few times, until softened and starting to turn golden. Add the cumin and coriander seeds and cook for 1 minute, then add the split peas, tomatoes, ham hock, and the stock—you want it to just barely cover the ham hock. Increase the heat, bring to a boil, then decrease the heat to medium-low. Simmer for 1¾ hours, covered. Lift the ham out of the soup and transfer to a plate to cool slightly, then add ½ teaspoon of salt (ham hock can vary in saltiness, so adjust the seasoning accordingly) and a good grind of pepper. Remove the bay leaves and then, using an immersion blender (or in batches in an upright blender or a food processor), blend the soup until it's as smooth as you like.

While the soup is cooking, make the sauce. Place a small frying pan on medium heat and add 1 teaspoon of the olive oil, the pumpkin seeds, and a pinch of salt. Toast the seeds for 4–5 minutes, stirring regularly, until they start to puff up slightly and pop. Set aside to cool. Put the whole mint leaves into the small bowl of a food processor, along with the dried mint, 1 cup/150g of the peas, half the pumpkin seeds, ½ cup/120ml of the oil, and ¾ teaspoon of salt. Process to form a rough purée, then scrape into a small bowl. Add the remaining ¼ cup/60ml of olive oil, the chopped mint, lime juice, and the rest of the peas. Stir to combine and set aside until serving.

When the ham is cool enough to handle, remove the fat and discard, then shred or chop the meat into bite-size chunks. At this stage the ham can either be stirred back into the soup or served on top, along with a couple of spoonfuls of the sauce and a sprinkle of toasted pumpkin seeds.

Matza ball soup

Hawaij spice mix (optional)
1 tbsp coriander seeds
2 tsp cumin seeds
2 whole cloves
seeds from 8 cardamom pods
½ tsp fenugreek seeds
¼ tsp black peppercorns
½ tsp ground turmeric

Chicken stock
4 small carrots, 2 thinly sliced,
  2 cut into big chunks
  (2⅓ cups/300g)
2 lb 2 oz/1kg chicken legs
1 large parsnip, quartered
  (6 oz/175g)
2 celery stalks, roughly chopped
  (1⅓ cups/135g)
1 onion, quartered (6⅓ oz/180g)
2 bay leaves
¾ oz/20g parsley stalks
⅓ oz/10g dill stalks (keep the fronds
  for serving)
4 garlic cloves, peeled and
  smashed
⅛ tsp ground turmeric
¼ tsp black peppercorns
3½ tsp salt
2 tsp hawaij spice mix (optional:
  store-bought or see above)

Matza balls
**1 cup/115g fine or medium
  matza meal**
½ tsp baking powder
3 eggs
¼ cup/60ml sunflower oil
1 garlic clove, crushed to a paste
salt and black pepper

Helen's family loves matza balls so much that they don't just wait for Passover to have them. They prefer a lighter, less dense version of the balls. Yotam's family—with his late aunt having the strongest opinions on the matter—prefer a denser ball. This is the Goldilocks version, where the matza balls, neither too fluffy nor too dense, sit nicely somewhere between the two.

Getting ahead: Both the stock and the matza balls can be made up to a day ahead.

Ingredients note: Hawaij means mixture in Arabic. It's a Yemeni spice blend, heavy on the cumin. It's not a traditional addition to matza ball soup but brings an incredibly warm aroma. Leave it out if you prefer.

Serves 4

For the hawaij, if making, place all the ingredients, except the turmeric, in a small dry saucepan on medium heat. Toast for 3–5 minutes, or until fragrant. Transfer to a spice grinder (or a mortar and pestle) and blitz to a smooth powder. Stir in the turmeric and transfer to a clean sealed jar, where it will keep for up to 6 months.

For the chicken stock, add the chunks of carrot to a large pot for which you have a lid. Add the remaining stock ingredients (but not the sliced carrots). Pour in 2½ quarts/liters of water and bring to a boil, skimming off any scum. Decrease the heat to low and cook at a bare simmer, covered, for 1½ hours.

Meanwhile, make the matza balls. Place the matza meal and the baking powder in a medium bowl, along with ¾ teaspoon of salt and ¼ teaspoon of freshly ground pepper. Put the eggs into a separate bowl, along with the oil and garlic. Whisk to combine, then pour into the matza meal mixture. Using a fork, stir the mix lightly and gently, raking it through to break up any clumps. Cover and refrigerate for at least 1 hour (or up to 24 hours) to firm up.

Toward the last 15 minutes of the stock cooking time, start making the matza balls. Lightly rake through the mix again, then shape into roughly ¾ oz/20g balls. Set aside on a plate.

Remove the chicken pieces from the stock and set aside. Strain out the vegetables, and discard. Bring the stock back up to a boil and add the reserved sliced carrots and matza balls. Turn the heat to medium-low and, with the lid partially on, simmer for 45 minutes (making sure the soup is not simmering too furiously). Remove the skin and bones from the chicken, then shred the meat and add it to the soup. Divide the balls among four bowls and ladle in the broth. Sprinkle with some hawaij, if using, and the dill fronds.

Cheesy bread soup with Savoy cabbage

5 tbsp/75ml olive oil
2 tbsp unsalted butter
3 onions, thinly sliced
(3¾ cups/450g)
4 garlic cloves, 2 thinly sliced and
2 left whole
7 anchovies, finely chopped
3 tbsp thyme leaves, finely chopped
1 bay leaf
¾ cup plus 2 tbsp/200ml dry
white wine
1 Savoy cabbage, leaves roughly
torn (2¾ cups/250g)
1 bunch of cavolo nero, leaves
roughly torn (2¼ cups/150g)
¼ tsp ground nutmeg
¾ oz/25g parsley, roughly chopped
9 slices of sourdough or rye,
cut ½ inch/1cm thick (1 lb/450g)
9 oz/250g fontina (or Gruyère or
Comté) cheese, coarsely grated
(2⅓ cups)
1¾ oz/50g parmesan, finely grated
(6 tbsp)
8½ cups/2 liters hot chicken
(or beef) stock, well seasoned
salt and black pepper

This feels like what would happen if a French onion soup, a cheese fondue, and a raclette got together after a day's hiking in the snow. Pure melted-cheese-sweet-onion comfort. In the absence of any mountains, this works just as well on any cold day when fresh air has been had and the need for a hearty dish is there.

Ingredients note: The quality and strength of the ingredients are important here: the stock should be strong, well seasoned, and flavorful, the bread should be robust and rustic, and the cheese should be nutty and smooth.

Serves 6–8

Put 2 tablespoons of the oil and 1 tablespoon of the butter into a large cast-iron casserole pan, and place on medium heat. Add the onions and cook for about 15 minutes, stirring regularly, until soft and beginning to brown. Lower the heat slightly and add the sliced garlic, anchovies, thyme, and bay leaf. Cook for 2 minutes, stirring once or twice. Don't worry if the bottom of the pot sticks a little. Add the wine, return the heat to medium, and let it bubble for 2 minutes. Add both cabbages, along with the remaining 1 tablespoon of butter, the nutmeg, 1 teaspoon of salt, and a good grind of pepper. Cook for about 6 minutes, stirring regularly, until the cabbage is softened. Transfer the mix to a separate bowl, stir in the parsley, and set aside.

Preheat the oven to 400°F.

Toast 6 slices of the bread until lightly golden brown on both sides, then rub the whole garlic cloves liberally on both sides of each piece. Tear the toast into 3–4 pieces and place enough pieces in your large casserole pan to cover the bottom—you should use about half. Spoon half the cabbage mix over the top, drizzle with 1 tablespoon of the oil, and scatter a third of both cheeses. Sprinkle with some pepper, then cover with the remaining toast pieces, to form an even layer. Follow this with the remaining cabbage mix, the remaining 2 tablespoons of olive oil, half the remaining cheese, and some more pepper. Finally, roughly tear the remaining 3 slices of (untoasted) bread and place these on top. Carefully ladle 6⅓ cups/1½ liters of the hot stock over the casserole, then press the bread down to make sure that it is soaked. Scatter the remaining cheese and bake for 30 minutes, until the cheese is golden brown. Allow to stand out of the oven for 10 minutes before scooping out into bowls. Ladle in the remaining stock to serve.

Hummus

2 x 25-oz/700g jars of good-quality
  chickpeas, drained and rinsed
2 tsp ground cumin
2 small, hot red chiles, thinly sliced
4 tsp apple cider vinegar
¾ cup plus 2 tbsp/250g tahini
¾ cup plus 2 tbsp/200ml water
4 lemons: 2 left whole and 2 juiced
  to get ¼ cup/60ml
2 large garlic cloves, crushed to
  a paste
3 tbsp olive oil, plus extra to finish
4 ice cubes (1¾ oz/50g)
½ tsp cumin seeds, toasted and
  roughly crushed
¼ cup/5g parsley leaves, chopped
salt

To serve (any or all of the following)
warm pita bread
hard-boiled eggs
sliced green onions
pickles

Many words have been written and spoken about hummus: a Palestinian staple, an Israeli staple, the center of much argument and discord. For the sake of *Comfort* and comfort, we'd like to put these aside here. This star dish of both nations is what Yotam sees in his mind's eye when he thinks of home, not in the sense of the house he grew up in—hummus isn't often made at home in Jerusalem—but the dish around which friends get together to eat in public. Fresh hummus, served in one of the city's many eateries specializing in this dish, isn't only insanely delicious, it's an experience like no other: warm, smooth, lemony, and rich, the ultimate source of warmth and solace. To this day, a hummus restaurant is the first stop on any visit to Israel for Yotam, Karl, and their boys. *Pictured on page 64.*

Serves 6–8, as a starter or as part of a spread

Put the chickpeas into a medium saucepan, along with the ground cumin and ½ teaspoon of salt. Pour in 3¼ cups/750ml of water and bring to a boil on high heat. Decrease the heat to medium-low and simmer for 10 minutes, until the chickpeas are super soft. Drain, discarding the cooking water.

Meanwhile, mix the chiles with the vinegar and a pinch of salt and set aside.

Make a tahini sauce by whisking together the tahini, water, ¼ cup/60ml of lemon juice, half the crushed garlic, and ½ teaspoon of salt.

Use a sharp knife to peel and segment the 2 whole lemons, then chop the segments and put them into a medium bowl, squeezing in any juice left in the lemon. Take half the drained chickpeas and add them to the chopped lemon. Add the olive oil and ½ teaspoon of salt and stir.

Put the remaining chickpeas into a food processor. Remove ¼ cup/70g of the tahini sauce and set aside to finish. Add the remaining tahini sauce to the food processor, along with the remaining crushed garlic, the ice cubes, and ¾ teaspoon of salt. Process for 2–3 minutes, until aerated and completely smooth.

Spread the hummus on a serving platter. Spoon the chickpea and lemon mixture over the top, then the reserved tahini sauce. Finish with the sliced chile and vinegar, a sprinkle of cumin seeds, the parsley, and a drizzle of oil. Serve with whichever extras you're having.

Hummus by way of southern France
(aka chickpea and fennel purée)

6 tbsp/90ml good-quality olive oil

1 large onion, cut into ½-inch/1cm
dice (1⅓ cups/200g)

1 large fennel bulb, cut into
½-inch/1cm dice (3 cups/275g),
any fronds saved to garnish

4 garlic cloves, crushed to a paste

2 tsp fennel seeds, lightly toasted
and roughly crushed

3 tbsp dry vermouth (or Pernod)

**1 x 25-oz/700g jar of good-quality
chickpeas**, drained and rinsed

3 tbsp lemon juice

½ cup/10g basil leaves, to garnish

Tomato, olive, and bell pepper topping

1 large red bell pepper, halved and
seeded (about 5¼ oz/150g)

2 tbsp plus 1 tsp olive oil

5¼ oz/150g cherry tomatoes, halved

1 small garlic clove, crushed with the
side of a knife

⅓ cup/50g pitted olives (preferably
black Niçoise style), roughly
chopped

1 tsp red wine vinegar

salt and black pepper

Traditional hummus this is not! A favorite item on the catering menu in Helen's café (so long ago now that the origin of the recipe is lost in time), where it was paired with grilled fish. The inclusion of vermouth, olive oil, and fennel in place of tahini gives this hummus a southern French note. The tomato, olive, and bell pepper topping continues the sun-drenched theme. Serve warm for a wonderful first course, mopped up with baguette—in keeping with the Provençal vibe—or with pita bread as a nod to its Levantine routes. *Pictured on page 65.*

Serves 6, as a starter or as part of a spread

Preheat the oven to 450°F.

First make the topping. Place the bell pepper halves on a small parchment-lined baking sheet, skin side up. Drizzle with 1 teaspoon of the olive oil and roast for 15 minutes, until softened and slightly wrinkly. Transfer to a bowl and set aside, tightly covered, to steam and help the skin loosen. Once cool, peel off the skins, then slice the bell peppers into thin strips and return them to the bowl.

Add the tomatoes to the same sheet, along with the garlic, 1 tablespoon of oil, ¼ teaspoon of salt, and a few grinds of pepper. Mix to combine and roast for 5 minutes, until the tomatoes just start to collapse. Remove from the oven and add to the bowl with the bell peppers, along with the olives, vinegar, and the remaining 1 tablespoon of oil.

To make the chickpea and fennel purée, put ¼ cup/60ml of the oil into a large sauté pan and place on low heat. Add the onion, fennel, and ½ teaspoon of salt and cook for about 7 minutes, until the vegetables begin to soften. Add the garlic and 1½ teaspoons of fennel seeds and cook for 7–8 minutes, until the vegetables are completely soft and beginning to color. Add the vermouth—it will evaporate quickly—then add the chickpeas and ¼ teaspoon of salt. Cook for 2–3 minutes, over medium heat, until the chickpeas are completely warmed through, then transfer to a food processor. Add the lemon juice and a good grind of pepper—about 1 teaspoon. With the machine running, dribble in 1 tablespoon of oil and process to a fine purée.

To serve, transfer the purée to a serving plate. Spoon the tomato topping over the top and garnish with the basil, fennel fronds, and the remaining ½ teaspoon of fennel seeds. Drizzle with the remaining 1 tablespoon of oil. Serve warm or at room temperature.

Fritters and other fried things

Easy, cheesy rice cakes

1 cup/200g **sushi rice**, soaked for
½ hour
1 cup/240ml **water**
⅛ tsp **ground turmeric**
4–5 **green onions**, finely chopped
(mounded ½ cup/50g)
3 tbsp **Greek yogurt**
2 tsp **nigella seeds (or black
sesame seeds)**
¾ cup/125g **frozen peas**, defrosted
3½ oz/100g **block of low-moisture
mozzarella**, finely grated (1 cup)
3 oz/80g **feta**
2 tbsp **ghee (or butter)**, for frying
salt and black pepper

Quick sweet chile sauce
2 **small, hot red chiles**, seeded and
finely chopped (2 tbsp/20g)
1 **garlic clove**, crushed to a paste
1½ tsp **fish sauce**
2 tbsp **honey**
1½ tsp **lime juice**

Easy, cheesy (and also peas-y), these are great to snack on before supper, as well as an absolute winner—kids love them—for supper itself. If anyone doesn't want the chile sauce, that's fine—just add a squeeze of lemon.

Don't be shy about giving these rice cakes plenty of time in the pan with the ghee. The crispy edges are reminiscent of the wonderful tahdig-style rice, where the bottom of the rice crisps up and colors as it cooks. *Pictured on page 70.*

Getting ahead: The rice cakes can be assembled in full a few hours before frying. Just cover them with a clean damp tea towel to prevent them from drying out. Once fried, the cakes are best eaten on the day. The chile sauce will keep for 3 days in the fridge. Double the batch, if you like—it's great mixed with a bit of mayo in a sandwich.

Serves 4

Drain the rice and transfer it to a small saucepan, for which you have a lid, along with the water, turmeric, and ½ teaspoon of salt. Bring to a simmer, then decrease the heat to low and cook for 15 minutes, covered. Remove from the heat and set aside to rest, still covered, for 10 minutes.

Put all the ingredients for the chile sauce, except for the lime juice, into a small saucepan. Bring to a simmer on medium heat, then let simmer for 3 minutes, until the mixture thickens slightly and turns glossy. Add the lime juice and remove from the heat. Set aside to cool.

Put the cooked rice into a medium bowl, along with the green onions, yogurt, nigella seeds, peas, both cheeses, and ¼ teaspoon of salt. Mix until combined. Have ready a bowl of cold water and, using wet hands, weigh out about 2¼ oz/60g of the rice mixture and roll into a ball, squeezing firmly to make sure the mixture stays together. Flatten to form a round disc and set aside while you continue with the remaining rice.

Put a third of the ghee into a large frying pan and place on medium-high heat. Once hot, add the rice cakes—4 or 5 at a time—and fry for about 6 minutes, turning halfway through so that both sides are nice and crispy. Transfer to a plate lined with paper towels and repeat with the remaining ghee and rice cakes. (If you want to keep the cooked cakes warm, pop them into a 350°F oven until serving.) Serve warm, with the chile sauce on the side.

Mung bean and kimchi "falafel"

⅔ cup/130g mung beans, soaked
  in plenty of water overnight
3½ oz/100g kimchi, drained and
  roughly chopped
3½ oz/100g white cabbage
  (not Napa or Chinese),
  roughly chopped
2 green onions, finely sliced
  (¼ cup/25g)
⅓ oz/10g cilantro, roughly chopped
sunflower oil, for frying
salt and black pepper

Kimchi dipping sauce
3½ oz/100g kimchi, blitzed to
  a purée
1 tbsp soy sauce
1½ tbsp rice vinegar
1½ tbsp honey
1½ tsp sesame oil
1 tbsp fish sauce

These started out as a Korean-style pancake fritter, but we were so taken by the crunchy, falafel-like exterior that we decided to see what would happen if we turned them into balls to deep fry. Turns out, to no one's surprise, it was then hard to imagine them any other way. *Pictured on page 71.*

Getting ahead: As with dried chickpeas in regular falafel, the mung beans do not get cooked before frying, but they do need their overnight soak. The mixture can be made a day ahead, if you like. It will exude liquid as it sits, so just drain before forming into balls and frying.

Serves 4–6

Combine all the ingredients for the dipping sauce and set aside.

Drain the mung beans, then transfer to a food processor and blitz well to form a smooth paste. Add all the remaining ingredients (except the oil), along with 1 teaspoon of salt and a good grind of pepper. Pulse a few times, to roughly chop, then scrape into a large bowl.

Line a baking sheet with a few layers of paper towels. Using a 1-tablespoon measuring spoon, take scoops of the mung bean mixture and roll to form small balls—about ¾ oz/20g each. Place on the lined sheet—you should have about 24 balls.

When ready to fry, pour enough of the oil into a medium sauté pan so that it rises up 1½ inches/4cm and place on medium-high heat. When hot enough (you can test if it's ready by placing a chopstick, or the end of a wooden spoon, in the oil: it should form tiny bubbles around the tip), carefully drop in the balls, a few at a time, and cook for about 4 minutes, until browned. Using a slotted spoon, lift them out and transfer to a wire rack lined with paper towels. Repeat with the remaining mixture and serve warm, with the dipping sauce alongside.

Cauliflower and butternut pakoras

¾ cup/100g all-purpose flour
1 cup/100g chickpea (gram) flour
1 tsp baking powder
1 tsp ground turmeric
1 tsp ground coriander
½ tsp chile powder
1½ tsp cumin seeds, lightly toasted
2 tsp black mustard seeds, lightly
    toasted
1 cup/240ml cold water
2 garlic cloves, crushed to a paste
⅓ oz/10g ginger, peeled and
    finely chopped
¾ oz/20g cilantro, roughly chopped
1 small red onion, thinly sliced
    (¾ cup/100g)
¼ butternut squash, peeled and
    grated (1½ cups/200g)
½ small cauliflower (11 oz/310g),
    leaves removed and roughly
    torn, florets cut into 1¼–1½-inch/
    3–4cm chunks
about 1 quart/liter sunflower oil,
    for frying
salt

Tamarind sauce
1½ tbsp tamarind purée
1 garlic clove, crushed to a paste
3 tbsp lime juice
1½ tbsp light brown sugar
1½ tsp fish sauce
2 tsp chile flakes

Ask Yotam what's his equation for comfort food, and it would look something like: vegetables + batter + fried + street food + eaten by hand = pakoras. They're the ultimate snack food, eaten for lunch or snacked on before supper.

See this as a fridge-raid recipe: if you have any carrots, sweet potatoes, parsnips, beets, or zucchini that need using up, these would work well instead of (or in addition to) the butternut. Broccoli can be used instead of the cauliflower. Use up what you have around, keeping the total weight the same. Once cooked, leftover pakoras can be kept in the fridge in an airtight container, reheated the next day.

Serves 4–6

Get all your vegetables chopped before you make the batter, so that you are ready to fry. The batter doesn't improve from sitting around.

Place all the ingredients for the sauce in a screw-top jar, shake to combine, and set aside until ready to serve.

Mix together both flours in a large bowl with the baking powder, spices, and 1¼ teaspoons of salt. Pour in the water and stir gently to form a thick batter. Add the garlic, ginger, cilantro, onion, squash, and cauliflower florets and leaves, and stir to combine.

Add enough oil to the pan so that it rises 2 inches/5cm up the sides, and place on medium-high heat. When hot (you can test if it's ready by placing a chopstick, or the end of a wooden spoon, in the oil: it should form tiny bubbles around the tip), use two spoons to scoop up about 2½ oz/70g of the pakora mix—you don't want to compact the mixture, so use large spoons or a ladle to keep it rounded. Carefully drop it into the oil and fry for about 4 minutes, turning halfway through. You should be able to fry 4 at a time. Using a slotted spoon, transfer the pakoras to a baking sheet lined with paper towels. Sprinkle very lightly with salt and set aside while you continue with the remaining batter. Serve with the tamarind sauce alongside, for dipping.

Cucur udang (shrimp spoon fritters)

12¼ oz/350g fresh or frozen shrimp, shell removed (but tail intact): set aside 12, remove the tails from the rest and chop into small pieces

about 2 cups/480ml sunflower oil, for frying

Batter
1 cup plus 3 tbsp/150g all-purpose flour
½ tsp granulated sugar
½ tsp fast-acting dried yeast
¼ tsp baking powder
½ tsp ground turmeric
4–5 green onions, finely sliced (½ cup/45g), plus extra to garnish
1 small, hot green chile, finely chopped
1½ tsp fish sauce
½ tsp sesame oil
⅔ cup/160ml water
salt and ground white pepper

Chile dipping sauce
2 small, hot red chiles, seeded and roughly chopped
⅓ oz/10g ginger, peeled and roughly chopped
2 garlic cloves, peeled and left whole
2½ tbsp granulated sugar
2 tbsp lime juice
½ tsp sesame oil
¼ cup/60ml water

Cucur udang are sold streetside all over Malaysia for drivers to pull over for a pick-me-up. Helen could not resist them as a kid and would beg her parents to stop every time they drove past a stall. They are devilishly good as a snack anytime. Traditionally, they're made with a ladle, but we use a long-handled, stainless-steel cooking or serving spoon. The long handle is important, though—without it, the spoon will be too hot to handle.

Serves 4

Put all the ingredients for the batter into a medium bowl, along with ½ teaspoon of salt and ¼ teaspoon of white pepper. Mix well to combine. Cover the bowl with a plate and set aside for 1 hour (not for much longer, though, as it may over-rise).

In the meantime, place all the ingredients for the chile sauce in a blender, along with 1 teaspoon of salt. Blitz to a runny sauce, then transfer to a small serving bowl and set aside.

When ready to cook, pour enough of the oil into a large saucepan so that it rises 1½ inches/4cm up the sides. Place on medium heat and place a large, long-handled stainless-steel serving spoon in the oil, for it to heat up. Gently fold the chopped shrimp into the batter. When the oil is ready (an easy way to check is to place a chopstick, or the end of a wooden spoon, in the oil: if it forms tiny bubbles around the tip, it is ready), remove the spoon from the oil and, using a separate spoon, scoop about 1 oz/30g of the batter and place it on the hot spoon. Place a whole shrimp in the center, pressing it in, then immediately lower it into the hot oil. Fry for 1 minute, until the fritter detaches itself from the spoon. Cook for 2–2½ minutes—flipping the fritter over for the last 30 seconds—until golden brown. Repeat with the remaining batter, frying 3 fritters per batch to make 12 in total. Drain the fritters on a plate lined with paper towels.

Pile up on a platter, scatter the extra green onions over the top, and serve with the chile dipping sauce alongside.

Spiced chicken sando with harissa mayonnaise

1¾ cups/400g plain yogurt
  (or buttermilk)
2 tbsp baharat
1 tsp ground cinnamon
½ tsp granulated sugar
4 small boneless, skinless chicken
  breasts (about 4½ oz/125g each)
6 oz/175g white cabbage,
  finely sliced
5 green onions, finely sliced
  (mounded ½ cup/50g)
2¼ cups/125g panko breadcrumbs
vegetable oil, for frying
8 thick slices of soft white
  sandwich bread (brioche buns
  work really well too)
salt

Harissa mayonnaise
2 tbsp rose harissa paste
½ cup/125g mayonnaise
2 tsp lime juice

It feels like everyone knows someone who knows *someone* who makes the best fried chicken sandwiches in town. This is what we'd set up our stall with: a North African version of katsu sando—the incredibly popular Japanese sandwich in which two slices of soft white milk-bread hold together the winning combination of fried pork (or chicken), tonkatsu sauce, and Kewpie mayonnaise.

Getting ahead: The chicken needs to marinate for at least 4 (and up to 24) hours ahead of when you are going to fry it.

Ingredients note: The bread really needs to be super-soft, white sandwich bread. Ottolenghi readers: no sourdough or artisan alternative allowed!

Makes 4

Put the yogurt, baharat, cinnamon, sugar, and 1 teaspoon of salt into a large bowl. Stir to combine and set aside.

One at a time, place the chicken breasts on a chopping board and, using a rolling pin, pound them very lightly to even them out. Add them to the bowl of spiced yogurt and mix gently. Cover and refrigerate for at least 4 hours (or up to 24 hours).

Mix together all the ingredients for the harissa mayonnaise in a small bowl and keep in the fridge.

In a separate bowl, toss together the cabbage and green onions.

When ready to cook, spread the breadcrumbs out on a small baking sheet. Line another sheet with parchment paper and set aside. One at a time, lift the chicken breasts out of the marinade (discarding the leftover yogurt) and place on the breadcrumbs. Turn over so that both sides are coated. Transfer to the lined baking sheet and repeat with the rest of the chicken.

Pour enough of the oil into a large frying pan so that it rises ¾ inch/2cm up the sides. Place on medium heat and, when hot, carefully lower 2 of the chicken breasts into the pan. Fry for about 4 minutes per side, until both sides are golden brown. Transfer to a plate lined with paper towels, sprinkle with salt, and set aside while you continue with the remaining chicken breasts.

When ready to assemble, spread one side of each slice of bread liberally with the harissa mayonnaise. Place a chicken breast on top of half of the slices, followed by a large handful of the cabbage and green onions. Top with the remaining slices, cut the sandwiches in half, removing the crusts, and serve.

Salmon fishcakes with chermoula remoulade

1 large sweet potato (9¾ oz/280g)
2 russet (or other floury)
   potatoes (9¾ oz/280g)
1 tsp olive oil
1 lb 2 oz/500g salmon fillets,
   skinless and boneless, cut into
   roughly 1½-inch/4cm chunks
4–5 green onions, thinly
   sliced (½ cup/45g)
½ oz/15g chives, finely chopped
1 tsp finely grated lime zest
3 tbsp store-bought chermoula
¼ cup/30g panko breadcrumbs
1 egg
½ cup/120ml sunflower oil,
   for frying
1 lime, cut into wedges, to serve
salt and black pepper

Remoulade
1½ tbsp store-bought chermoula
⅓ cup/75g mayonnaise
1 tbsp Greek yogurt
1 oz/30g sweet dill pickles,
   finely chopped
¼ oz/5g chives, finely chopped

Fishcakes can tip too far in one direction—too much fish or too much potato. We think these strike the right balance. As with most things potatoey and fried, these are a family-dinner-winner, served with a simple salad, or piled into a brioche bun or baguette for lunch.

Serving suggestion: The cakes also work as a canapé (served in a little gem lettuce leaf with a dot of the remoulade) or else as a nibble before the main meal. If you do this, just shape them into much smaller patties and decrease the frying time to 3–4 minutes.

Getting ahead: The fishcakes can be made up to a full day ahead before frying and kept refrigerated. The remoulade keeps for up to 2 days in the fridge.

Serves 4

Preheat the oven to 400°F.

Pierce both types of potatoes a few times with a fork and rub them with the olive oil. Place them on a baking sheet and roast for 1 hour and 20 minutes, until soft. Carefully split the potatoes in half and set aside to cool.

Make the remoulade by mixing together all the ingredients in a small bowl. Set aside in the fridge.

Place the salmon in a food processor and pulse 2–3 times, until very roughly chopped. Transfer to a large bowl and set aside. Scoop out the flesh from all the potatoes and add it to the salmon bowl, along with the green onions, chives, lime zest, chermoula, breadcrumbs, and egg. Add ¾ teaspoon of salt and a good grind of pepper and, using your hands, gently mix together, breaking up the potato as you go, then shape into 12 patties, about 3 oz/85g each and ¾ inch/2cm thick.

Heat the sunflower oil in a large frying pan, about 11 inches/28cm wide, and place on medium-high heat. Fry half the fishcakes for about 7 minutes, turning halfway through, until golden-brown. Transfer to a plate lined with paper towels while you continue with the rest. Serve warm, with the remoulade and lime wedges alongside.

Meatballs with nuoc cham, cucumber, and mint

Meatballs
2 garlic cloves, crushed to a paste
1 shallot, finely chopped (⅓ cup/50g)
1 oz/30g cilantro, stems finely
   chopped (save the leaves to serve)
½ cup/10g mint leaves, finely
   chopped, plus a few extra
   leaves to serve
1½ tbsp fish sauce
1 tbsp granulated sugar
½ cup/100g leftover cooked rice
1 lb 2 oz/500g ground pork
5 tbsp/75ml vegetable oil, for frying
salt and ground white pepper

Nuoc cham
2 garlic cloves, roughly chopped
1 small red bird's-eye chile, roughly
   sliced
1 large mild red chile, roughly sliced
¼ tsp flaked sea salt
2 tbsp roughly chopped palm sugar
   (or granulated sugar)
2 tbsp lime juice
¼ cup/60ml fish sauce
¼ cup/60ml rice wine vinegar

To serve
1 small iceberg lettuce, separated
   into leaves/cups
½ cucumber, thinly sliced
   (1 cup/150g)

Versions of these meatballs appear all over Vietnam and Thailand, usually skewered and grilled over an open flame. Delicious though they are, our pan-fried version removes the need for either skewers or an open flame. It also allows us to eat them with our hands in lettuce cups, which we love.

Playing around: These are lovely as a group snack, with everyone helping themselves and making up their own wraps. They also work well served with some blanched rice vermicelli noodles in a bowl, tossed with the salad, along with the herbs and with the nuoc cham dipping sauce poured over the top.

Serves 4

Place the first six ingredients for the meatballs in a medium bowl, with ¼ teaspoon of salt and ¾ teaspoon of ground white pepper. Stir well to combine, until the sugar dissolves, then add the rice and meat. Mix well, then form into roughly 1 oz/30g balls—you should make around 24. Flatten them slightly and place on a baking sheet. Keep in the fridge until ready to cook.

Next make the nuoc cham. Put the garlic, chiles, and flaked salt into a mortar and pestle and pound to form a wet paste—the chiles won't break down completely. Add the remaining ingredients, then transfer to a screw-top jar. Shake vigorously, and keep in the fridge until ready to serve. If you don't have a mortar and pestle, place all the ingredients in a food processor and pulse until the chiles and garlic are broken up.

When ready to serve, prepare the salad platter by stacking the lettuce cups on the side of the plate and strewing the cucumber and reserved herbs around. Pour the nuoc cham into small serving bowls so each person has their own little dipping sauce.

Put half the oil into a large frying pan and place on medium-high heat. Add half the patties and cook for 4–5 minutes, turning them halfway, until cooked through. Add the rest of the oil to the pan and continue with the remaining batch. Transfer to the salad platter and serve warm or at room temperature.

Comfort veg

Caponata with celery and burrata

3 **eggplants**, skin peeled in
   alternating strips, flesh cut into
   roughly 1-inch/2½cm cubes
   (9½ cups/800g)
9 **tbsp/135ml olive oil**
4–5 **celery stalks** (8 oz/225g):
   6⅓ oz/180g cut into ½-inch/1½cm
   dice, the rest thinly sliced at an
   angle, reserving any leaves
1 **large onion**, cut into roughly
   1-inch/2½cm dice (1⅓ cups/200g)
2 **garlic cloves**, crushed to a paste
¾ **tsp dried oregano**
⅛ **tsp chile flakes**
1 x 14-oz/400g **can of diced
   tomatoes**
1 **tbsp tomato paste**
1 **tbsp honey**
scant 1 cup/120g **pitted
   Kalamata olives**
½ cup/50g **small capers**
3 **tbsp red wine vinegar**
¾ cup/15g **basil leaves**
10½ oz/300g **burrata**
salt and black pepper

Caponata is the quintessential Sicilian dish, in which small cubes of fried eggplant and other vegetables sit in a sweet-sour salad—or is it a relish?!—with tangy capers, olives, celery, sometimes raisins, lots of olive oil, and tomato sauce. It feels like one of those recipes we should all be inheriting from someone-who-knows-someone who knows the Sicilian granny who makes the best caponata in town. People swear by their own versions—the addition of the pine nuts, for example, the raisins, cinnamon, or herbs—as we do ours. It's less sweet than is often found, and we prefer to roast (rather than fry) the eggplant. It pairs wonderfully with burrata, but also works really well with some jammy soft-boiled eggs, pulled apart like the burrata, dotted on top just before serving, and crusty bread or toast alongside. *Pictured on page 88.*

Getting ahead: The caponata can be made up to 3 days ahead and kept in the fridge. Just bring it back to room temperature before serving.

Serves 6, as a starter

Preheat the oven to 450°F.

Toss the eggplants with 2 tablespoons of the oil, 1 teaspoon of salt, and a good grind of pepper, then spread out on a large parchment-lined baking sheet. Roast for about 30 minutes, until golden, then remove from the oven and set aside.

Put 5 tbsp/75ml of oil into a medium sauté pan, for which you have a lid, and place on medium heat. Add the diced celery and the onion and cook for 10 minutes, stirring from time to time, until softened but not taking on too much color. Add the garlic, oregano, chile flakes, ¾ teaspoon of salt, and a good grind of pepper and cook for 2–3 minutes, stirring frequently. Add the tomatoes, tomato paste, and honey. Bring to a simmer, then cook on medium-low heat for about 10 minutes, partially covered, stirring from time to time. Add the olives, capers, vinegar, and roasted eggplants and cook, partially covered, over low heat for about 20 minutes, still stirring from time to time, until the vegetables are soft and the sauce has thickened and lightly coats the vegetables. Remove from the heat, stir in the basil, and set aside to cool.

When ready to serve, spoon the caponata into a shallow serving bowl. Gently pull apart the burrata and place big chunks on top. Mix the sliced celery with the remaining 2 tablespoons of oil and spoon on top, followed by the reserved celery leaves and a grind of pepper. Serve at room temperature.

Creamy eggplant Caesar dip

2 eggplants, pricked a few times with a fork (about 1 lb 2 oz/515g)
3 green onions (⅓ cup/30g)
5¼ oz/150g Padrón peppers
⅓ cup/80ml olive oil
6 garlic cloves, thinly sliced
6 anchovies (¾ oz/20g)
1 lemon: finely shave the peel to get 3 strips, then juice to get 1½ tsp
⅓ cup/75g plain yogurt
2 tsp English mustard
1½ oz/40g parmesan, finely grated (⅓ cup)
salt and black pepper

Maple mustard croutons
3 thick slices of sourdough, crusts removed and bread torn into roughly 1½-inch/4cm pieces (3½ cups/140g)
2½ tbsp olive oil
2 tsp English mustard
2 tsp maple syrup
1 tbsp sesame seeds

To serve
3½ oz/100g radishes
2 little gem lettuces, large outer leaves discarded, each lettuce cut lengthwise into quarters
1 small radicchio, leaves pulled apart

The starting point for this dip was the eggplant cream in Yotam and Ixta Belfrage's book *Flavor*. With its Dijon mustard and lemon juice, it always reminded us of a Caesar salad. Here we add anchovies and parmesan to take it one step closer to the Caesar salad theme. *Pictured on page 89.*

Getting ahead: The eggplant cream keeps well in the fridge for 3 days. Tara has a batch at the ready in her fridge on a near-permanent basis, ready to spoon alongside most meals. No chicken salad is complete without!

Serves 4

Heat a griddle pan until very hot, add the eggplants and cook for about 45 minutes, turning throughout, so that all sides are completely charred and collapsing. Transfer to a colander and set aside. Add the green onions to the pan and cook for a couple of minutes, until charred in places. Roughly chop and set aside. Finally, in a small bowl, toss the Padrón peppers in 1 teaspoon of the oil, a pinch of salt, and a couple of grinds of pepper. Add them to the griddle and cook for 3–4 minutes, until charred and blistered in places. Set aside.

Once the eggplants are cool enough to handle, remove and discard the skins and let the flesh drain for about 20 minutes—it should weigh about 4½ oz/130g. Set aside.

Meanwhile, put the remaining 5 tbsp/75ml of oil into a small frying pan, along with the garlic, anchovies, and lemon strips, and place on medium heat. Once it comes to a simmer, decrease the heat to medium-low and cook for about 12 minutes, until the garlic and lemon are soft but have not taken on any color. Remove from the heat and set aside to cool.

Preheat the oven to 350°F.

Put the pieces of sourdough on a parchment-lined baking sheet. Whisk together the olive oil, mustard, and maple syrup and pour over the sourdough. Sprinkle with the sesame seeds, along with ¼ teaspoon of salt and a good grind of pepper, and toss well. Bake for about 25 minutes, stirring once or twice, until golden and crisp. Set aside.

Put the drained eggplant into the small bowl of a food processor with the green onions, yogurt, mustard, ¼ cup/25g of the parmesan, the lemon juice, ½ teaspoon of salt, and a good grind of pepper. Add the garlic-anchovy-lemon oil (including the strips of lemon) and blitz until smooth. Transfer to a bowl and keep in the fridge until ready to serve.

Arrange the croutons, Padrón peppers, radishes, lettuce leaves, and radicchio on a large platter and serve alongside the dip. The remaining parmesan can go in a separate little bowl, for the crudités to get a second snowy coating, or can just be sprinkled on top of the vegetables.

Silky zucchini and salmon salad

¼ cup/30g pine nuts

Quick-pickled shallots
2 large shallots, thinly sliced
 (⅔ cup/80g)
⅓ cup/80ml lemon juice
1 tsp salt

Zucchini
6 large zucchini, coarsely
 grated (about 10 cups/1kg)
¼ cup/60ml olive oil
salt and black pepper

Salmon
4 x 4½ oz/130g salmon fillets,
 skin on
1½ tbsp olive oil
4 cups/80g arugula

This is a dish that is more than the sum of its parts. It's the way the zucchini are cooked—well salted and cooked low and slow in plenty of olive oil—that makes them a rich and silky star. The end result is as good for a summer party lunch as it is for a simple midweek meal.

Getting ahead: Both the salmon and the zucchini can be made a few hours ahead of eating, ready to assemble before serving. The zucchini last a couple of days in the fridge, so make more than you need! The color will dull a little but all the flavor will still be there.

Serves 4

Preheat the oven to 350°F.

Spread the pine nuts on a baking sheet and roast for 10–12 minutes, until lightly toasted. Remove from the oven and set aside.

Place the shallots and lemon juice in a small bowl or jar, along with the salt. Stir to combine and dissolve the salt, then set aside.

Place the zucchini in a large bowl and mix in 2 teaspoons of salt. It will seem like a lot, but much of it gets released when the liquid is squeezed out. Tip the zucchini into a colander, sitting on top of a mixing bowl (or in the sink) to catch the juices. Let rest for about 30 minutes, then squeeze firmly to remove excess juice—you should get around ¾ cup plus 2 tbsp/200ml of liquid, which can be discarded.

Put the oil into a medium saucepan and place on medium heat. Add the drained zucchini and cook for about 5 minutes. Decrease the heat to low and cook for 15 minutes—stirring regularly and adding a good crack of pepper during the last 5 minutes of cooking—until the zucchini turn into a loose, silky paste.

Increase the oven temperature to 400°F.

Place the salmon on a parchment-lined baking sheet, skin side down. Drizzle with the oil and season with ½ teaspoon of salt (in total) and a good grind of pepper. Bake for about 8 minutes, or until the fillets are just cooked through (or a couple of minutes longer, if you prefer), then remove from the oven. Set aside for about 15 minutes—the salad is best eaten warm or at room temperature (rather than piping hot).

When ready to serve, scatter the arugula over the bottom of a large serving plate. Spoon about three-quarters of the zucchini on top, then, breaking it up as you go, add the salmon. Spoon the remaining zucchini around the salmon and gently scatter the shallots over the salad. Sprinkle with the toasted pine nuts and serve.

Rice vermicelli with turmeric fish, dill, and green onion

1 lb 5 oz/600g cod (or other firm white fish) fillets, sliced into 2-inch/5cm strips
2 tbsp peanut (or sunflower) oil
7 oz/200g dried rice vermicelli noodles
12–14 green onions, green and white parts cut into 2-inch/5cm lengths (slice the white stems lengthwise if they are very thick) (1¾ cups/125g)
1¾ oz/50g dill sprigs, tough stalks removed but kept as sprigs
2 bird's-eye chiles, thinly sliced
⅓ cup/40g roasted salted peanuts, roughly chopped
salt

Marinade
1 large shallot, roughly chopped (¼ cup/45g)
¾ oz/20g ginger, peeled and roughly chopped
2 garlic cloves, roughly chopped
1 tbsp fish sauce
1 tbsp peanut (or sunflower) oil
1 tsp ground turmeric
1 tsp medium or hot curry powder

Nuoc cham
2 garlic cloves, roughly chopped
1 small red bird's-eye chile, roughly sliced
1 large mild red chile, roughly sliced
¼ tsp flaked sea salt
2 tbsp roughly chopped palm sugar (or granulated sugar)
2 tbsp lime juice
¼ cup/60ml fish sauce
¼ cup/60ml rice wine vinegar

This is one of those back-pocket recipes that, if you've made the marinade and dipping sauce in advance, feels pretty much like fast food when it comes to cooking. The noodles are near-instant, and the green onions and dill take as little time to chop and wilt as the fish takes to broil. A total treat on the table in 15 minutes. *Pictured on page 94.*

Getting ahead: The paste for the marinade can be made up to 3 days ahead and kept refrigerated. Don't mix it with the fish more than an hour before broiling, though—if you do, the fish will start to break down.

Serves 4

Put all the ingredients for the marinade into the small bowl of a food processor. Blend to form a smooth paste, then transfer to a medium bowl. Add the fish, toss gently to coat, then keep in the fridge, covered, for about (but not much longer than) 30 minutes.

Meanwhile, make the nuoc cham. Put the garlic, chiles, and flaked salt into a mortar and pestle and pound to form a wet paste: the chiles won't break down completely. Add the remaining ingredients, then transfer to a screw-top jar. Shake vigorously, and keep in the fridge until ready to serve. If you don't have a mortar and pestle, place all the ingredients in a food processor and pulse until the chiles and garlic are broken up.

When ready to serve, preheat the oven broiler to its highest setting and position a rack in the upper third of the oven. Cover a large baking sheet with foil and brush lightly with 1 tablespoon of the oil. Spread the fish out on the sheet and broil for about 8 minutes, carefully turning it over halfway through so that both sides are golden brown. Switch off the broiler and place the sheet on the lowest rack of the oven to keep the fish warm. Leave the oven door ajar.

While the fish is cooking, put the noodles into a large bowl and cover with just-boiled water. When softened (3–5 minutes, depending on the brand), drain in a colander and set aside.

Put the remaining 1 tablespoon of oil into a large frying pan (or wok) and place over medium-high heat. When hot, add the green onions and ⅛ teaspoon of salt. Stir-fry for 1 minute, then add the dill sprigs and toss and fry for another 30 seconds or so, until they just wilt and turn bright green. Remove the pan from the heat, leaving the greens in the pan.

When ready to serve, divide the rice noodles among four bowls. Top with the fish, followed by the green onions and dill. Pour 2–3 tablespoons of the nuoc cham over the top, then scatter some sliced chiles and chopped peanuts. Serve warm or at room temperature, with the remaining nuoc cham in a bowl for everyone to help themselves.

Silky steamed eggplant

1 large eggplant, peeled
   (about 12¾ oz/360g)
1 tbsp Chinkiang (or malt) vinegar
2 tbsp Shaoxing wine
1 tbsp light brown sugar
1 tbsp light soy sauce
4 tsp sesame oil
2 tbsp peanut (or sunflower) oil
3 green onions, finely sliced
   (⅓ cup/30g)
⅓ oz/10g ginger, peeled and
   julienned
1 small, hot red chile, finely sliced
   (seeded if you like less heat)
2 garlic cloves, finely sliced
1 tsp toasted sesame seeds
¼ cup/5g cilantro leaves
1–2 tbsp tahini
salt

For those who are used to cooking eggplants "the Ottolenghi way" (either in a hot oven, with plenty of olive oil, or over an open flame, for plenty of charring), steaming them will be a bit of a revelation. No oil, for starters, and then a 25-minute steam, with the most silky soft of results. We couldn't resist the addition of a bit of tahini, though, drizzled over at the end—the creaminess works so well. This is a vegan meal in itself, served warm with jasmine rice, or it works at room temperature, as part of a spread. *Pictured on page 94.*

Playing around: The soy dressing is also really good drizzled on a slab of cold silken tofu if you are looking for something else to pair it with.

Serves 2, or 4 as a side

Slice the eggplant lengthwise into ½-inch/1½cm-thick slices and then again into ½-inch/1½cm strips. Place in a colander (set over a bowl or in the sink), sprinkle with 2 teaspoons of salt, and let drain. After 10 minutes, rinse the eggplant to remove the salt, then drain well and spread out on a clean tea towel to dry.

Once dry, arrange the eggplant in a stainless-steel steamer and steam for 25 minutes, until a knife inserted goes in really easily—there should be no resistance.

Meanwhile, put the vinegar, Shaoxing wine, sugar, soy sauce, and 1 teaspoon of the sesame oil into a small saucepan. Stir to combine, bring to a simmer on medium heat, and simmer for 1–2 minutes, until slightly syrupy. Remove from the heat and set aside. When the eggplants are ready—and still warm—pour the syrup all over them and set aside.

Wipe the small saucepan clean with paper towels—there is no need to wash it—then add the peanut oil and the remaining 1 tablespoon of sesame oil. Place on medium heat and, when hot, add the green onions, ginger, chile, and garlic. Cook for 3 minutes, until slightly softened and smelling aromatic. Pour immediately onto the eggplants and sprinkle with the sesame seeds and cilantro. Finish with a drizzle of tahini.

Vegan creamed spinach and artichokes

3 small, hot red chiles: 2 sliced into thin rounds (seeds included), 1 seeded and finely chopped

2 tbsp lemon juice

7 tbsp/100ml olive oil

1 large onion, finely sliced (scant 2 cups/220g)

3 garlic cloves, crushed to a paste

¾ oz/25g cilantro, stalks finely chopped and leaves roughly chopped

scant ½ cup/100g grilled artichokes in olive oil, drained and roughly chopped

14 oz/400g frozen spinach, defrosted and well squeezed, then roughly chopped (8 oz/220g)

3 tbsp capers, roughly chopped

6 green onions, finely sliced (¾ cup/65g), plus extra to garnish

1 lb 5 oz/600g silken tofu, drained

3½ tbsp nutritional yeast flakes

1 slice of sourdough, crusts removed and bread torn into small pieces (1 cup/40g)

salt and black pepper

lemon wedges, to serve

Vegans must roll their eyes every time they hear someone's surprise that a dish that doesn't seem like it's vegan is, in fact, vegan. But, here, it's true! Make it for your vegan friends, make it for your non-vegan friends, make it for everyone, and remark upon the wonders of silken tofu and nutritional yeast flakes. Celebrating their ability to bring a cheesy, creamy depth of flavor to a vegan dish is worth risking the eye-roll for. This is a wonderfully versatile side, working as well with some rice and firm baked tofu as it does alongside a roasted chicken.

Ingredients note: We've used frozen spinach here but starting with fresh leaves also works: in order to get the 8 oz/220g required, you'll need to start with about 1 lb 5 oz/600g.

Serves 6, as a side

Place the sliced chiles in a small bowl with the lemon juice and ⅛ teaspoon salt, and set aside to pickle.

Put ¼ cup/60ml of the oil into a large, ovenproof sauté pan and place on medium heat. Add the onion and cook, stirring often, for 15–18 minutes, until soft and caramelized. Add the chopped chile, garlic, and cilantro stalks and cook for 2 minutes. Add the artichokes, spinach, capers, and green onions, along with ½ teaspoon of salt and a good grind of pepper. Stir to combine, warm through for 1 minute, and then remove from the heat.

Preheat the broiler to 475°F (or to its highest setting).

Put the tofu into a food processor, along with 3 tablespoons of the yeast flakes, ½ teaspoon of salt, and a good grind of pepper. Blitz until smooth, then, with the motor running, slowly stream in 2 tablespoons of olive oil until glossy.

Add the tofu mix to the spinach mixture and stir well to combine. Smooth the top and clean the sides of the pan.

In a small bowl, mix together the pieces of bread with the remaining ½ tablespoon of yeast flakes and the remaining 2 tsp/10ml of olive oil. Sprinkle evenly over the spinach and place under the hot broiler for about 6 minutes, until golden brown. Sprinkle with the extra green onions, the cilantro leaves, and the pickled, drained chiles. Serve hot or just warm, with lemon wedges alongside for squeezing.

All-purpose mushroom ragù

½ oz/15g dried porcini mushrooms
1 cup/240ml boiling water
1 lb 14 oz/850g fresh mixed
  mushrooms, small ones left
  whole, larger ones roughly
  torn in two
¼ cup/50g unsalted butter
2 tbsp olive oil
2 onions, thinly sliced
  (2⅔ cups/320g)
½ large celery root, peeled and
  cut into ¾-inch/2cm chunks
  (2⅓ cups/360g)
4 garlic cloves, crushed to a paste
1¼ tsp Urfa chile flakes
  (or ½ tsp regular chile flakes)
1½ tbsp white miso
1 preserved lemon, quartered,
  flesh and seeds discarded, skin
  cut into thin strips (½ oz/15g)
1½ tbsp sherry (or red wine) vinegar
1½ tbsp all-purpose flour
1⅔ cups/400ml chicken
  (or vegetable) stock
2 tbsp heavy cream
⅓ oz/10g tarragon, leaves roughly
  chopped, plus a few extra leaves
  to garnish
salt

A pre-made batch of this ragù is a bit of a secret kitchen weapon. Knowing that it's there, in the fridge or freezer, means that you are only ever minutes away from the most satisfying of meals. Stir it into pasta, top it with mash for an impromptu veggie shepherd's pie, serve it alongside polenta or rice, or just eat a bowl of it as it is, with a crisp green salad alongside.

Getting ahead: This will keep for up to 3 days in the fridge.

Serves 4

Preheat the oven to 400°F.

Place the dried mushrooms in a small liquid measuring cup and pour in the boiling water. Set aside to soak for 30 minutes, then drain over a bowl (keeping the liquid to use later), roughly chop, and set aside.

Meanwhile, place the fresh mushrooms on a large parchment-lined baking sheet (as they are—no need to season or toss in oil) and roast for 25 minutes, giving them a stir halfway through, until the mushrooms have shriveled significantly and have lost a lot of moisture. Remove from the oven and set aside.

Put the butter and oil into a large sauté pan, for which you have a lid, and place on medium-high heat. Add the onions, celery root, and ½ teaspoon of salt and cook for 15–20 minutes, stirring frequently, until nicely caramelized. Add the garlic, roasted mushrooms, and chopped mushrooms and cook for 3 minutes, stirring. Add the Urfa, miso, preserved lemon, and vinegar and cook for 30 seconds or so. Stir in the flour and cook for 30 seconds, then add the stock, the reserved mushroom-soaking liquid, and ¾ teaspoon of salt. Bring to a simmer, then decrease the heat to low and cook for 25 minutes, covered, until the celery root is tender, but still holding its shape. Remove the lid, stir in the cream, and let it bubble away for 5 minutes.

Remove the pan from the heat, stir in the tarragon, and serve with the extra tarragon leaves sprinkled over the top.

Butter beans with roasted cherry tomatoes

1 lb 2 oz/500g cherry tomatoes
5 tbsp plus 2 tsp/85ml olive oil
1 onion, finely diced (1 cup/150g)
2 garlic cloves, thinly sliced
2 tsp dried oregano
2 tsp thyme leaves, roughly
  chopped, plus a few whole
  thyme leaves to garnish
1 tsp fennel seeds, toasted and
  lightly crushed
1 fresh bay leaf
⅓ cup/80ml dry white wine
2 tsp smoked paprika
1 x 25-oz/700g jar of good-quality
  butter (lima) beans, drained and
  rinsed
salt and black pepper

To serve
¼ cup/75g Greek yogurt
thick slices of sourdough (or any
  crusty) bread, toasted (optional)

Source the larger butter beans (lima beans), or judiones, for this, if you can. They're softer, more buttery, and much creamier than the smaller ones (that come in a can). This dish works well as part of a mezze spread, or can be eaten as it is, with something like crumbled feta or olives on top.

Keeping notes: Once made, the beans keep for up to 3 days in the fridge: just bring them back to room temperature before serving. The crispy tomato skins are a great thing to have around as well, to add to salads and pasta dishes. The recipe comes from a restaurant called Bar Rochford in Canberra, Australia, where they're served with fresh green beans. They keep for 1 week in a sealed jar.

Serves 4

Preheat the oven to 450°F.

Toss the tomatoes with 2 teaspoons of the oil and spread them on a parchment-lined baking sheet. Roast for 20 minutes, until the skins have loosened and the tomatoes are soft and have shrunk a little. Remove from the oven and transfer the tomatoes, along with all their juices, to a shallow bowl to cool.

Re-line the baking sheet with a fresh sheet of parchment paper and decrease the oven temperature to 250°F.

Once cool enough to handle, pinch the skins off the tomatoes and place the skins on the lined baking sheet. Return the sheet to the oven for about 45 minutes, until the skins are dry and crisp, giving them a good stir a couple of times during baking. Set the skinless tomatoes aside.

Put the remaining 5 tbsp/75ml of oil into a medium saucepan and place on medium heat. Add the onion, garlic, oregano, thyme, fennel seeds, and bay leaf and cook for 10–12 minutes, until the onion has softened but has not taken on too much color. Add the wine, simmer for 2 minutes to reduce, then add the paprika. Cook for 1 minute, then add the reserved tomato flesh, along with 1 teaspoon of salt. Simmer gently for about 15 minutes, stirring often so that the tomatoes break down. Add the beans and a good grind of pepper and stir to combine. Cook for a couple of minutes, just to warm through, then remove from the heat. Spread the yogurt over a serving plate and then pile the beans on top. Crumble the dried tomato skins over the top, finish with a sprinkling of thyme leaves, and serve with the toasted sourdough (if you like).

Green beans on toast

7 tbsp/100ml olive oil
2 shallots, thinly sliced (½ cup/75g)
4 garlic cloves, thinly sliced
10½ oz/300g French green
   beans, trimmed
10½ oz/300g runner beans,
   trimmed and cut on the diagonal
   into ¾-inch/2cm strips
3½ oz/100g cherry tomatoes, halved
1½ tsp dried oregano
½ tsp chipotle chile flakes
1½ tbsp lemon juice
1½ tbsp fresh oregano, roughly
   chopped, plus extra leaves
   to garnish
½ cup/10g basil leaves, roughly
   torn, plus extra to garnish
3½ oz/100g feta, roughly crumbled
½ cup/100g mascarpone
4 thick slices of sourdough,
   toasted (7–8 oz/200–225g)
salt and black pepper

Cooking green beans like this—in plenty of olive oil and for quite a long time—makes them meltingly soft and incredibly comforting. It's the way they are cooked across Turkey, where they're usually eaten warm (rather than piping hot) or at room temperature, as part of a spread. A batch of these cooked beans is one of Verena's fridge staples—they keep in the fridge for up to 3 days—and Claudine, who tests our recipes at home, says she is never cooking beans any other way again!

Serves 4

Put the oil into a large sauté pan, for which you have a lid, and place on medium heat. Add the shallots, garlic, beans, tomatoes, dried oregano, chile flakes, 1 tablespoon of the lemon juice, ¾ teaspoon of salt, and a good grind of pepper. Stir to combine, and cook, covered, for 35–40 minutes, stirring from time to time, until the beans have really softened (and lost all their vibrant green color) and the shallots have started to stick and caramelize in places. Take off the heat, add the fresh oregano, basil, and the remaining ½ tablespoon of lemon juice, and stir to combine. Set aside until ready to serve.

Meanwhile, combine the feta and mascarpone in a small bowl and mash together with a fork—don't worry about trying to make it smooth—a rough/curd-like texture works well. Set aside.

Divide the feta-mascarpone mix among the slices of toast and, using the back of a spoon, smear it all over. Arrange the beans on top, along with their oily juices. Scatter the reserved oregano and basil leaves and serve.

Slow-roasted celery root with Gorgonzola cream

⅔ cup/160ml olive oil
2 lemons: thinly shave the zest to get about 6 strips, then juice to get 3 tbsp/45ml
6 garlic cloves, lightly smashed
1 tbsp cumin seeds, roughly crushed
1 large (or 2 small) celery root(s), peeled and cut into 6–8 wedges (2 lb 2 oz/1kg)
scant 1½ cups/200g roasted red bell peppers (from a jar), drained
⅓ cup/50g blanched hazelnuts, roasted, plus 1 tbsp/10g extra, roughly chopped, to garnish
2 tsp pomegranate molasses
1 tsp Aleppo chile flakes
1 tbsp red wine vinegar
1¾ oz/50g Gorgonzola
⅓ cup/80g sour cream
¼ oz/5g chives, finely chopped
¼ cup/5g parsley leaves, to garnish
salt and black pepper

Slow-cooking celery root in oil gives it a wonderfully soft, buttery texture—the result is incredibly soft and comforting to eat. The sauce is somewhere between a muhammara dip (without the breadcrumbs) and Romesco sauce (made with hazelnuts instead of the traditional almonds). Serve warm or at room temperature either as a standalone dish or as a side to something like a roasted chicken.

Getting ahead: The Gorgonzola cream can be made up to 2 days ahead and kept in the fridge. If you want to make more of this, it's a wonderful addition to a baked potato. Once assembled, the dish doesn't benefit from sitting around.

Serves 4

Preheat the oven to 375°F.

Put the oil, lemon strips and juice, garlic, and 2 teaspoons of crushed cumin seeds into a 9 x 13-inch/23 x 33cm baking pan, along with 1 teaspoon of salt. Stir to combine, then add the celery root wedges. Turn to coat them in the oil, then arrange them in a single layer in the pan, lying flat on their sides. Cover the pan tightly with foil and bake for 1½ hours, turning the celery root over halfway through. Increase the temperature to 400°F, remove the foil, and return to the oven for 30 minutes, until golden and tender. Transfer the wedges to a serving plate and set aside.

Measure out 6 tbsp/90ml of the cooking oil in the pan and put this into a food processor. Fish out the garlic cloves and lemon peel and add these as well, along with the bell peppers, hazelnuts, pomegranate molasses, chile flakes, vinegar, the remaining 1 teaspoon of cumin seeds, ½ teaspoon of salt, and a good grind of pepper. Blitz until smooth.

Mash the Gorgonzola with the sour cream, then add the chives, ⅛ teaspoon of salt, and some pepper. Keep in the fridge until ready to use.

Spoon about two-thirds of the red pepper sauce over the celery root wedges and dollop spoonfuls of the Gorgonzola cream in between the wedges. Sprinkle with the parsley and remaining hazelnuts. Serve with any remaining sauce and/or Gorgonzola cream alongside.

Roasted carrots with curry leaf dukkah

2 lb 2 oz/1kg bunch of thin
  carrots, trimmed to remove all
  but ½ inch/1cm of the green tops
  and peeled (1 lb 10 oz/750g);
  if starting with thicker carrots,
  slice them in half lengthwise
2 tsp lemon juice
1 cup plus 2 tbsp/320g Greek
  yogurt (or labneh), to serve
salt and black pepper

*Curry leaf dukkah: a mix of any/all
of the four nuts (just keep the total
weight of 3½ oz/100g the same)*
3 tbsp/25g cashews
3 tbsp/25g raw (aka skinless)
  peanuts
3 tbsp/25g blanched almonds
3 tbsp/25g blanched hazelnuts
1 tbsp coriander seeds
¼ cup/60ml vegetable oil
⅓ oz/10g curry leaves
⅓ cup/25g store-bought crispy
  fried shallots
½ tsp chile flakes
¼ tsp salt

On vacation in Sri Lanka a few years ago, Helen got very into the little pot of dukkah mix that was often on her table in the evening. So into it was she that there soon appeared two pots each night. On the last night of her vacation, the chef—Madhura Geethanjana—scribbled the recipe down on Helen's napkin, calling it his "nut crumble." It's such a lovely image and act of sharing—a recipe being written on a napkin, continuing its journey. Dukkah keeps well in the fridge for 5 days (or longer in the freezer), so make more than you need. It's lovely sprinkled over all sorts of things: soups, roasted vegetables, chicken (see page 128), grilled fish, leafy salads.

Serves 4–6, as a side

Preheat the oven to 350°F.

First, make the dukkah. Spread the nuts and coriander seeds on a parchment-lined baking sheet and roast for 8–10 minutes. Remove from the oven and set aside to cool.

Increase the oven temperature to 450°F.

Put the oil into a small frying pan and place on medium-low heat. Add the curry leaves—stand back: they will splutter!—and cook for about 30 seconds, until the leaves are crisp. Drain in a small sieve placed over a small bowl, keeping the flavored oil. Tip the leaves out onto a plate lined with paper towels and set aside to cool. Once cool, set about 10 leaves aside and transfer the remainder to a food processor. Add all the roasted nuts and coriander seeds, along with the crispy fried shallots, chile flakes, and salt. Pulse to form a rough crumble and transfer to a small bowl until ready to use.

Spread the carrots out on a large parchment-lined baking sheet and drizzle with 3 tablespoons of the reserved curry leaf oil. Sprinkle with ¾ teaspoon of salt and a few cracks of pepper, then drizzle with the lemon juice. Toss lightly and roast for about 30 minutes, until the carrots are cooked and slightly charred at the edges. Remove from the oven and set aside for at least 5 minutes—they want to be served just warm or at room temperature.

When ready to serve, mix the yogurt with ¼ teaspoon of salt and spread it over the bottom of a plate. Arrange the carrots on top, then sprinkle 3–4 tablespoons of the dukkah directly on top of the carrots. Scatter the reserved fried curry leaves on top, spoon the remaining curry leaf oil over the top, and serve.

Butter-braised kohlrabi with olive chimichurri

¼ cup/50g unsalted butter
2½ lb/1.2kg kohlrabi (about 4),
    peeled and cut into ½-inch/1½cm
    batons (1 lb 15 oz/885g)
1 tsp lemon juice
½ cup/130g crème fraîche

Chimichurri
7 tbsp plus 1 tsp/105ml olive oil
¼ cup/40g pumpkin seeds
⅓ cup/50g pitted green olives
1 green jalapeño, seeded and
    roughly chopped
1 garlic clove, crushed to a paste
½ oz/15g parsley, roughly chopped,
    plus extra leaves, to garnish
¼ oz/5g chives, chopped
1½ tbsp capers
1 tbsp lemon juice
1 tsp Dijon mustard
1 tsp maple syrup
salt and black pepper

We had you at butter-braised, right? Don't get lost at kohlrabi! We love this vegetable in all its forms—raw or roasted, for example—but cooking it as we do here makes it unusually silky and melt-in-the-mouth. Other root vegetables also work well: carrot, for example, rutabaga, or turnip. Serve it as it is, with some bread alongside to make it into a meal, or as part of a spread.

Getting ahead: The chimichurri can be made a day ahead and kept refrigerated: it will start to discolor but will still taste good. It's a lovely addition to all sorts of roasted veg, meat, and fish.

Serves 4

First make the chimichurri. Put 1 teaspoon of the oil into a large sauté pan, for which you have a lid, and place on medium-high heat. Add the pumpkin seeds and ⅛ teaspoon of salt, and cook for about 5 minutes, stirring a few times, until the seeds are well toasted and starting to pop. Transfer half the seeds to the small bowl of a food processor and put the other half on a plate lined with paper towels.

Add the remaining ingredients for the chimichurri to the seeds in the processor, along with the remaining 7 tbsp/100ml of olive oil. Add ⅛ teaspoon of salt and a good grind of pepper and blitz until finely chopped. Set aside (or keep in the fridge) until ready to serve.

Put the butter into the sauté pan and add the kohlrabi, along with ¾ teaspoon of salt and a good grind of pepper. Place on high heat, covered, then—as soon as the butter starts to bubble—give everything a good stir. Decrease the heat to medium and cook for 15–20 minutes, still covered, stirring occasionally at the beginning and then more toward the end, until the kohlrabi has fully cooked and caramelized in places but still holds its shape. Stir in the lemon juice and set aside.

Put the crème fraîche into a small bowl and season with ⅛ teaspoon of salt and plenty of pepper. Spread out on a large serving plate and arrange the kohlrabi on top. Spoon on some of the chimichurri and scatter the remaining toasted pumpkin seeds. Garnish with the parsley leaves and serve with the rest of the chimichurri alongside.

Charred sprouts with olive oil and lemon

2 lb 2 oz/1kg Brussels sprouts, trimmed and halved lengthwise

12 garlic cloves, peeled and left whole

1 small, hot green chile, pierced a few times with a small sharp knife (½ oz/15g)

8 tbsp/120ml olive oil

2 onions, finely chopped (2 cups/300g)

1 cup/240ml vegetable (or chicken) stock

2 lemons: finely grate the zest to get 2 tsp, then juice to get 3 tbsp

⅓ oz/10g tarragon leaves, roughly chopped

⅓ oz/10g dill fronds, roughly chopped

⅓ oz/10g parsley, roughly chopped

1¼ oz/35g preserved lemon (1–2), flesh and seeds discarded, skin julienned

salt and black pepper

Is it possible to write a recipe for Brussels sprouts and *not* say that this is the one to convert all sprout-doubters? We suspect not! But this *is* the one! The combination of charring and then slow-braising the sprouts makes them so very soft and sweet. The lemon and herbs then do their job to make the dish both vibrant and comforting.

Getting ahead: These can be made in advance, if you want to get ahead (or even the day before). Simply hold back on the fresh herbs and stir these in just before serving.

Serves 6, as a side

Place a large sauté pan, for which you have a lid, on high heat. Once smoking, add a quarter of the sprouts and cook for about 5 minutes, tossing the pan occasionally, until they are charred in places. Transfer to a baking sheet and continue in batches with the remaining sprouts. Add the garlic and chile to the pan and cook in the same way, until charred all over—about 5 minutes—then add to the sheet with the sprouts. Set the pan aside to cool slightly.

Add 6 tbsp/90ml of the oil to the pan and place on medium-high heat. Once hot, add the onions and cook for about 10 minutes, stirring occasionally, until soft and golden brown. Add the charred sprouts, garlic and chile, the stock, 1½ teaspoons of salt, and a good grind of black pepper. Bring to a simmer, lower the heat to medium-low, and cook for about 20 minutes, covered, until the sprouts are very soft. Stir in the lemon zest and juice.

Meanwhile, put the herbs, preserved lemon, the remaining 2 tablespoons of oil, ¼ teaspoon of salt, and plenty of pepper into a small bowl and mix to combine.

When ready to serve, stir the herb mixture into the sprouts, to just incorporate. Serve warm, or at room temperature.

Roasted beets with tarragon and walnut tarator

2 bunches of beets (2 lb 2 oz/1kg), peeled and quartered (larger beets cut into 6 wedges) (1¾ lb/800g)
2 tbsp olive oil
salt and black pepper

Tarragon dressing
1½ tsp Dijon mustard
1½ tbsp red wine vinegar
½ tsp granulated sugar
¼ cup/60ml olive oil
⅓ oz/10g tarragon leaves, half finely chopped and the remainder to garnish

Tarator
3 slices of soft white bread (2½ oz/75g), crusts removed and bread roughly torn
2 tbsp lemon juice
8–9 tbsp/120–135ml water
1 cup/95g walnuts
3 garlic cloves, peeled and left whole
¼ cup/60ml olive oil
½ cup/10g mint leaves: set aside just a few leaves to garnish and finely chop the rest

There's always something very comforting about roasting root vegetables. There's just so much sweetness there, ready to be coaxed out through long and slow cooking. So too with beets. A few pieces of rindless goat cheese, dotted on top (either instead of or along with the tarator), also work really well. Serve with some warm pita or toasted sourdough, or as a side to grilled, oily fish.

Storing notes: Both the tarragon dressing and the tarator keep for 3 days in the fridge. You'll make a bit more tarator than you need here, but it's lovely to have around as a dip for crudités or to spoon over other roast veg, or chicken or fish.

Serves 4

Preheat the oven to 400°F.

Place the beet wedges on a large parchment-lined baking sheet, about 16 x 12 inches/40 x 30cm. Drizzle with the oil and sprinkle with ¾ teaspoon of salt and a good grind of pepper. Toss to combine, then roast for about 50 minutes, stirring halfway through, until the beets are tender.

Meanwhile, place all the ingredients for the tarragon dressing in a jar, along with ¼ teaspoon of salt and some pepper. Shake to combine and set aside.

When the beets are cooked, transfer them to a mixing bowl and, while still warm, pour three-quarters of the dressing over them. Toss gently to combine and set aside to cool to room temperature.

Next, make the tarator. Put the bread, lemon juice, and ¼ cup/60ml of the water into a food processor and let rest for 2–3 minutes, until the bread is evenly moistened. Add ¾ cup/80g of the walnuts—roughly chop the rest to serve—along with the garlic, oil, ½ teaspoon of salt, and a few grinds of pepper. Process to form a smooth paste, then, with the machine still running, pour in the remaining 4–5 tbsp/60–75ml of water and process until the mix has the consistency of thick yogurt. Scrape into a medium bowl and fold in the chopped mint.

Spread half the tarator over a serving plate and place the roasted beets on top. Dollop the remaining half over the beets and spoon the remaining tarragon dressing around. Scatter with the extra tarragon, mint, and chopped walnuts, and serve.

Parmesan and black pepper roasted parsnips

1 lb 5 oz/600g parsnips,
  unpeeled, trimmed, and
  cut in half lengthwise
3 tbsp olive oil
¾ tsp freshly cracked black pepper
2 tsp maple syrup
¾ oz/20g parmesan
1 lemon, cut into 4 wedges, to serve
salt

This is a very quick and easy side dish to serve alongside a weekend (or festive) roast. Serve the parsnips as soon after roasting as possible, while they're still crispy.

Serves 4, as a side

Preheat the oven to 450°F.

Fill a medium saucepan with 6⅓ cups/1½ liters of water and bring to a boil on medium-high heat. Once boiling, salt the water with 1 tablespoon of salt. Add the parsnips and cook for 5 minutes, until the tip of a small sharp knife easily slides through but the parsnips are not falling apart.

Drain the parsnips in a colander, then transfer to a large baking sheet. Add 2 tablespoons of the oil, ½ teaspoon of the pepper, and all the maple syrup and toss gently to combine. Roast for 20 minutes, until lightly golden. Remove from the oven, finely grate half the parmesan on top, and return the sheet to the oven for a final 5 minutes, or until the parmesan is golden brown.

Spoon the remaining 1 tablespoon of oil over the top and grate the remaining parmesan on top for a snow-like effect.

Sprinkle with the remaining ¼ teaspoon of pepper and serve with the lemon wedges alongside for squeezing.

Roasted chicken and other sheet pan dishes

Roasted chicken with Auntie Pauline's marinade

1 whole chicken (3⅓–3¾ lb/1.5-1.7kg), spatchcocked (ask your butcher to do this for you or look online for a tutorial)

Marinade
5 garlic cloves, roughly chopped
½ oz/15g ginger, peeled and roughly chopped
3 tbsp light soy sauce
6–7 limes, juiced to get 7 tbsp/110ml
2 oz/55g palm sugar, roughly chopped (or light brown sugar)
5 tbsp/75ml peanut (or sunflower) oil (we like Lion peanut oil)
1¾ tsp chile powder
4 tsp ground coriander
1 oz/30g cilantro: stems roughly chopped (¾ oz/20g), leaves roughly chopped to serve (½ cup/10g)
½ cup plus 2 tbsp/150ml coconut milk
2 tbsp fish sauce
salt

As with all the best aunties, Auntie Pauline wasn't *really* an auntie. She was a friend of Helen's family who migrated to Australia from Malaysia at the same time as them. They would meet in the park, play cricket, and barbecue meat on the public grills. What was being grilled varied—chicken wings or thighs were a favorite, shrimp also—but the marinade was too good to change. Make more of the marinade than you need, if you like—it freezes well for future use. Serve this with a big, green salad, some bok choy, or the pineapple slaw suggested on the next page also works really well.

Serves 4

Place all the ingredients for the marinade in a blender or food processor, along with ¾ teaspoon of salt. Blend well, until completely smooth. Place the chicken in a large container for which you have a lid, pour in the marinade, and chill in the fridge overnight. Turn the chicken once or twice as it marinates, so that all sides get coated.

Preheat the oven to 400°F.

Place the chicken, along with half the marinade, in a roughly 9 x 13-inch/23 x 33cm baking pan. Roast for 30 minutes, basting once or twice. After 30 minutes, spoon the remaining marinade over the top and continue to cook for 25–30 minutes. Turn off the oven but leave the chicken inside to rest for 15 minutes, with the oven door slightly open.

Transfer the chicken to a serving dish and pour the roasting sauce into a serving bowl. Sprinkle the cilantro leaves over the chicken and serve, with the sauce alongside.

Chicken with Steph's spice

1 tsp **whole allspice berries** (aka pimento)
2 **bay leaves**, roughly torn
1½ tsp **chile powder**
1½ tsp **paprika**
½ tsp **ground cinnamon**
½ tsp **pumpkin pie spice**
2 tbsp **light brown sugar**
1½ tbsp **honey**
1–2 **green jalapeños**, finely chopped
1–2 **red Scotch bonnet (habanero) chiles**, finely chopped
1 **small red onion**, cut into ½-inch/1cm dice (¾ cup/100g)
3 **green onions**, finely chopped (⅓ cup/30g)
3 tbsp **olive oil**
2 lb 2 oz/1kg **chicken thighs**, bone in, skin on
2 tbsp **white wine vinegar**
salt

Steph was a Jamaican chef Helen worked with many years ago in Melbourne. A lot of time has passed since the recipe for Steph's roasted jerk-spiced meats was handed on—passed around the kitchen, scribbled down on a scrap of paper—but it's been with Helen ever since. Recipes, like postcards, flying around the world with the scent of a place on one side, scribbled greetings on the other.

We served the chicken with a simple slaw made with half a small cabbage and a quarter of a pineapple, both thinly sliced, some freshly flaked coconut, sliced jalapeño, green onion, cilantro, and mint. It's dressed with olive oil, lime juice, and maple syrup.

Serves 4, with rice and salad

Put the allspice and bay leaves into a dry pan and toast them for 1–2 minutes, until the bay leaves have blistered. Using a mortar and pestle, crush to a powder, then tip into a large bowl along with all the remaining ingredients except the chicken and vinegar. Add 1 teaspoon of salt, mix well to combine, then add the chicken. Massage well so that all the thighs are coated, then keep in the fridge, covered, for at least 6 hours (or overnight).

Half an hour before you are going to cook the chicken, take it out of the fridge, add the vinegar, and toss to combine.

Preheat the oven to 400°F.

Spread the chicken out on a large parchment-lined baking sheet, skin side up. Bake for about 45 minutes, rotating the sheet halfway through, until crisp and golden brown. Remove from the oven and allow to rest for 10 minutes before serving.

Coconut rice with peanut sauce and cucumber relish

Cucumber and ginger relish

½ cup/120ml **rice (or other white) vinegar**

6 tbsp/80g **granulated sugar**

½ **cucumber**, quartered lengthwise, seeded and thinly sliced (1⅓ cups/200g)

¾ oz/20g **ginger**, peeled and julienned

1 small, **hot red chile (or 2 bird's-eye chiles, if you like the heat)**, halved, seeded, and thinly sliced lengthwise

⅓ oz/10g **cilantro**, stems finely chopped, leaves roughly torn

1 **lime**, cut into wedges, to serve

salt

Peanut sauce

1½ cups/200g **unsalted roasted peanuts**

1 **onion**, roughly chopped (1 cup/150g)

4 **garlic cloves**, roughly chopped

3–4 **lemongrass stalks**, white part only, sliced (¼ cup/20g)

⅓ oz/10g **ginger**, peeled and sliced

¼ cup/60g **sambal oelek**

½ cup/120ml **vegetable oil**

1¾ cups/450ml **water**

2 tsp **paprika**

1 tsp **ground coriander**

¼ cup/50g **granulated sugar**

3 oz/80g **tamarind purée** (use either liquid tamarind concentrate from a jar or make your own from a block)

Coconut rice

2½ cups/500g **jasmine rice**

1 x 13.5-oz/400ml can of **coconut milk**

6 fresh **lime leaves**, stalks removed, leaves cut thinly

There are peanut sauces and there are peanut sauces. Then there is Helen's peanut sauce. It takes a bit longer to make than versions that use peanut butter, but it's worth it. Make more than you need, ready to have with grilled or roasted chicken (we suggest the sambal spiced chicken on page 125), shrimp, tofu—or to dress raw or lightly blanched vegetables. As it is here—served with rice—the dish makes a hearty vegan main. *Pictured on page 126.*

Getting ahead: The peanut sauce can be made up to 5 days ahead if kept in the fridge, or longer if frozen. The relish keeps well in the fridge for up to 2 days.

Serves 4

First make the relish. Put the vinegar and sugar into a small saucepan, along with ¼ cup/60ml of water and ¼ teaspoon of salt. Bring to a boil, then simmer for 1 minute, stirring once or twice, until the sugar has dissolved. Remove from the heat and, once cool, add the cucumber, ginger, chile, and cilantro stems. Transfer to a sealed container and keep in the fridge.

Next make the peanut sauce. Place the peanuts in a food processor and blitz until finely chopped: pulse them well but not into a powder. Set aside for now.

Place the onion, garlic, lemongrass, ginger, and sambal oelek in a blender or food processor. Blitz well to form a fine purée.

Put the oil into a medium sauté pan and place on medium heat (it looks like a lot of oil but it's okay). After 1 minute, add the lemongrass purée, then decrease the heat to medium-low and cook for 25 minutes, stirring frequently, until the sauce deepens in color and starts to stick to the bottom of the pan. Add the chopped peanuts, along with the water, and bring to a boil on medium-high heat. Decrease the heat to medium-low and simmer for 15 minutes, until a slick of oil starts to float to the top. Add the paprika, coriander, sugar, tamarind purée, and ½ teaspoon of salt, and cook for 5 minutes. Remove from the heat, set aside to cool, then transfer to a bowl. Keep in the fridge until ready to serve.

Put the rice, coconut milk, and lime leaves into an 11-inch/28cm nonstick sauté pan (for which you have a tight-fitting lid) with 3 cups/700ml of water and 1¼ teaspoons of salt. Place on high heat and bring to a boil, stirring from time to time. As soon as it starts to boil, decrease the heat to its lowest setting and cook for 30 minutes, covered. Increase the heat to high and continue to cook, still covered, for 15 minutes, until the rice forms a golden crust at the bottom. Remove the pan from the heat and let the rice cool and set for 5 minutes, undisturbed. To unmold it, run a flexible spatula all around the edges of the pan, then place a large plate on top and carefully turn the rice out.

Strain the relish—the liquid can be discarded—and fold in the cilantro leaves. Warm up the peanut sauce and spoon it over the rice. Top with the relish and serve with wedges of lime alongside.

Sambal spiced chicken

8 chicken thighs, bone in, skin on, and lightly scored (2 lb 2 oz/1kg)

Spice rub
2 tbsp ground coriander
1½ tsp ground cumin
1½ tsp ground turmeric
1 tsp fennel seeds, finely crushed
2 tbsp maple syrup
2 tbsp lime juice
1 tbsp sambal oelek
1½ tsp peanut (or vegetable) oil
salt

To serve
peanut sauce (see page 124)
1 lime, cut into wedges

Pictured on page 127.

Serves 4

Combine all the ingredients for the spice rub, along with 1½ teaspoons of salt, in either a large zip-lock bag or a large container, for which you have a lid and into which the chicken will fit in a single layer. Add the chicken, seal the bag (if using), and squish together (or if using a container, use your hands to give everything a good squish), so that the chicken is coated. Keep in the fridge for at least 4 hours (or up to 24 hours), giving it a couple of turns as it marinates, if possible.

An hour before cooking, take the chicken out of the fridge.

Preheat the oven to 400°F.

Spread the chicken on a large parchment-lined baking sheet, skin side up, and roast for about 40 minutes, basting a couple of times, until golden brown. Serve with the warmed-up peanut sauce drizzled over the top, and extra to serve alongside, plus the lime wedges.

Roasted chicken with curry leaf dukkah

Curry leaf dukkah: a mix of any/all of the four nuts (just keep the total weight of 3½ oz/100g the same)

3 tbsp/25g cashews
3 tbsp/25g raw (aka skinless) peanuts
3 tbsp/25g blanched almonds
3 tbsp/25g blanched hazelnuts
1 tbsp coriander seeds
¼ cup/60ml vegetable oil
⅓ oz/10g curry leaves
⅓ cup/25g store-bought crispy fried shallots
½ tsp chile flakes
¼ tsp salt

Roasted chicken
3 onions, sliced into ¾-inch/ 2cm-thick rings (1 lb 3 oz/540g)
7 tbsp/100g unsalted butter, at room temperature
1 small chicken (about 2¾ lb/1.3kg)
2 limes, quartered
1 small head of garlic, unpeeled and cut in half horizontally
salt and black pepper

Discovering a new way to roast a chicken—the ultimate home cooking comfort food—always feels like a joy. Serve this with those roasted carrots (see page 106) or any other root veg. Some buttered Savoy cabbage is also a lovely accompaniment.

Serves 4

Preheat the oven to 350°F.

First make the dukkah. Spread the nuts and coriander seeds on a large parchment-lined baking sheet and roast for 8–10 minutes. Remove from the oven and set aside to cool.

Put the oil into a small frying pan and place on medium-low heat. Add the curry leaves—they will splutter!—and cook for 30 seconds, until crisp. Drain in a small sieve placed over a bowl, keeping the flavored oil (this is great for dressings or for drizzling over roasted veg). Tip the leaves out on to a plate lined with paper towels and set aside. Once cool, reserve 10 leaves, to garnish, and transfer the remainder to a food processor. Add all the nuts and coriander seeds, along with the crispy fried shallots, chile flakes, and salt. Pulse to form a rough crumble and transfer to a small bowl.

Increase the oven temperature to 400°F.

Place the sliced onions on a medium baking sheet or casserole dish, sitting in a single layer.

Put 3½ oz/100g of the dukkah into a medium bowl with all the butter and beat together with a wooden spoon until well combined.

Gently separate the skin of the chicken from the flesh with your fingers, or use a small spoon, curved side up, to gently slide over the breasts, then the legs. Push small clumps of the softened dukkah butter into the cavities, then use your fingers to massage the skin and spread the butter out. Sprinkle the chicken with 1¼ teaspoons of salt and a few generous grinds of pepper all over. Put half the lime quarters and both the garlic halves inside the cavity, then sit the chicken on top of the onions.

Roast for 1 hour and 10 minutes—covering with foil, if necessary—until golden brown. Switch the oven off, leaving the chicken in there for 15 minutes (with the oven door closed). Transfer to a serving plate, sprinkle with the reserved curry leaves and serve, with the remaining wedges of lime and the rest of the dukkah alongside.

Summer chicken cacciatore with herb sauce

2 lb 2 oz/1kg chicken thighs,
  bone in, skin on
½ tsp dried oregano
½ tsp dried thyme
1 tbsp olive oil
**14 oz/400g datterini (or cherry)
  tomatoes**, cut in half
7 oz/200g Roma tomatoes,
  quartered
1 tbsp white wine vinegar
½ sourdough loaf, sliced,
  crusts removed, toasted, then
  torn into 1½-inch/4cm pieces
  (3⅔ cups/150g)
salt and black pepper

Herb sauce
2 tbsp toasted sesame seeds
½ tsp dried oregano
½ tsp dried thyme
¾ oz/25g parsley, roughly chopped
¾ oz/25g chives, cut into
  ½-inch/1cm lengths
3 garlic cloves, crushed to a paste
7 tbsp/100ml olive oil
⅓ cup/50g pitted green olives,
  halved
½ cup/10g mint leaves, roughly
  chopped
1 lemon: finely grate the zest to get
  1½ tsp, then juice to get 1 tsp

Thanks to Jake Norman in the Ottolenghi test kitchen for this dish. Jake took inspiration from a couple of places. From Italy it's their cacciatore—or "hunter's chicken"—a humble stew of tomatoes and olives. Another inspiration was panzanella, Italy's wonderful tomato and bread salad. The herb sauce is a fresh and minty take on the dried spice mix za'atar. We've suggested both cherry and Roma tomatoes here, but use any combination you like or can find. Serve alongside a leafy salad or boiled potatoes, or both. *Pictured on page 131.*

Serves 4

Preheat the oven to 400°F.

Place the chicken in a large bowl and rub with the dried herbs and ¾ teaspoon of salt. Place a large, high-sided ovenproof sauté pan or casserole dish, for which you have a lid, over high heat. Add the oil, tomatoes, and ¼ teaspoon of salt. Fry for 5 minutes, stirring occasionally, until the tomatoes begin to break down and release their juices. Place the chicken on top of the tomatoes, skin side up, and add the vinegar. Cover and bake for 40 minutes. After 40 minutes, increase the oven temperature to 425°F, remove the lid, and bake for 20 minutes. Remove the pan from the oven and transfer the chicken to a plate to rest. Return the pan to the oven for a final 10 minutes, until the sauce has reduced slightly and the tomatoes are charred.

Meanwhile, make the herb sauce. Combine all the ingredients in a medium bowl, along with ¼ teaspoon of salt and a good crack of pepper. Mix to combine, then set aside.

Remove the pan from the oven and stir in the toasted sourdough. Place the chicken on top and baste the skin with some of the juices. Sprinkle with a good grind of pepper, spoon the sauce over the top, and serve.

Cheeseball lemon rice with chile butter

8 **cloves**
6 **cardamom pods**, bashed
1 **lemon**: shave the zest into
   strips, then juice to get 2 tbsp
½ **cup/125g ricotta**
5¼ **oz/150g feta**, crumbled
4½ **oz/125g low-moisture
   mozzarella**, shredded
   (mounded 1 cup)
¾ **oz/25g parmesan**, grated (¼ cup)
1 **egg**, beaten
2 **cups/400g basmati rice**, rinsed
   and drained well
½ **cup/75g pitted green olives**,
   cut in half
7 **tbsp/100g unsalted butter**
½ **tsp chile flakes**
¾ **tsp Aleppo chile flakes**
½ **tsp sumac**
5 **green onions**, sliced on the
   diagonal into ½-inch/1cm pieces
   (mounded ½ cup/50g)
salt

There's something really reassuring about a baked rice dish. Add the right amount of water, seal the dish well, pop it into the oven, and forget about it. This is as comforting and delicious as you'd expect cheesy, briny, chile-butter-doused rice to be. It's the perfect side to something simple like a roasted chicken, or can be eaten as a main, with some wilted greens. *Pictured on page 135.*

Getting ahead: The rice wants to be eaten fresh out of the oven but can be taken up to the point just before the hot water and aromatics are added, if you want to get ahead.

Serves 6

Preheat the oven to 425°F.

Pour 3¼ cups/750ml of water into a medium saucepan and add the cloves, cardamom pods, lemon strips, and 1½ teaspoons of salt. Place on medium-high heat, bring to a simmer, then remove from the heat.

Meanwhile, put the four cheeses and the egg into a medium bowl and mix well. Using your hands, divide the mixture into 12 portions and roll them roughly into balls, approximately 1½ oz/40g each. They don't need to be perfect, as they will spread once in the rice.

Scatter the rice on the bottom of a high-sided baking dish, 9 x 13-inch/23 x 33cm (or an 11-inch/28cm ovenproof sauté pan, for which you have a lid), and scatter the olives. Pour in the hot water and aromatics. Shake the dish gently to spread the rice evenly, then deposit the cheese balls in the rice. Cover the dish tightly with foil (or lid), to keep the steam in, and bake for 25 minutes. Remove from the oven and allow to settle, covered, for 10 minutes.

While the rice is resting, melt the butter in a medium saucepan on medium heat. Add the chile flakes, Aleppo flakes, and sumac and cook for 2–3 minutes. Add the green onions and cook for 20 seconds. Remove from the heat, add the lemon juice, and set aside.

Uncover the rice and spoon the chile butter all over just before serving.

White-poached chicken with Chinese cabbage and peanut rayu

4 small boneless, skinless chicken
  breasts (1 lb 5 oz/600g)
4 tsp Shaoxing wine
⅓ oz/10g ginger, peeled and
  finely grated
2 tsp peanut oil
1 large Chinese (aka napa or
  wombok) cabbage, thinly
  sliced (4½ cups/400g)
1 cup/20g basil leaves, torn
6 green onions, finely sliced on the
  diagonal (¾ cup/60g)
1–2 limes, cut into wedges, to serve
salt

Peanut rayu
1 cup/240ml peanut (or other
  flavorless) oil
3 tbsp chile flakes (Korean
  gochugaru, ideally, or an equal
  mix of regular chile flakes and
  Aleppo pepper flakes)
scant 1 cup/120g unsalted roasted
  peanuts, roughly chopped in
  a food processor
4 large garlic cloves, chopped
¼ cup/35g sesame seeds
2 tbsp soy sauce
2 tbsp granulated sugar
1 tsp flaked sea salt

"White-cooking" is a term used to describe food, usually a whole chicken, poached in a simple stock of Chinese rice wine and aromatics. It's a brilliant and really simple way of subtly flavoring the meat as well as keeping it tender.

The key to success for this technique is all in the temperature of the chicken when it goes into the just-boiled water—it needs to be out of the fridge, at room temperature, for 30 minutes. If it's too cold when it goes in, it will not properly cook.

Getting ahead: Ideally, the peanut rayu should be made a day ahead of serving for the flavors to infuse. If you need to make it on the day that's okay—even a couple of hours will help. It keeps for up to 2 weeks in the fridge and is great spooned over all sorts of things: crispy fried eggs, noodles, plain rice, stalks of celery.

Serves 4

To make the rayu, put the oil and chile flakes into a small pan and place on medium-low heat. When the oil starts simmering, add the peanuts, garlic, and sesame seeds, cook for 2 minutes, then remove from the heat. Add the soy sauce, sugar, and flaked sea salt and set aside to cool, then decant into a sealed jar.

Half an hour before you are going to start cooking the chicken, remove it from the fridge.

When you are nearly ready to cook, fill a large pot (for which you have a tight-fitting lid) with 6⅓ cups/1½ liters of water. Bring to a boil on medium-high heat and, when it begins to boil, add the chicken breasts, stir quickly, then immediately put the lid on and turn off the heat. Allow it to sit, undisturbed, for 1 hour, then strain the chicken, discarding the poaching liquid.

When cool enough to handle, tear the chicken into long shreds—discarding the skin first—and place in a large mixing bowl. Add the Shaoxing wine, ginger, peanut oil, and ½ teaspoon of salt and set aside for at least 5 minutes. Just before serving, add the cabbage leaves and most of the basil and toss to combine. Transfer to a large serving plate and spoon the rayu on top. Finish with the green onions and the remaining basil and serve with the lime wedges alongside.

Shawarma meatloaf with caramelized onions

Meatloaf
2 onions, grated (1¾ cups/265g)
3 eggs, lightly beaten
3 garlic cloves, crushed to a paste
1 tbsp ground cumin
1 tbsp paprika
1½ tsp ground allspice
1¼ tsp ground turmeric
¼ tsp cayenne pepper
⅔ cup/125g bulgur
**1 lb 10 oz/750g ground lamb
   (or beef)**, 20% fat
1 large zucchini, grated
   (2 cups/200g)
½ oz/15g cilantro, leaves and
   stems finely chopped, plus
   ¼ cup/5g extra leaves to serve
¾ cup/15g mint leaves, finely
   chopped, plus ¼ cup/5g extra
   leaves to serve
3 tbsp olive oil
salt and black pepper

Caramelized onion topping
3 tbsp olive oil
3 onions, thinly sliced (4 cups/480g)
1 tsp granulated sugar
2 tbsp pomegranate molasses
½ tsp ground cinnamon
½ tsp ground allspice

Pomegranate yogurt
1 tbsp pomegranate molasses
**1 cup plus 1 tbsp/300g
   Greek yogurt**
2 tbsp pomegranate seeds,
   to serve (optional)

Meatloaf: is it the texture that makes it so comforting, the memory of eating it as kids, or the relative ease—mix it all together and bake—with which it's made? As ever, it's a little bit of everything. This particular meatloaf is a bit of a double-whammy for Yotam in terms of food-as-memory-as-comfort. As well as eating a lot of meatloaf growing up, he also ate a lot of shawarma. With all the flavor of a shawarma but in easy meatloaf form, the result is a complete trip down memory lane.

Getting ahead: The meatloaf can be made and sitting ready in the pan for up to 1 day before baking. Once baked, it keeps for a couple of days in the fridge. Bring it back up to room temperature or warm through before serving.

Serves 6

To make the meatloaf, put the onions, eggs, garlic, spices, and bulgur into a medium bowl. Set aside in the fridge for 1 hour, to soak and bloom. Add the lamb, zucchini, cilantro, mint, 2 tablespoons of the oil, 1½ teaspoons of salt, and a good grind of pepper and mix well to combine.

Meanwhile, make the caramelized onions. Put the oil into a medium saucepan and place on medium-low heat. Add the onions, sugar, ¾ teaspoon of salt, and some pepper and cook for 15–20 minutes, stirring often, until slightly caramelized. Add the molasses and spices and cook for 5 minutes. Remove from the heat.

Swirl the pomegranate molasses into the yogurt and set aside.

Preheat the oven to 400°F.

Place an 11-inch/28cm cast-iron overproof sauté pan on high heat and, when hot, add the remaining oil and spread it in the pan. Add the meatloaf mixture and, using your fingers, quickly pat down and immediately place in the oven. Bake for 20 minutes. Spread the caramelized onion topping evenly on top and bake for 10–12 minutes. Remove from the oven and set aside for 15 minutes, to rest.

Sprinkle with the extra mint and cilantro leaves and the pomegranate seeds, if using. Serve warm or at room temperature, with the pomegranate yogurt alongside.

Roasted hispi cabbage with miso butter

½ cup plus 1 tbsp/125g unsalted
  butter, at room temperature
1 garlic clove, peeled and left whole
2 tsp white miso paste
½ oz/15g ginger, peeled and
  finely grated
2 tsp toasted sesame oil
1 tsp rice vinegar (or lemon juice)
2 tbsp toasted sesame seeds, plus
  1 tsp extra to garnish
½ tsp chile flakes
1 tbsp light soy sauce
4 green onions, thinly sliced
  (½ cup/45g)
2–3 hispi (aka sweetheart)
  cabbages (they vary a lot in size),
  quartered lengthwise (about
  3⅓ lb/1.5kg)
salt

There is no secret as to what allows wedges of cabbage to become so comforting here: a lot of butter. No apologies. Serve with steamed rice or noodles, or as a side to roasted meats.

Getting ahead: The miso and sesame butter can be made in advance, if you want to get ahead, and kept in the fridge. Just bring it back to room temperature before spreading it on the cabbage.

Serves 4

Preheat the oven to 400°F.

Place the first eight ingredients in the small bowl of a food processor, along with 2 teaspoons of the soy sauce, half the green onions, and ¾ teaspoon of salt. Blitz until smooth, then divide the mixture equally between the cabbage wedges, spreading it all over the cut sides.

Place the cabbages, cut side up, in a parchment-lined baking sheet or dish, about 14 x 10 inches/35 x 25cm. Cover the dish tightly with foil and roast for 50-60 minutes. Remove the foil and increase the oven temperature to 425°F. Mix the remaining 1 teaspoon of soy sauce with 1 tablespoon of water and add to the pan. Roast for 15-20 minutes, until nicely browned.

Transfer the cabbages to a serving plate and serve, with the remaining green onions and sesame seeds scattered over the top.

Hawaij-roasted cauliflower with gribiche sauce

6 tbsp/90ml olive oil
1 large cauliflower, broken into
    large florets (1½ lb/675g),
    leaves reserved
3–4 large shallots, quartered
    (8 oz/225g)
salt and black pepper

Hawaij spice mix
1½ tbsp coriander seeds
1 tbsp cumin seeds
¾ tsp fenugreek seeds
3 whole cloves
seeds from 12 cardamom pods
¾ tsp ground turmeric
¼ tsp granulated sugar

Gribiche
¼ cup/25g golden raisins
2 tbsp apple cider vinegar
¼ cup/60ml olive oil
1½ tsp Dijon mustard
1 tsp honey
1 tsp hawaij (see above)
½ oz/15g dill, finely chopped, plus
    a few extra fronds to garnish
⅓ oz/10g parsley, finely chopped,
    plus a few extra leaves to garnish
1 oz/30g cornichons, thinly sliced
4 medium-boiled eggs, cooled,
    peeled, and roughly chopped

Hawaij is an intense and warming Yemeni spice blend. It's usually used in soups and stews but pairs really well with gribiche, a mayonnaise-like sauce made with medium-boiled eggs. We find that 7–8 minutes, for a room-temperature egg going into boiling water, is hard to beat for jamminess. The raisins are an untraditional, but welcome, addition.

Storing notes: You'll make more of the hawaij than you need here, but it keeps well. Try it out with other roasted vegetables, too.

Serves 4

Preheat the oven to 475°F.

Put all ingredients for the hawaij, except for the turmeric and sugar, into a small saucepan and place on medium heat. Toast for 3–5 minutes, until fragrant, then transfer to a spice grinder (or a mortar and pestle) and blitz to a smooth powder. Stir in the turmeric and sugar, then put 1 tablespoon of the mix into a large bowl.

Add the 6 tbsp/90ml of olive oil to the hawaij in the bowl, along with 1 teaspoon of salt and a really good grind of pepper. Stir, then add the cauliflower florets. Using your hands, turn to coat in the oil, then spread on a parchment-lined baking sheet. Add the shallots to the bowl, turn to coat in the oil, and add to the sheet. Add the cauliflower leaves to whatever oil is left, turn them until covered, and set aside.

Roast the cauliflower and shallots for 15 minutes, until starting to color. Remove the sheet and turn the cauliflower and onions over. Add the cauliflower leaves and return to the oven for 10 minutes, until everything is deeply golden and caramelized in places.

Meanwhile, make the gribiche. Put the raisins, vinegar, and 1 tablespoon of water into a small pan over high heat. Bring to a boil, then set aside to cool.

Strain the raisins (setting them aside for later) and put the vinegar into a medium bowl, along with the oil, mustard, honey, 1 teaspoon of hawaij, ¼ teaspoon of salt, and a good grind of pepper. Whisk together until combined. Add the dill, parsley, cornichons, and chopped eggs. Stir together gently.

Tip the cauliflower and shallots onto a serving platter and spoon the gribiche sauce on top. Scatter the soaked raisins and garnish with the extra dill and parsley. Serve warm or at room temperature.

Cheesy baked rice with okra and tomato

1 lb 9 oz/700g okra, stems trimmed (without exposing the seeds); half chopped into 1¼-inch/3cm pieces, the remainder left whole

1 lb 5 oz/600g cherry tomatoes: half sliced in half, the remainder left whole

1¼ cups/250g basmati rice, covered with water and soaked for 30 minutes

2 whole cloves

1 cinnamon stick

4 tbsp/50g unsalted butter, cut into ¾-inch/2cm cubes

1¾ cups/425ml boiling water

¼ cup/60ml olive oil

2 onions, thinly sliced (2½ cups/300g)

1¼ tsp ground cardamom

2 tsp ground cumin

1½ tsp granulated sugar

5 garlic cloves, crushed to a paste

1 small, hot green chile, seeded and finely chopped

¾ oz/20g cilantro, leaves and stems separated

1 tbsp tomato paste

1½ tbsp red wine vinegar

1¼ cups/300ml chicken (or vegetable) stock

7 oz/200g buffalo mozzarella, roughly torn

5¼ oz/150g mature cheddar, grated (1⅓ cups)

⅓ cup/20g panko breadcrumbs

salt and black pepper

Helen used to own a café in Melbourne, Mortar and Pestle, and this dish is inspired by one that featured on its menu. It was layered, set in a springform pan, and unmolded like a cake—it was the 90s! While the presentation now seems a bit passé, the appeal of a cheesy rice bake is timeless—comforting and just-one-more-bite all the way.

Playing around: If you don't have (or don't like!) okra, then French or flat runner beans work really well. Treat them the same way as the okra, with half chopped and the remainder left whole.

Serves 6

Preheat the oven to 450°F.

Place a large sauté pan, for which you have a lid, over high heat. When it's really hot, add the whole okra—you'll need to do this in two batches—and char for about 5 minutes, until blackened in places. Transfer to a plate and set aside. Add the whole cherry tomatoes to the pan and char for about 3 minutes, until blackened in places. Add these to the okra and wipe the pan clean.

Drain the rice and place in a separate large ovenproof sauté pan, for which you have a lid (or a 9 x 13-inch/23 x 33cm ovenproof dish). Add the cloves, cinnamon stick, 3 tbsp/40g of the butter, ¾ teaspoon of salt, and a good grind of pepper. Pour in the boiling water and give everything a good stir. Cover and bake for 25 minutes. Remove from the oven but keep covered for 10 minutes to steam. Keep the oven on.

Meanwhile, add the olive oil to the wiped-clean pan and place on medium heat. Add the onions and cook for 20–25 minutes, stirring from time to time, until starting to caramelize. Add the cardamom, cumin, sugar, garlic, chile, cilantro stems, tomato paste, 1½ teaspoons of salt, and some pepper, and cook for 2 minutes. Add the vinegar and let it bubble for 30 seconds, then add the chopped okra and the halved cherry tomatoes. Cook for 5 minutes, then pour in the stock. Bring to a simmer, then decrease the heat to medium-low and cook for 15 minutes, covered, stirring occasionally. Return the charred okra and tomatoes to the pan and stir them in. Simmer for 5 minutes, covered, then for another 5 minutes uncovered.

Uncover the rice, discard the whole spices, and fluff with a fork. Tuck the mozzarella into the rice and sprinkle with half the grated cheddar. Place the remaining cheese in a small bowl and add the panko breadcrumbs and remaining 1 tbsp/10g of butter. Mix to combine.

Spoon the okra and tomato stew over the rice and cover with the breadcrumb mix. Bake for 15 minutes, until golden brown. Let cool for 10 minutes, then scatter the cilantro leaves and serve.

Braised fennel and cod with black-eyed peas and 'nduja butter

¼ cup/60ml olive oil

2–3 large fennel bulbs, trimmed, halved, and each half cut into 2–3 wedges, depending on size (1 lb 5 oz/600g)

3 large shallots, quartered lengthwise (6⅓ oz/180g)

1 head of garlic, unpeeled and cut in half crosswise

1 x 15-oz/425g can of black-eyed peas (or cannellini beans), drained and rinsed

½ cup plus 2 tbsp/150ml chicken stock (or water)

½ cup/120ml dry vermouth (or white wine)

4–5 white fish fillets (such as cod, haddock, or hake), skinless and boneless (about 1 lb 2 oz/500g)

3 tbsp crème fraîche

¼ oz/5g chives, finely chopped

1 lemon, cut into wedges, to serve

salt and black pepper

'Nduja butter

3 tbsp unsalted butter

2 tbsp 'nduja paste (from a jar or fresh)

¾ tsp Urfa chile flakes

¾ tsp chipotle chile flakes

½ tsp smoked paprika

Vegetables and fish braised in a beany broth make the most comforting of dishes. This is where a weeknight sheet pan dish gets dialed right up. Use whatever fish you have on hand or prefer: salmon, for example, is as good as white fish. For anyone who eats fish but not meat, look out for a jar of store-bought vegan 'nduja. Some of them are really great and make a brilliant alternative. *Also pictured on page 151.*

Getting ahead: The 'nduja butter can be made up to 3 days in advance and kept in the fridge. Just melt it gently again before using.

Serves 4

Preheat the oven to 450°F. Cut a piece of parchment paper into a roughly 10½-inch/27cm-wide circle.

Put the olive oil into an 11-inch/28cm shallow casserole dish, for which you have a lid, and place on medium-high heat. Add the fennel, shallots, and garlic and sauté for about 6 minutes, until the vegetables are starting to stick in places. Add the peas, stock, vermouth, 1 teaspoon of salt, and a few really good grinds of pepper. Stir gently and bring to a simmer. Place the parchment circle on top of the vegetables, clamp on the lid, and transfer the pan to the oven. Bake for 30 minutes, until the vegetables are cooked through and soft. Remove the lid and parchment, add a splash of water or more stock if it's looking dry, and bake for 10–15 minutes, until the vegetables have browned in places.

Meanwhile, combine all the ingredients for the 'nduja butter in a small saucepan and place on medium-low heat. Bring to a gentle simmer, stirring and smooshing the 'nduja with the back of a spoon to incorporate it into the butter, then remove from the heat.

Season the fish with ½ teaspoon of salt (in total, not each fillet!) and a few grinds of pepper, and drizzle 1½ teaspoons of the 'nduja butter over each fillet. Remove the pan from the oven, arrange the fish on top and return to the oven, uncovered, for a final 7-10 minutes, until the fish is just cooked through.

Remove the pan from the oven and let it rest for 5 minutes, then dollop spoonfuls of the crème fraîche among the fennel and fish. Drizzle with the remaining 'nduja butter and finish with a sprinkling of chives. Serve with the lemon wedges alongside.

151

Puttanesca-style sheet pan salmon

7 oz/200g haricots verts, trimmed
7 green onions, cut crosswise
  into thirds (2½ oz/75g)
7 oz/200g mixed cherry tomatoes,
  halved
6 salmon fillets, skin on
  (about 1 lb 9 oz/720g)
salt and black pepper

Tomato anchovy oil
⅓ cup/80ml olive oil
8 anchovies, finely chopped
2½ tbsp tomato paste
1 tsp chile flakes
2 tsp coriander seeds, lightly
  bashed in a mortar
8 garlic cloves, very thinly sliced
2 preserved lemons, flesh and
  seeds discarded, skin finely
  chopped (2 tbsp/20g)
2 tsp maple syrup

Sauce
**½ cup/60g pitted Kalamata
  olives**, halved
½ cup/60g capers, roughly chopped
1 preserved lemon, flesh and
  seeds discarded, skin thinly
  sliced (1 tbsp/10g)
½ cup/10g basil leaves,
  roughly chopped
½ cup/10g parsley leaves,
  roughly chopped
2 tbsp olive oil
2 tsp lemon juice

If you make the tomato anchovy oil a day ahead here, you can then delight in the fact that a midweek supper can be on the table within 20 minutes. The fuss-free cooking method—all hail the sheet pan!—plus the dialed-up flavors—all hail puttanesca!—makes such a winning combination.

Serves 4

First make the tomato anchovy oil. Put the oil, anchovies, and tomato paste into a small sauté pan and place on medium heat. Once the mixture starts to simmer, cook for 5 minutes, stirring from time to time. Add the chile flakes and coriander seeds and cook for 1 minute, until fragrant. Remove from the heat and add the garlic, preserved lemon, and maple syrup. Stir to combine, then set aside to cool.

Preheat the oven to 450°F.

Place the beans, green onions, and tomatoes on a large, parchment-lined baking sheet. Drizzle with 3 tablespoons of the tomato anchovy oil, along with ¼ teaspoon of salt and a good grind of pepper. Toss to combine and place in the oven for 12–13 minutes, until the beans and tomatoes are starting to soften and taking on a little color. Meanwhile, arrange the salmon fillets on a plate and, using a spoon, drizzle the remaining tomato anchovy oil (as well as all the solids) evenly over the fillets. Once the beans and tomatoes have had their time in the oven, nestle the salmon fillets among them and bake for 8 minutes. Set aside for 5 minutes, out of the oven, to rest.

While the salmon is baking, mix all the ingredients for the sauce in a small bowl and season with a good grind of pepper. Spoon half the sauce over the salmon and serve the fish warm (or at room temperature, which works just as well), with the rest of the sauce in a bowl on the side.

Dals, stews, curries

Red lentil dal with potato and fennel

2 tsp black or brown mustard seeds

2 tsp cumin seeds

2 tsp fennel seeds

1 tsp nigella seeds (or black sesame seeds)

½ tsp fenugreek seeds

3 whole dried red chiles

3 garlic cloves, peeled and left whole

⅓ oz/10g ginger, peeled and roughly chopped

1 small, hot green chile, roughly chopped

1 onion, roughly chopped (mounded 1 cup/180g)

4 tbsp/60g ghee (or olive oil to keep the whole dish vegan)

20 curry leaves

1 large fennel bulb, cut into 1-inch/2½cm dice (3½ cups/300g)

2 russet (or other floury) potatoes, peeled and cut into 1-inch/2½cm dice (1¼ cups/300g)

2 large tomatoes, cut into ¾-inch/2cm dice (⅔ cup/120g)

1 tsp ground turmeric

¾ cup/150g red split lentils (masoor dal), well rinsed and soaked in plenty of water for an hour or two, then drained

⅔ cup/130g split mung beans (moong dal), well rinsed and soaked in the same bowl as the red split lentils, then drained

¾ cup plus 2 tbsp/200ml coconut milk, plus 2–3 tbsp extra for drizzling

3⅓ cups/800ml water

1 tbsp lime juice

½ cup/10g cilantro leaves, roughly chopped, plus extra whole leaves to garnish

salt

To serve

1 lime, cut into wedges

cooked rice or roti

Dals are one of those dishes where everyone has their own, honed over the years, yet familiar enough to be made slightly differently every time depending on what's in the pantry. The combination of fennel and potato is one that Helen has held onto from the curries of Malaysia with its significant Indian population. The combination of two types of lentils works really well, with the red lentils collapsing and the moong dal retaining a bit of a bite. Serve with rice or roti.

Getting ahead: The dal can be made up to 3 days ahead and kept in the fridge, ready to warm through. It will thicken once cooled, so just add a little water, when reheating, to loosen it up. Tarka—the infused oil or ghee, poured over the dal just before serving—always needs to be made at the last minute, so it's hot and fresh.

A note on soaking: If you want to soak the lentils and split beans overnight, then do—it will only add to the softness of the end result. It's also absolutely fine to soak for just an hour or two.

Serves 6

Combine the mustard, cumin, fennel, nigella, and fenugreek seeds in a small bowl and add the dried chiles.

Place the garlic, ginger, green chile, and onion in the small bowl of a food processor and pulse until finely chopped.

Put 3 tablespoons of the ghee into a large sauté pan, for which you have a lid, and place on medium-high heat. Add the spices, reserving 2 teaspoons to serve, and half the curry leaves and cook for 1–2 minutes, stirring, until fragrant.

Decrease the heat to medium and add the onion mixture to the pan, along with the fennel. Cook for 20 minutes, stirring regularly, until the fennel is almost translucent and beginning to color. Add the potatoes, tomatoes, turmeric, lentils, and beans. Gently stir, cook for 2 minutes, then add the coconut milk, water, and 2¼ teaspoons of salt. Stir, bring to a boil, then decrease the heat to low. Simmer gently, covered, for about 45 minutes, stirring occasionally. Remove the lid, increase the heat a little to bring to a gentle simmer, then continue to cook for 15 minutes, stirring regularly, until the lentils are completely soft and the dal has thickened. Stir in the lime juice and cilantro and set aside.

Just before serving, put the remaining 1 tablespoon of ghee into a small frying pan and add the reserved spices and remaining curry leaves. Cook for 1 minute, until fragrant, then pour over the dal. Drizzle with the reserved coconut milk, scatter the reserved cilantro leaves, and serve with a good squeeze of lime.

Oyakodon: mother and child

3 tbsp/50ml sunflower oil
3 onions, sliced ½ inch/1cm thick
    (1 lb 2 oz/500g)
1¾ lb/800g skinless and boneless
    chicken thighs, cut into
    1½–2-inch/4–5cm pieces
3 garlic cloves, crushed to a paste
1 oz/30g ginger, peeled and
    finely grated
⅔ cup/160ml Shaoxing wine
⅓ cup/80ml mirin
¾ cup plus 3 tbsp/220ml dashi
    (or chicken stock)
7 tbsp/100ml soy sauce
6 eggs
5 green onions, thinly sliced
    (mounded ½ cup/50g)
½ cup/10g cilantro leaves
1 sheet of nori, crumbled (optional)

To serve
cooked short-grain rice
¾ oz/20g ginger, peeled
    and julienned
shichimi togarashi

In Japanese, oya means parent, ko means child, and don is the abbreviation of donburi, which means bowl. Put the three together and you have pure Japanese soul food—as comforting as the combination of eggs + rice + chicken soup + eating from a bowl would suggest. The "mother and child"—the chicken and the egg—are cooked together in the pan, which also makes this an easy one-pot dish. *Also pictured on page 160.*

Serves 4–6

Put the oil into a large sauté pan, for which you have a lid, and place on high heat. Add the onions and cook for about 5 minutes, stirring frequently, until they begin to turn translucent. Add the chicken and cook for 8–10 minutes, stirring occasionally—you want to seal the chicken without it taking on too much color. Add the garlic and ginger, continue to cook for 1 minute, and then pour in the Shaoxing wine. Stir and scrape up any brown bits that have become stuck to the bottom of the pan.

Whisk together the mirin, dashi, and soy sauce and add to the pan. Bring the liquid to a boil, decrease the heat to medium-low, and simmer for about 25 minutes, uncovered and stirring occasionally, until the chicken is tender.

Stir the eggs with a knife—you want to break up the yolks and whites so that some of them are mixed but some are still distinct. Gently pour this over the simmering chicken, onions, and broth, being careful not to mix them—the eggs should float on top like a raft. Cook for 1 minute, then cover and cook for 2 minutes, until the egg is just barely set. It should be streaky white and yellow in parts, so not totally scrambled.

Switch off the heat and allow to rest for a couple of minutes, covered, before scattering the green onions, cilantro, and nori (if using).

Divide the rice among individual bowls, then use a large serving spoon to scoop out the chicken and broth. Spoon directly on the rice, trying to keep the egg on top. Sprinkle with the ginger, along with a good sprinkle of shichimi togarashi.

Soy-braised pork belly with eggs and tofu

1 lb 5 oz/600g **pork belly**, skin on, cut into ¾-inch/2cm cubes (keeping the layers of fat and meat together)

2 tbsp vegetable oil

3 green onions, halved crosswise (1½ oz/45g)

1 head of garlic, cloves peeled and lightly smashed

½ oz/15g ginger, unpeeled and thinly sliced lengthwise

1 cinnamon stick

2 whole star anise

1 bay leaf

1 tsp Chinese five-spice

1½ tbsp Shaoxing wine

¼ cup/60ml light soy sauce

2 tbsp dark soy sauce

4 eggs

2 tbsp maple syrup

1 tbsp rice (or other white) vinegar

3½ oz/100g fried tofu puffs, cut into 1-inch/2.5cm pieces (or 7 oz/200g firm tofu, diced)

steamed jasmine rice, to serve

salt and black pepper

Quick-pickled cucumber

1 cucumber, halved lengthwise, seeded and thinly sliced (1⅓ cups/200g)

2 tsp rice wine vinegar

2 tbsp mirin

2 green onions, finely sliced (¼ cup/20g)

¼ cup/5g mint leaves, roughly chopped

¼ cup/5g cilantro leaves, roughly chopped

This is a one-pot meal for the family and a staple in every Chinese household, served with steamed jasmine rice. The soy base is familiar and comforting for children, while the infusion of aromatics adds flavor and interest. Slowly cooked, the fat from the belly pork melts and emulsifies, enriching the sauce.

Getting ahead: Not only can this be made a day or two ahead of serving, it actually benefits from this. Keeping it in the fridge overnight will mean a layer of fat will form on the surface—just skim this off, if you like, before reheating.

Serves 4

Fill a medium pot with about 2¾ cups/650ml of water, then add the pork and bring to a boil. Lower the heat to medium-low. Simmer for 5 minutes, skimming away any scum that forms, then, in a colander set over a bowl—you want to reserve the liquid—drain the pork.

Put the oil into a medium casserole dish (or sauté pan), for which you have a lid, and place on medium-high heat. Add the drained pork and cook for 5 minutes, turning occasionally, until golden all over. Add the green onions, garlic, ginger, cinnamon stick, star anise, bay leaf, and ½ teaspoon of freshly cracked pepper. Cook for 1 minute and then add the five-spice and Shaoxing wine. Cook for a few seconds and then add both the soy sauces, ½ teaspoon of salt, and the reserved poaching liquid—you should have 2½ cups/600ml. Bring to a boil, then decrease the heat to very low. Simmer gently, covered, for about 2 hours, until the pork is super tender. The sauce should be brothy (rather than thick).

Meanwhile, place the eggs in a small saucepan and cover with cold water. Bring to a boil over medium-high heat and, when it comes to a boil, set a timer for 4 minutes. Drain the eggs and run under cold tap water until cool enough to peel.

Add the maple syrup and rice vinegar to the pork, stir to combine, then add the tofu and peeled eggs—don't cut the eggs in half. Stir very gently, tucking the eggs in so that they are covered in the liquid. Cook, partially covered, over low heat for 20 minutes, basting the eggs from time to time. The liquid will reduce but should still be very brothy.

Meanwhile, make the quick-pickled cucumber. Mix together the cucumber, rice wine vinegar, and mirin in a small bowl with ¼ teaspoon of salt. Just before serving, stir in the green onions, mint, and cilantro.

Remove the braised pork from the heat and let it stand for 10 minutes, then serve with the rice, if you like. The aromatics are not edible, so either leave them in—they look good but should not be eaten!—or discard them.

Butternut, tamarind, and coconut stew

⅓ cup/80ml vegetable
  (or coconut) oil
1 tsp black mustard seeds
2 large onions, finely diced
  (2⅔ cups/400g)
¼ oz/5g curry leaves
6 garlic cloves, crushed to a paste
1 green jalapeño, finely chopped
  (2 tbsp/20g)
1 tsp ground turmeric
1 tsp chile powder
1 tsp paprika
1½ tsp ground coriander
1 large butternut squash,
  peeled, seeded, and cut into
  roughly 1½-inch/4cm chunks
  (5⅓ cups/750g)
½ cup/120ml tamarind
  concentrate, mixed with
  1 cup/240ml just-boiled water
⅔ cup/160ml coconut milk
¾ oz/25g jaggery, coarsely grated
  (or dark muscovado sugar)
¼ cup/5g cilantro leaves, roughly
  chopped, to serve
salt

There's a different type of comfort food for each season, but there's something *particularly* comforting about the dishes that make most sense in the autumn. Here, the butternut, tamarind, and coconut play really well together. Sweet and soft from the seasonally colored squash, tangy from the tamarind, and—rolling with the alliteration—creamy from the coconut, it makes a perfectly comforting autumn stew. Serve with either flatbread (see page 165) or naan, or with some plain, steamed basmati rice. *Pictured on page 166.*

Getting ahead: As with so many stews, this keeps well for a day or two, with the flavors actually improving thanks to having time to mingle.

Serves 4

Put the oil into a large sauté pan, for which you have a lid, and place on medium-high heat. Add the mustard seeds and, when the seeds begin to pop, add the onions and curry leaves. Cook for 20–25 minutes—the onions need this long to turn really golden brown—stirring from time to time and lowering the heat if they start to stick. Add the garlic, jalapeño, and spices and cook for about 2 minutes, until fragrant.

Add the butternut, tamarind water, and 1 teaspoon of salt. Give everything a gentle stir and cook for about 45 minutes, covered, on low heat, until the chunks of butternut are soft but have not broken down. Add the coconut milk and jaggery, stir gently to combine, and cook for 5–10 minutes, uncovered, or until some, but not all, of the butternut begins to break down. Sprinkle with the chopped cilantro and serve.

Cumin and coriander flatbreads

2 cups/250g all-purpose flour, plus extra for dusting

½ cup/50g whole wheat flour

1¼ tsp cumin seeds, toasted and roughly crushed

1¼ tsp coriander seeds, toasted and roughly crushed

½ cup/115g ghee (or butter), ¼ cup/50g cut into roughly ¾-inch/2cm pieces, and ¼ cup/50g melted for brushing

¾ cup/180ml just-boiled water

salt

Whipping up a flatbread is, truly, such an easy thing to do. It's a relatively quick process (due to the short resting time needed and quick cooking on the stovetop in a pan) and, once you get into the habit of making them, it becomes second nature. They're such a useful addition—they're a wrap! they're a mop!—to all sorts of meals. These are delicious with the butternut, tamarind, and coconut stew, page 164. *Pictured on page 167.*

Makes 6

Put both flours and the spices into a medium bowl along with ¾ teaspoon of salt. Whisk to combine, then add the ¼ cup/50g of roughly cut ghee. Pour the hot water directly over the ghee, so that it starts to melt. Using a fork, gently mix to combine—the flour should be evenly moistened—then, using your hands, gather up the dough. Knead once or twice to bring it together and shape it into a ball. Return the dough to the bowl, cover with a clean tea towel or reusable plastic wrap, and set aside to rest at room temperature for a minimum of 30 minutes (and up to 4 hours).

Divide the dough into 6 equal pieces and shape each piece into a rough ball. Cover and allow to relax while you preheat your pan.

Place a large, heavy-duty nonstick (or cast-iron) frying pan on high heat. Have a wire rack ready, with a clean tea towel draped on top.

Working with one ball at a time, roll out on a lightly floured surface to form a roughly 8-inch/20cm-wide circle.

Place in the now very hot pan and cook for 2–3 minutes, or until you see bubbles of varying sizes appear on the surface. Flip the flatbread over—it should have some nice brown/blackish spots in places—then brush with the melted ghee, and cook for 20–30 seconds.

Place the hot flatbread on the tea towel and roughly fold over the edges of the towel to keep the bread warm. Repeat with the remaining dough balls and serve as fresh from the pan as you can.

Fresh turmeric and peppercorn curry with shrimp and asparagus

1 x 5.4-oz/160ml can of
  coconut cream
1 x 13.5-oz/400ml can of
  coconut milk
¾ oz/25g palm sugar, roughly
  chopped (or light brown sugar)
4 tsp fish sauce
1 lb 2 oz/500g asparagus, cut into
  1¼-inch/3cm lengths, keeping
  the tips separate
1 lb 2 oz/500g peeled raw
  large shrimp
steamed jasmine rice, to serve

Cucumber and ginger relish
¼ cup/60ml water
½ cup/120ml rice (or other white)
  vinegar
7 tbsp/80g granulated sugar
½ cucumber, quartered lengthwise,
  seeded, and thinly sliced
  (1⅓ cups/200g)
¾ oz/20g ginger, peeled and
  julienned
1 small, hot red chile (or 2 bird's-eye
  chiles, if you like the heat), halved,
  seeded, and thinly sliced
  lengthwise
⅓ oz/10g cilantro, stems finely
  chopped, leaves roughly torn
1 lime, cut into wedges, to serve
salt

Spice paste
¼ oz/5g dried red chiles
  (or more, if you like)
½ tsp whole white peppercorns,
  toasted and coarsely ground
2 tsp coriander seeds, toasted
  and coarsely ground
1 shallot, roughly chopped
  (⅓ cup/60g)
4 garlic cloves, roughly chopped
¾ oz/20g cilantro stems, roughly
  chopped
⅓ oz/10g fresh turmeric, peeled and
  roughly chopped

This is everything we want from a curry: bright (from the turmeric), hot and aromatic (from the peppercorns), substantial (from the shrimp), and fresh (from the asparagus). The recipe uses a traditional method of cooking Thai curries called "cracking." This is where the spice paste is simmered in coconut cream for so long that it splits and the oil separates out. This then creates a rich base for a deeply flavored curry. Swap the shrimp for chicken or tofu, or make a vegetarian version with your favorite vegetables, omitting the fish sauce.

Getting ahead: The relish is best made a day ahead of serving and kept refrigerated. Hold back on the cilantro leaves, though, stirring these in just before serving.

Serves 4

First make the relish. Put the vinegar and sugar into a small saucepan, along with the water and ¼ teaspoon of salt. Bring to a boil, then simmer for 1 minute, stirring once or twice, until the sugar has dissolved. Remove from the heat and, once cool, add the cucumber, ginger, chile, and cilantro stems. Transfer to a sealed container and keep in the fridge.

To make the spice paste, place the dried chiles in a small bowl, cover with boiling water, and set aside for a few minutes. Put the ground white peppercorns and coriander seeds into the small bowl of a food processor, along with the shallot, garlic, cilantro stems, turmeric, 1 tablespoon of the coconut cream, soaked chiles, and 1 tablespoon of the chile-soaking liquid. Blend to form a smooth purée, scraping down the sides of the bowl a few times.

Put the remaining ½ cup plus 2 tbsp/145ml of coconut cream into a medium saucepan and place on medium-high heat. When it begins to simmer, add the spice paste and cook for 15–20 minutes, stirring frequently until thick, clotted, and oily. Add the coconut milk, sugar, fish sauce, and ¼ teaspoon of salt. Stir gently, then bring to a simmer. Add the asparagus stalks, cook for 4 minutes, then add the shrimp and asparagus tips. Cook for 3–5 minutes, until the shrimp are just cooked through, and serve with the rice, if you like.

Lemongrass and galangal tuna curry

2½ cups/600ml coconut milk
1 cup/240ml water
1 lb/450g baby bok choy
1 lb/450g tuna (from a jar or a can, drained weight)

Spice paste
3–4 stalks of lemongrass, white parts roughly chopped (¼ cup/25g), fibrous stalks set aside for the curry
2 shallots, roughly chopped (¾ cup/100g)
¾ oz/25g ginger, peeled and roughly chopped
¾ oz/20g galangal, peeled and roughly chopped (or ⅓ oz/10g extra ginger)
¾ oz/20g fresh turmeric, peeled and roughly chopped
3 garlic cloves, peeled and left whole
8 large lime leaves, tough center ribs removed from 4 and the remainder left whole and set aside for the curry
¾ oz/25g palm (or light brown) sugar
2 small, hot red chiles, seeded and roughly chopped
1¾ oz/50g cilantro, roughly chopped
2 tbsp lime juice
2 tbsp peanut (or vegetable) oil
salt

To serve (any or all of the following)
kicap manis (or sweet soy sauce)
hot chile sauce
⅓ cup/30g store-bought crispy fried shallots
½ cup/10g cilantro leaves, roughly chopped
steamed jasmine (or basmati) rice
1 lime, cut into wedges

Canned tuna and curry might not sound like an obvious fit to some, but try it! It was first introduced to Helen by a kitchen porter named Andreas who worked in her café in Melbourne. Everyone took their turn to make staff meals. While most meals stayed there—feeding and fueling the staff—Andreas's meal (a dish his Indonesian mum used to cook for him) was so good that it got promoted to the café menu. *Also pictured on page 172.*

Batch-making: Helen and her café team used to batch-make the spice paste (that they nicknamed "noodle gloop"!), ready to be deployed in all kinds of dishes. It was the base for stir-fried noodles (hence the nickname); it was folded into ground chicken for chicken burgers; it was added to the mixture for fishcakes. Even if you're not running your own café, it's really worth batch-making the spice paste as well, to use in other similar ways.

Serves 4

Place all the ingredients for the spice paste in a blender or food processor, along with 1½ teaspoons of salt and 3 tablespoons of water. Blitz to form a fine paste. The texture won't be as fine when done in a food processor, but it will still be okay.

Transfer to a large sauté pan and add 1 cup/240ml of the coconut milk. Bring to a simmer on medium-high heat, decrease the heat to medium-low, and gently simmer for 45–50 minutes, uncovered, stirring from time to time (especially toward the end) until the paste is thick. Add the 1 cup/240ml of water, the remaining 1½ cups/360ml of coconut milk, the lemongrass stalks, and the 4 whole lime leaves. Stir, bring to a gentle simmer, and continue to cook, uncovered, stirring every now and then, for 10 minutes.

Meanwhile, bring a pot of salted water to a boil and add the bok choy. Cook for 1 minute, drain, then add to the curry, along with the tuna. Simmer gently for 2 minutes, just to heat through. Spoon the curry into bowls and drizzle with kicap manis, hot chile sauce, and a little pinch of salt. Scatter the crispy shallots and cilantro leaves and serve, with the steamed rice and a wedge of lime on the side.

Chicken and lime leaf curry with noodles

3 tbsp Malay chicken curry powder (or mild Madras curry powder)
1 tbsp paprika
½ tsp chile powder
7 tbsp/100ml cold water
2 tbsp sunflower oil
1 onion, thinly sliced (1½ cups/180g)
4 garlic cloves, finely sliced
⅓ oz/10g ginger, peeled and finely grated
½ oz/15g cilantro stems, finely chopped (save leaves to garnish)
2 tsp belacan powder (or 1 tsp belacan paste or 2 tbsp fish sauce)
1 lb 9 oz/720g skinless and boneless chicken thighs, cut into 1½–2-inch/4–5cm pieces
8 fresh lime leaves
2 cups plus 2 tbsp/500ml coconut milk (if you need to open a second can, what you don't use can be frozen)
½ oz/15g jaggery, coarsely grated (or 2 tsp dark muscovado sugar)
salt

To serve
4½ oz/120g trimmed French green beans, cut in half on the diagonal
1 cup/100g fresh bean sprouts
15 oz/425g fresh thick egg (aka Hokkien) noodles
¼ cup/20g store-bought crispy fried shallots
2 limes, cut into wedges

Every Malaysian household has a version of this curry. It's usually cooked with bone-in chicken pieces, potatoes, and curry leaves, and served with steamed rice. Our version uses lime leaves instead—they make the curry bright and zesty rather than earthy—and noodles instead of the rice. Leftovers are delicious the next day, best eaten with a slice of toasted fresh white bread.

Ingredients note: Belacan in powder form is by far the easiest way to use this funky ingredient, as it just needs to be added to the curry. It's more readily available as a paste in a small tub, though, and needs to be toasted before use. To do this, wrap it tightly in foil and heat in the oven. Alternatively, use fish sauce.

Serves 4

Put the curry powder, paprika, and chile powder into a small bowl. Add the water, stir to form a thick paste, and set aside.

Put the oil into a wok or large pan, for which you have a lid, and place on medium heat. Add the onion, garlic, ginger, and cilantro stems and cook for 10–12 minutes, stirring regularly, until softened but not colored. Add the curry paste and belacan and cook for 1 minute, stirring continually, then add the chicken and lime leaves. Increase the heat to medium-high and cook for 5 minutes, stirring frequently, until the chicken pieces are well coated with the spice mix. Add enough cold water to just cover the chicken—around 1¼ cups/300ml—then decrease the heat to medium-low. Simmer, partially covered, for 40 minutes, or until the chicken is tender. Stir in the coconut milk, jaggery, and 2 teaspoons of salt. Cook for 5 minutes, then remove from the heat.

When ready to serve, bring a large pot of water to a boil and add the beans. Blanch for 3 minutes and then, using a large slotted spoon, remove them from the water. Keeping the pan on the heat, blanch the bean sprouts for 30 seconds and add to the beans. Leaving the water at a boil, add the noodles, blanch for 1 minute (or according to package instructions if using dried), and drain.

Divide the noodles among pasta bowls, spoon on the chicken curry, then top with the bean sprouts and beans. Sprinkle with some crispy fried shallots and serve, with a lime wedge alongside to squeeze over the top.

Chicken meatballs, potatoes, and lemon

Meatballs
4 green onions, roughly chopped
   (½ cup/40g)
¾ cup/15g mint leaves
½ oz/15g cilantro (leaves and stems)
2 garlic cloves, crushed to a paste
1 lb 2 oz/500g ground chicken
1 egg, beaten
15 oz/425g red-skinned potatoes,
   peeled and finely grated and
   wrung dry in a clean tea towel
   (about 1 heaping cup/250g)
1 tsp ground cumin
¼ cup/30g breadcrumbs
   (fresh or panko)
2 tbsp olive oil, for frying
salt and black pepper

Yogurt sauce
½ cup/150g Greek yogurt
½ cup/10g mint leaves
⅓ oz/10g cilantro
   (leaves and stems)

Broth
3 tbsp olive oil, plus extra to finish
1 large onion, thinly sliced
   (1¾ cups/200g)
4–5 celery stalks, cut into
   ¾-inch/2cm chunks
   (2 cups/200g), leaves roughly
   chopped (2 cups/40g)
2 lemons: shave the zest to
   get 2 strips, then juice to get
   ¼ cup/60ml
1 lb 3 oz/550g red-skinned
   potatoes, peeled and cut
   into 1¼-inch/3cm chunks
   (2 cups/450g)
8 garlic cloves, thinly sliced
½ tsp ground turmeric
1 tbsp ground cumin
1½ tsp ground cinnamon
2 cups/480ml chicken stock
   (or water)
1 tsp granulated sugar
¾ oz/20g cilantro (leaves and
   stems), roughly chopped

Yotam's idea of comfort can easily be embodied in a meatball, or a whole load of meatballs, to be precise. The Hebrew word *ktsitsa* covers meatballs, patties, fritters—anything, really, that's ground or finely chopped into a sticky mass, shaped into balls or patties, and then cooked. A *ktsitsa* can be veggie or meaty, poached or fried, stuffed into pita or served on a plate. In all of these cases, it's the bouncy texture of the meatball, the slight give that's created by the addition of starch to the mix, that is crucial (otherwise it would be a burger). Serve with rice, bulgur, or couscous.

Getting ahead: The meatballs can be made and kept in the fridge to firm up the day before, then cooked along with everything else on the day. Leftovers are great reheated the next day—the broth will just be that bit thicker from the potatoes, so add a splash of water or stock when heating, if you like.

Serves 4

First make the meatballs. Place the green onions, mint, cilantro, and garlic in the small bowl of a food processor and blitz until finely chopped. Scrape out into a medium bowl and add the remaining meatball ingredients, except for the oil, along with 1½ teaspoons of salt and plenty of pepper. Mix well and, with wet hands, shape into 16 balls, roughly 1¾ oz/50g each. Refrigerate for 30 minutes to firm up.

Meanwhile, put all the ingredients for the yogurt sauce into the same small food processor bowl, along with ¼ teaspoon of salt and a little pepper. Blitz until smooth. Transfer to a small serving bowl and set aside in the fridge.

Put the 2 tablespoons of oil into a large sauté pan, for which you have a lid, and place on medium-high heat. Once hot, sear the meatballs well on all sides for 10 minutes. Remove from the pan, and set aside.

To the same pan, add 3 more tablespoons of olive oil for the broth. Add the onion, celery chunks, lemon strips, 1 teaspoon of salt, and a good grind of pepper. Sauté for 7 minutes, to soften, then add the potatoes and garlic and sauté for another 7 minutes, until beginning to brown. Add the spices and cook for 1 minute, then add the lemon juice, chicken stock, sugar, and the celery leaves. Bring to a simmer, then carefully place the meatballs in the broth. Simmer on low heat, covered, for 25–30 minutes, until the meatballs are cooked through and the liquid has thickened slightly. Remove from the heat, carefully stir in the cilantro, and set aside to rest for 5 minutes.

To serve, drizzle the meatballs with oil and spoon some of the yogurt sauce on top, serving the rest on the side.

Braised lamb with butter beans and yogurt

2 tsp coriander seeds, toasted and roughly crushed

2½ tsp cumin seeds, toasted and roughly crushed

¼ tsp flaked sea salt

1¾ lb/800g lamb neck, cut against the grain into roughly ¾-inch/2cm chunks

¼ cup/60ml olive oil

2 onions, quartered (10 oz/285g)

2 bay leaves

1 lemon: finely shave the zest to get 6–7 strips, then cut into wedges to serve

6 garlic cloves, lightly smashed

4 anchovies, finely chopped

1 tbsp thyme leaves, finely chopped

1 tbsp rosemary leaves, finely chopped

9 oz/250g cherry tomatoes

⅓ cup/80ml white wine

2 cups/480ml chicken stock

1 x 25-oz/700g jar of good-quality butter beans (lima beans), drained and rinsed

½ cup/150g Greek yogurt

⅓ oz/10g parsley, roughly chopped, to garnish

salt and black pepper

Comfort, for some, will always be about texture. From there, it's often about things that are soft and falling apart. It's like the opposite of uptight; very much the case here with a slow-cooked stew of falling-apart lamb and soft and creamy butter beans. Serve with a simple green salad and the requisite crusty bread.

Getting ahead: This can be made in full a day or two in advance—the flavors only improve—and gently reheated to serve.

Serves 4

Preheat the oven to 375°F.

Mix all of the coriander seeds and 2 teaspoons of the cumin seeds in a small bowl and set aside. Put the remaining cumin into a separate small bowl, along with the flaked sea salt, and set aside.

Put the lamb into a large bowl with ½ teaspoon of salt and a good grind of pepper. Stir to combine.

Put 2 tablespoons of the oil into a large cast-iron sauté pan, for which you have a lid, and place on medium-high heat. When hot, add half the lamb—don't overcrowd the pan—and cook for about 6 minutes, turning so that all sides form a crust. Transfer to a plate, add another 1 tablespoon of oil, and repeat with the remaining lamb.

Add the remaining 1 tablespoon of oil to the pan, decrease the heat to medium, and add the onions, bay leaves, lemon strips, and garlic. Cook for 6 minutes, stirring a few times, until the onions have taken on some color. Add the anchovies, the coriander-cumin mix, the thyme, rosemary, and half the tomatoes. Cook for 1 minute, then return the lamb to the pan. Cook for another minute, then add the wine. Let it bubble away for 30 seconds, then add the stock, ¾ teaspoon of salt, and a good grind of pepper. Stir, increase the heat to medium-high, and bring to a simmer. Cover with the lid and place in the oven for 1½ hours, until the lamb is very soft and the liquid has reduced by quite a bit.

Remove the lamb from the oven and add the butter beans and remaining tomatoes. Stir, cover, and return to the oven for a final 20 minutes. Remove the pan from the oven and set aside to rest for 15 minutes.

When ready to serve, give the stew a good stir before spooning dollops of the yogurt on top. Sprinkle with the cumin salt and finish with the parsley. Serve the lemon wedges alongside.

Sausage and lentils with mustard crème fraîche

1½ cups/300g dried Puy lentils
3 tbsp olive oil
1 lb 5 oz/600g cooked Polish
   smoked sausages
1 large onion, finely chopped
   (1¼ cups/180g)
2 celery stalks, finely chopped
   (1½ cups/150g)
1 green bell pepper, seeded and cut
   into ½-inch/1cm dice (1 cup/140g)
3 garlic cloves, crushed to a paste
1 tbsp thyme leaves, roughly
   chopped
1 bay leaf
2 bunches of Swiss chard, stalks
   cut into ½-inch/1cm dice, leaves
   roughly torn (14 oz/400g)
1 tbsp tomato paste
2 tsp ground cumin
1 quart/1 liter chicken stock
¾ oz/20g parsley, roughly chopped
⅔ cup/50g store-bought crispy
   fried onions, to serve (optional)
salt and black pepper

Mustard crème fraîche
⅓ cup/75g crème fraîche
1½ tsp Dijon mustard
1½ tsp whole grain mustard

This classic combination of lentils and sausages is often made with herby Italian sausages. We love using the smoked Polish sausages, though, which impart their smoky flavor to the whole dish.

Getting ahead: This keeps well for a day or two, if you want to either get ahead or have leftovers for the next few days.

Serves 6

Rinse the lentils well, cover with plenty of cold water, and set aside, soaking, until needed.

Mix together all the ingredients for the mustard crème fraîche and keep in the fridge until ready to use.

Put ½ tablespoon of the oil into a Dutch oven and place on medium-high heat. Add the sausages and cook for 5 minutes, uncovered, turning so that all sides are browned. Transfer to a plate. Leave the oil in the pan.

Add the remaining 2½ tablespoons of oil to the pan and, keeping it on medium heat, add the onion, celery, and green bell pepper. Cook for 12–15 minutes, stirring from time to time, until the vegetables are starting to turn golden. Add the garlic, thyme, bay leaf, and chard stalks (the leaves are for later) and continue to cook for 2–3 minutes. Add the tomato paste and cumin and cook for 1 minute or so.

Drain the lentils and add them to the pot, along with the stock, 1½ teaspoons of salt, and a really good grind of pepper. Bring to a boil, then decrease the heat to low and cook for 30 minutes, covered, until the lentils are just cooked through. Using an immersion blender, blitz the lentils on one side of the pot for about 30 seconds, to break some of them up. Add the chard leaves to the pot and stir to combine.

Return the sausages to the pot and simmer for 10 minutes, until the leaves have wilted and the sausages are warmed through. Stir in the parsley and divide among six bowls. Spoon the mustard crème fraîche on top, followed by the crispy onions, if using, and serve.

Noodles, rice, tofu

Green tea noodles with avocado and radish

¾ oz/25g dried wakame seaweed (or a package of sea vegetable salad)

7 oz/200g dried green tea (or soba) noodles

2 tsp sesame oil

1 ripe avocado, peeled and sliced

4 green onions, thinly sliced (½ cup/45g)

½ cup/10g basil leaves

1 tbsp sesame seeds (a mix of black and white looks great), toasted

Sake-pickled radishes

3 oz/80g radishes, thinly sliced

2 tbsp rice (or white) wine vinegar

1 tbsp granulated sugar

2 tsp sake (or Shaoxing) wine

salt

Lemon soy dressing

3 tbsp lemon juice

3 tbsp rice (or white) wine vinegar

⅓ cup/80ml light soy sauce

2 tbsp mirin

½ oz/15g ginger, peeled and finely grated

1 garlic clove, crushed to a paste

Cold noodles on a warm day are as comforting as warm noodles on a cold day. It's the way they are eaten—holding the bowl with one hand, chopsticks or fork in the other, head slightly lowered; it's their texture—slippery and substantial; it's their receptiveness to all the other textures and flavors going on in the same bowl.

Getting ahead: All the components can be made in advance here—the noodles and radishes up to 2 days ahead, the dressing up to 3 days—kept separate, in the fridge, ready for the dish to be assembled in just a minute.

Ingredients note: Wakame has an interestingly oceanic flavor, which works so well against the avocado. The texture is also great: slippery, crunchy, and chewy at once. It's widely available but, as an alternative, packages of sea vegetable salad also work well.

Serves 4

Pickle the radishes up to 2 days (or at least 30 minutes) ahead of eating. Place them in a medium bowl and add ¾ teaspoon of salt. Using your hands, gently massage for a minute or two, then add the remaining pickle ingredients. Transfer to a small bowl or jar and keep in the fridge until ready to use.

Rehydrate the seaweed: this takes 30 minutes in cold water (which is the best option) or 10 minutes in hot water. Once rehydrated, drain and roughly tear any very large pieces and set aside in the fridge.

Place all the ingredients for the lemon soy dressing in a large screw-top jar and shake to combine. Keep in the fridge until ready to use.

Bring a large pot of water to a boil. Add the noodles, stir, then cook for 3 minutes. Add enough cold water to stop the boiling process and continue to cook for another 2 minutes. Drain in a sieve and rinse under cold running water. Drain well again, then transfer to a large bowl and add the sesame oil, mixing it with your hands. Cover and keep in the fridge until cold.

When ready to serve, use your hands to loosen and separate the noodles and add all the dressing, the drained radishes, wakame, avocado, green onions, and basil. Toss gently to mix, then transfer to a rimmed serving platter or shallow bowl. Scatter the toasted sesame seeds and serve.

Nasi goreng with shrimp and green beans

3 tbsp **peanut oil**, plus ¼ cup/60ml extra for frying the eggs

7 oz/200g **French green beans**, trimmed and cut into 1¼-inch/3cm lengths

¼ tsp **granulated sugar**

2 large **shallots**, sliced into thin rings (1 cup/140g)

scant 4 cups/750g **cooked long-grain rice**

½ cup/10g **Thai basil leaves**, plus a few extra to garnish

4 **eggs**

⅔ cup/50g **store-bought crispy fried shallots**, to serve

Kicap
1½ tbsp **lime juice**
1½ tbsp **fish sauce**
3 tbsp **dark soy sauce**
3 tbsp **dark brown sugar**
2 **bird's-eye chiles**, seeded (if you prefer) and finely sliced
salt

Spice paste
2 long **mild red chiles**, seeded and roughly chopped (about ¾ cup/25g)
1 **shallot**, roughly chopped (½ cup/80g)
4 **anchovies**
3 **garlic cloves**, peeled and left whole
6 large **lime leaves**, ribs removed, rolled and cut into fine slivers
1 tbsp **granulated sugar**
1 tbsp **fish sauce**
1 tbsp **lime juice**
5¼ oz/150g **peeled raw shrimp**

The secret to any kind of fried rice dish is using cold, pre-cooked rice (and a fried egg on top, of course). It's perfect for using up leftover rice, but the increasingly available pouches of long-shelf-life rice make it even easier. Just tip into the hot pan straight out of the package.

Getting ahead: Both the kicap and the spice paste can be made up to 3 days ahead.

Serves 4

Place all the ingredients for the kicap in a screw-top jar, along with ⅛ teaspoon of salt. Shake to combine and set aside.

Place all the ingredients for the spice paste, except the shrimp, in the small bowl of a food processor, along with 1 teaspoon of salt. Blitz to a purée, then add the shrimp. Blitz until finely chopped, rather than completely smooth and uniform.

Next, make the rice. Place a large sauté pan or wok, for which you have a lid, over high heat. When very hot, add 1 tablespoon of the oil, followed by the green beans. Add ¼ teaspoon of salt and the sugar, toss once, and cook for 1 minute without stirring too much—you want the beans to char a little. Transfer the beans from the pan to a plate.

Decrease the heat to medium-high and place the pan back on the stove. Add the remaining 2 tablespoons of oil, then the shallots, and cook for 5 minutes, stirring regularly, until lightly browned. Add the spice paste and cook for 5 minutes, stirring occasionally. Keep the heat on high and add the cooked rice (don't microwave it first), and stir until the grains are evenly coated in the spice paste. Cook for 5 minutes, stirring from time to time, until the rice is starting to turn golden in places. Add the fried beans, along with the basil. Stir, cover, and keep warm while you fry the eggs.

Place a large, nonstick frying pan over medium-high heat. Add the oil and, when hot, fry the eggs until the edges are crispy and the yolk a little runny.

Divide the rice among four bowls, place a fried egg on top of each, and drizzle the kicap. Scatter a few torn basil leaves around the egg, add a sprinkling of crispy shallots, and serve.

Quick ramen noodles with mushrooms

10½ oz/300g **brown button mushrooms**, stalks trimmed, caps wiped and roughly broken into 4–5 pieces

1 tbsp **peanut (or sunflower) oil**

2 tbsp **Shaoxing wine (or sake)**

2 x 3 oz/85g nests of **dried instant ramen noodles**

2 small pieces of **snacking nori**, to serve

Green onion sauce

6 **green onions**, finely sliced (¾ cup/60g)

1 **garlic clove**, finely chopped

⅓ oz/10g **ginger**, peeled and finely chopped

1 tsp **shichimi togarashi** (or ½ tsp regular chile flakes)

3 tbsp **peanut (or sunflower) oil**

2 tbsp **dark soy sauce**

1 tbsp **honey**

1 tbsp **fish sauce**

1 tbsp **lime juice**

We wanted to call these "10-minute ramen noodles" but, even at our most ready-steady-cook, we were landing on around 15 minutes so couldn't quite pull it off! Either way, they're super quick and pack a real flavor punch. It's a dish we fall back on time and again. They're also lovely eaten cold.

Ingredients note: The dark soy sauce is important here—it's thicker, darker, and less salty than regular light soy.

Serves 2

First make the green onion sauce. Place the green onions, garlic, ginger, and togarashi in a small heatproof bowl. Put the oil in a small sauté pan and place on medium heat. Bring to smoking point—it should take around 2 minutes—then remove from the heat. Immediately (and very carefully) pour the oil into the green onion mixture and stir. Let rest for 10 minutes, for the mixture to infuse and bloom, then add the soy sauce, honey, fish sauce, and lime juice. Set aside.

Meanwhile, place the mushrooms in a food processor and pulse about ten times, until finely chopped—some uneven bits are fine.

Place a large sauté or frying pan on medium-high heat and add the oil, followed by the chopped mushrooms. Cook for 12–15 minutes, stirring frequently, until the mushrooms have softened and darkened and most of the moisture has evaporated. Add the wine—it will evaporate almost immediately—then switch off the heat.

Fill a medium pot half full with water and bring to a boil on high heat. When the water has come to a boil, add the noodles and cook for 2 minutes (or according to the package instructions), until just softened. Drain the noodles and add them directly to the mushrooms. Toss gently, then add the green onion sauce and turn the noodles in the sauce to coat.

Divide between two bowls. Crumble a piece of nori sheet over each portion and serve.

Gingery fish and rice

6 sea bass fillets (or other thinly
cut white fish), skin on, sliced
crosswise
1 tsp cornstarch
1 tbsp sesame oil
1 tbsp unsalted butter
7–8 green onions, white and green
parts thinly sliced (and kept
separate) (1¼ cups/95g)
¾ oz/20g ginger, peeled and half
finely chopped, half julienned
2 garlic cloves, finely chopped
1½ cups/300g jasmine rice
2 cups/480ml chicken stock
2 tbsp sunflower oil

Chile ginger sauce
3 small, hot red chiles, seeded and
roughly chopped
2 garlic cloves, peeled and
left whole
⅓ oz/10g ginger, peeled and
roughly chopped
2 tbsp granulated sugar
2 tbsp lime juice
3 tbsp water
1 tsp salt

Marinade for the fish
1 tbsp Shaoxing wine (or sake)
1 tbsp oyster sauce
1 tsp light soy sauce
2 tbsp water
¾ tsp granulated sugar
salt and ground white pepper

This one-pot meal is a lovely way to cook fish, which steams over the rice. Make both the sauces in advance and the whole thing comes together very quickly. Serve with some quickly sautéed greens.

Getting ahead: The chile ginger sauce can be made up to 3 days ahead, stored in a screw-top jar. It's the same chile ginger sauce as is used for the cucur udang (see page 76)—with the addition of a bit of sesame oil—in case you are menu planning and want to double up the batch.

Serves 4

Place all the ingredients for the chile ginger sauce in a small blender (or in the small bowl of a food processor). Blitz to form a runny sauce. Transfer to a bowl and set aside until ready to serve—you'll have more than you need, which is no bad thing.

Next make the marinade for the fish. Put the Shaoxing wine, oyster sauce, soy, water, sugar, ¼ teaspoon of salt, and ¼ teaspoon of ground white pepper in a small bowl and stir to dissolve.

Place the fish in a shallow bowl and spoon the marinade over the top. Add the cornstarch, stir so that the fish is coated, and set aside.

To prepare the rice, put the sesame oil and butter into a large sauté pan (about 10 inches/25cm wide), for which you have a tight-fitting lid. Place on medium-low heat, add the white parts of the green onions, the finely chopped ginger, and garlic, and cook for about 6 minutes, until softened and starting to take on some color. Add the rice and stir for a couple of minutes, then add the stock and 1 teaspoon of salt. Increase the heat to high, bring to a boil, stir, then immediately decrease the heat to its lowest setting. Steam for 15 minutes, tightly covered, until the rice is just set. Working swiftly, uncover the pan and carefully place the fish in one layer on top of the rice and drizzle over any remaining marinade. Return the lid and steam for 12 minutes, until the fish is just cooked. Remove from the heat and allow to sit for 5 minutes, covered.

Scatter the julienned ginger and green parts of the green onion on top of the fish. Just before serving, heat the sunflower oil in a small saucepan. When very hot, pour the oil over the fish, lightly cooking the green onions and ginger as you do. Serve the fish and rice with the chile sauce on the side.

Chilled tofu with spiced sesame dressing

⅓ cup/50g sesame seeds
2 tbsp granulated sugar
2 garlic cloves, finely chopped
7 tbsp/100ml light soy sauce
2 tbsp toasted sesame oil
1 tbsp Chingkiang black
   (or malt) vinegar
1 tbsp shichimi togarashi
3 green onions, finely sliced
   (⅓ cup/30g)
2 blocks of soft tofu

To garnish
1 green onion, finely sliced
   (2 tbsp/10g)
a few cilantro sprigs
1 mild red chile, thinly sliced
2 tbsp store-bought crispy fried
   shallots (roughly chopped
   salted peanuts or cashews
   also work well)

Slippery and cool, this light but flavorful dish is cold comfort on a hot summer's day. Serve as a first course or a vegan main course.

Ingredients note: Chinkiang black vinegar has a lovely sweet and malty undertone that adds complexity to this simple soy-based dressing, but malt vinegar also works well. If you shop in a Chinese supermarket, there'll be a big choice of tofu. If you see "soft" tofu, then do get this—it slices much more easily than silken, which can rather collapse.

Getting ahead: The dressing can be prepared up to 3 days ahead and kept refrigerated. From there, it is 5 minutes to get this on the table.

Serves 4

Put the sesame seeds into a small frying pan and place on low heat. Toast for about 6 minutes, shaking the pan regularly, until light golden brown. Transfer to a mortar and pestle (or a spice grinder), then add the sugar and pound until coarsely ground. Place in a medium bowl and add all the remaining ingredients except for the tofu (and the garnishes). Stir to combine.

Ease the tofu out of its container and onto a large, shallow serving bowl, then cut into large, flat, rectangular pieces or dice. Spoon the sauce over the top and garnish with the green onion, cilantro, chile, and crispy-fried shallots.

Poached chicken congee

Poached chicken and stock
1 small chicken (about 2 lb 7 oz/1.1kg)
1¾ oz/50g ginger, unpeeled and
lightly bashed
15 whole black peppercorns
3 shallots, peeled and halved
lengthwise (1¼ cups/170g)
5 garlic cloves, unpeeled and
lightly bashed
1 cup/20g cilantro stems (reserve
the leaves for the topping)
salt

Congee
1 cup/200g jasmine rice
2 tbsp toasted sesame oil
2 shallots, finely chopped
(1 cup/155g)
¾ oz/25g ginger, peeled and finely
grated to get 1 tbsp
3 garlic cloves, crushed to a paste
7¼ cups/1.75 liters chicken stock
(see above)
2 tbsp fish sauce

*For the toppings (any or all of the
following)*
4 green onions, finely sliced
(½ cup/40g)
**½ cup/40g store-bought crispy
fried onions**
3 tbsp toasted sesame seeds
¾ oz/20g cilantro leaves (from the
stems used above)
1 cup/100g bean sprouts
1 tsp crushed white peppercorns
(don't substitute ground white
pepper here)
1–2 small, hot red chiles, thinly
sliced
crispy chili oil (either store-bought,
or see page 136 for the recipe for
peanut rayu)
1 lime, cut into wedges, to serve

This is comfort food by so many measures. The soothing texture of
the chicken and porridge; the chicken-soup-for-the-soul; bowl food
eaten with a spoon or chopsticks. It's the sort of food we eat when
we are in need of something soothing and convivial, and is a dish
that takes Helen straight back home. Kids love it too—you might
just hold back on the sprinkle of peppercorns and chile at the end.

Getting ahead: The congee is best made fresh, but the chicken can
be poached and shredded the day before. You'll need to warm it
up before serving, or stir it into the hot congee, rather than placing
on top.

Serves 4

Place the chicken in a medium stockpot or deep Dutch oven, breast
side up. Add 3–3½ quarts/liters of water—you want the chicken to
be just covered. Add all the other poaching ingredients, along with
1 teaspoon of salt, and bring to a simmer on medium-high heat. Once
simmering, decrease the heat to low and cook gently for 1½ hours.
Skim a few times, and don't allow the stock to come to a boil at any
point. To check when the chicken is done, tug gently at one of the
drumsticks: it should start to detach. Turn off the heat, then, using
a large slotted spoon, lift the chicken out of the stock, and transfer
it to a large rimmed plate. Set aside to cool.

Place the rice in a sieve and rinse really well until the water runs
clear. Set aside to drain. Put the sesame oil into a large saucepan
and place on medium heat. Add the shallots and ginger and cook
for 5 minutes, stirring a few times, until softened. Add the garlic
and ¼ teaspoon of salt, cook for another 2 minutes, then add the
rice. Stir and then strain 7¼ cups/1.75 liters of the chicken stock
over the rice (the vegetables can be discarded and the remaining
stock can be used in other dishes or frozen). Cook on medium heat
for 30 minutes, uncovered and stirring regularly, until the rice is
soft and starting to break down—it should have the consistency
of oatmeal. Add the fish sauce.

While the congee is cooking, tear the chicken off the bones into
shreds.

To serve, divide the congee among four large soup bowls, then top
with the shredded chicken and the rest of the toppings. Serve with
a wedge of lime.

Mushroom and kimchi mapo tofu

10½ oz/300g **mixed mushrooms** (a mixture of brown button, shiitake, and oyster, for example), caps and stalks roughly broken into 3–4 pieces

2 tbsp **peanut (or sunflower) oil**

8 **green onions**, finely sliced (1 cup/85g), white and green parts kept separate

4 **garlic cloves**, finely chopped

¾ oz/20g **ginger**, peeled and finely chopped

2 tbsp **Shaoxing wine**

3 tbsp **doubanjiang** (aka chile bean sauce)

1½ tbsp **light soy sauce**

1 tbsp **dark soy sauce**

1¼ cups/300ml **vegetable stock (or water)**

1 tbsp **potato starch (or cornstarch)**, dissolved in 2 tbsp of water

1 cup/150g **kimchi**, roughly chopped

1¾ lb/800g **soft tofu** (not the silken variety), cut into roughly 1¼-inch/3cm squares

2 tsp **toasted sesame oil**

½ tsp **Sichuan peppercorns**, toasted and roughly crushed

steamed rice, to serve

Get your shopping and your chopping done and this is a fewer-than-15-minutes-to-the-table meal. In terms of effort-to-impact ratio, it's also a delight, with so much going on in terms of flavor (amplified) and texture (wonderfully soft). Traditionally, mapo tofu—the much-loved Sichuan dish—is made with ground beef or pork. Here we use mushrooms. It's a complex vegan meal, to be eaten with plenty of steamed plain or jasmine rice. Leftovers are great for the next couple of days so, even if you're cooking for just one or two, do make the whole recipe.

The name "mapo," so the story goes, comes from the wife of a late nineteenth-century Qing dynasty restaurateur, who used to cook big batches of tofu for passing workers. Her face, marked with smallpox scars, earned her the nickname *ma po*, "pock-marked woman." So there we go—hundreds of years later, versions of her street food live on.

Serves 4–6

Put the pieces of mushroom into a food processor and pulse about 10 times, until finely chopped.

Put the oil into a large nonstick sauté pan and place on medium heat. Add the white parts of the green onions, along with the garlic and ginger. Cook for 2–3 minutes, until softened, then add all the chopped mushrooms. Increase the heat to medium-high and cook for 8–9 minutes, stirring occasionally, until the mushrooms have softened and most of the moisture has evaporated.

Add the Shaoxing wine, doubanjiang, and the light and dark soy sauces. Bring to a simmer, then lower the heat and cook for 1 minute, stirring to combine. Add the stock, then the potato flour mixture, and simmer for 1 minute until slightly thickened. Add the kimchi, then gently fold in the tofu to warm through.

Transfer to a large serving bowl, drizzle the sesame oil over the top, and sprinkle with the Sichuan peppercorns and the reserved green parts of the green onions.

Pasta, polenta, potatoes

Pesto pasta with charred beans and potatoes

2¾ cups/55g **basil leaves**
⅓ cup/50g **pine nuts**
1 **garlic clove**, crushed to a paste
7 tbsp/100ml **olive oil**
1½ oz/40g **parmesan**, finely grated (⅓ cup)
6⅓ oz/180g **French green beans**, trimmed
1 **lemon**: finely grate the zest, then juice to get 1 tbsp
9 oz/250g **dried trofie (or orecchiette or cavatelli)**
10½ oz/300g **new potatoes**, peeled and sliced into roughly ¾-inch/2cm pieces
salt and black pepper

This is our test kitchen colleague Katja Tausig's twist on the classic Ligurian combination of pasta, pesto, green beans, and potatoes. Double carbs are the comfort; charring the beans is the twist.

Serves 4

To make the pesto, put 2¼ cups/45g of the basil into a food processor, along with the pine nuts, garlic, ⅛ teaspoon of salt, and a good grind of pepper. Pulse a few times, scrape down the sides of the bowl, and pulse again until you have a coarse paste. With the food processor running, slowly add ⅓ cup/80ml of olive oil, until just combined. Add three-quarters of the parmesan and pulse to combine. Set aside.

Heat a griddle pan on high heat. Place the beans in a bowl, along with ½ teaspoon of oil and ⅛ teaspoon of salt, and toss to combine. When the pan is very hot, add the beans—in 2–3 batches—and cook for about 5 minutes, turning so that all sides are charred and tender. Remove from the heat and, once cool enough to handle, cut the beans in half and transfer to a bowl. Add the remaining 1 tablespoon of olive oil, the lemon zest, juice, the remaining ½ cup/10g of basil leaves, and ⅛ teaspoon of salt.

Meanwhile, fill a medium saucepan three-quarters full with well-salted water and bring to a boil. Add the pasta to the boiling water, cook for around 5 minutes, then add the potatoes. Cook for 7 minutes, until the potatoes are cooked through and the pasta is al dente. Drain, reserving ¼ cup/60ml of the water. Return the pasta and potatoes to the pan, stir in the pesto and the reserved pasta water, and mix gently to combine.

To serve, transfer the pasta to a large serving bowl. Top with the beans, followed by the remaining parmesan, and serve.

Caramelized onion orecchiette with hazelnuts and crispy sage

7 tbsp/100ml olive oil
1 cup/20g sage leaves
2 onions, thinly sliced
(2⅔ cups/320g)
9 oz/250g dried orecchiette
(or casarecce or small conchiglie)
3 cups/700ml water, at room
temperature
1½ tbsp lemon juice
⅓ cup/50g hazelnuts, coarsely
chopped
salt and black pepper

This is one of those magic recipes that seems to come together when you haven't got much in the pantry. It also feels like so much more than the sum of its parts, making a quick and delicious weeknight supper.

Playing around: Other nuts work as well as the hazelnuts here—walnuts or almonds are particularly good—so use what you have in the pantry.

Serves 4

Put the oil into an 11-inch/28cm sauté pan, for which you have a lid, and place on medium-high heat. Once hot, add the sage leaves and fry for 4 minutes, stirring frequently, until the leaves are dark green and crispy. Drain the leaves in a sieve set over a small bowl. Spoon 2 tablespoons of the reserved oil into a small frying pan and set aside.

Return the sauté pan to medium heat, pour in the rest of the reserved oil and, once hot, add the onions. Cook for about 25 minutes, stirring frequently, until golden but not too dark. Add the pasta to the pan, along with the water, 1¼ teaspoons of salt, and ½ teaspoon of freshly cracked pepper. Mix well, then simmer gently, covered, for 20 minutes, until the liquid has been absorbed and the pasta is al dente. Drizzle with the lemon juice, finish with a good crack of pepper, and set aside.

Place the small frying pan (with its oil) on medium heat, then add the chopped hazelnuts and fry gently for 2–3 minutes, until golden. Spoon the hazelnuts and the oil on top of the pasta, sprinkle with the crispy fried sage leaves, and serve hot, straight from the pan.

Linguine with miso butter, shiitake, and spinach

7 oz/190g dried linguine
  (or spaghetti)
1 tbsp olive oil
7 tbsp/100g unsalted butter, fridge-
  cold, cut into ¾-inch/2cm cubes
1 shallot, finely chopped (½ cup/75g)
5¼ oz/150g fresh shiitake
  mushrooms, roughly sliced
3 garlic cloves, crushed to a paste
3 tbsp white miso paste
1 tsp light soy sauce
1 tbsp Chinkiang black (or malt)
  vinegar
5¼ oz/150g baby spinach leaves
salt and black pepper

To serve
shichimi togarashi (or chile flakes)
lemon or lime wedges

The butter, miso, and cooking water all combine to emulsify and coat the linguine here in the most comforting of all sauces. It's totally creamy without the use of any cream, and is perfect for an easy mid-week supper.

Ingredients note: The suggestion to add togarashi—the Japanese 7-spice mix—feels fusion and works well, but some regular chile flakes and a really (really!) good crack of black pepper works brilliantly too.

Serves 2

Bring a large saucepan with 8½ cups/2 liters of water to a boil. Add 1 teaspoon of salt, followed by the pasta, and cook until al dente. Drain, saving ¾ cup plus 2 tbsp/200ml of the cooking water.

Meanwhile, put the oil and 1 tbsp of the butter into a large sauté pan and place on medium-high heat. Add the shallot and cook for about 5 minutes, until soft but not taking on any color. Add the mushrooms, along with a good grind of pepper, and cook for about 7 minutes, until the moisture has evaporated and they are starting to brown. Add the garlic, miso, soy sauce, and vinegar and stir for about 30 seconds until combined. Add the reserved pasta-cooking water, mix well, and bring to a simmer. Decrease the heat to medium and, keeping the mixture at a good simmer, add the remaining 6 tbsp/85g of butter piece by piece, stirring constantly until the sauce has emulsified and thickened slightly—this should take about 3 minutes.

Return the cooked pasta to the pan, toss for 30 seconds, then add the spinach. Toss and turn for 1 minute, until it has wilted, then serve with a generous shake of shichimi togarashi (or chile flakes and a few extra grinds of pepper) and lemon or lime wedges alongside for squeezing.

Rigatoni al ragù bianco

½ oz/15g **dried wild mushrooms**, soaked in 1 cup/240ml boiling water for 30 minutes
1 tbsp **unsalted butter**
1 tbsp **olive oil**
1 **onion**, finely diced (1¼ cups/180g)
2 **carrots**, peeled and finely diced (1½ cups/180g)
2 **celery stalks**, finely diced (1 cup/100g)
14 oz/400g **ground beef**, 10–15% fat
14 oz/400g **ground pork**
1¼ cups/300ml **chicken stock**
12¾ oz/360g **dried rigatoni (or spirali)**
salt and black pepper

Potato paste
1 **small russet (or other floury) potato**, peeled and roughly diced (⅔ cup/160g)
2 **large garlic cloves**, roughly chopped
6 **sage leaves**, finely chopped
1 tbsp **rosemary leaves**, finely chopped
½ tsp **chile flakes** (optional)
4 **anchovies**, roughly chopped

To serve
1 tbsp **finely grated lemon zest** (from 2 lemons)
½ oz/15g **parsley**, finely chopped
¾ oz/20g **parmesan**, finely grated (3 tbsp)

Ask an Italian what their idea of comfort food is, and they might not know what you're talking about. "*All food is comfort food,*" they'll probably say. With a cuisine so rich in pasta, risotto, and polenta, it's easy to see where such thinking comes from. Still, if we take comfort food to mean food that sustains and nurtures, then *rigatoni al ragù bianco*—commonly made in the north of Italy (and often made by Yotam's Italian dad when the kids were growing up) counts as *particularly* comforting Italian food. It's low-key, easy, and restorative. Serve with pasta, as we do here, or on soft polenta (see page 220). *Pictured on page 208.*

Serves 4, generously

First make the potato paste. Put the potato, garlic, sage, rosemary, chile flakes, and anchovies into a food processor and process to form a coarse paste. Scrape into a bowl and set aside. Don't worry if it discolors a little.

Strain the mushrooms (saving the liquid), roughly chop, and set aside. Strain the reserved liquid (discarding any gritty sediment) and set aside, as well, for later.

Put the butter and oil into a medium pan, for which you have a lid, and place on medium heat. Once hot, add the onion, carrots, and celery and cook for 10 minutes, until softened. Increase the heat to high, add the ground beef and pork, and cook for 10–12 minutes, stirring gently, to brown. You don't want the meat to completely break up, so don't be too vigorous with the stirring. Add the potato paste, along with 1½ teaspoons of salt and a good grind of black pepper. Cook for 2 minutes, then add the mushrooms, along with their soaking liquid and the stock. Bring to a simmer, then decrease the heat to low and cook for 1½ hours, partially covered, until the sauce has thickened.

Cook the pasta in salted boiling water until al dente, then toss with the ragù. Combine the lemon zest and parsley and sprinkle on top. Finish with the parmesan.

Helen's Bolognese

⅓ cup/80ml peanut oil
1 onion, finely diced (1¼ cups/180g)
1 large carrot, peeled and finely
  diced (1 cup/125g)
1 celery stalk, finely diced
  (¾ cup/75g)
2 star anise
1 cinnamon stick
2 bay leaves
1½ tsp Sichuan peppercorns,
  roughly crushed in a mortar
  and pestle
1 tsp fennel seeds, roughly crushed
  in a mortar and pestle
1 lb 2 oz/500g ground pork
  (or beef, or a mixture of both)
3 garlic cloves, crushed to a paste
1½ oz/40g ginger, peeled and
  finely chopped
2 tbsp Shaoxing wine
7 tbsp/100g doubanjiang
  (aka chile bean paste)
3 tbsp light soy sauce
1¼ cups/300ml water
1 tbsp cornstarch
7 green onions, finely sliced
  (scant 1 cup/75g)
12¾ oz/360g dried pappardelle

Dressed cucumbers
1 large cucumber, cut into thin
  batons (2 cups/310g)
2 tbsp rice wine vinegar
1 tsp honey
1 tsp sesame oil
salt

To serve
¼ cup/5g cilantro leaves,
  roughly torn
1½ tbsp toasted sesame seeds

Pasta Bolognese: so many of us grow up on a particular version that then becomes the normal against which all others are measured. Anyone whose default is an Italian or Anglophone take on the dish will be delighted by Helen's Bolognese. Adapted from a noodle sauce in Carolyn Phillips' book, *All Under Heaven*, it gets a lot of its depth and deliciousness from doubanjiang—a spicy bean paste made from fermented soy beans, fava beans, and chiles. It is a key ingredient in a lot of Sichuanese food and readily available in Asian grocery stores or online. *Pictured on page 209.*

Serves 4

Put the oil into a medium saucepan, for which you have a lid, and place on medium-high heat. Once hot, add the onion, carrot, celery, star anise, cinnamon stick, and bay leaves. Cook for 5 minutes, stirring frequently, then add the Sichuan peppercorns and fennel seeds. Cook for another 5 minutes, stirring from time to time, until the vegetables take on some color. Take the pan off the heat and, using a slotted spoon, transfer the vegetables to a plate, leaving behind the oil and any sediments.

Keep the pan on medium-high heat and add the meat, garlic, and ginger. Cook for 5–7 minutes, stirring from time to time, until the meat is lightly browned. Add the Shaoxing wine, cook for 1 minute, then add the doubanjiang, soy sauce, and 1 cup/240ml of the water. Stir to combine, partially cover, and simmer on medium-low heat for about 25 minutes, stirring from time to time.

While the meat sauce is simmering, mix the cornstarch with the remaining ¼ cup/60ml of water and set aside.

Return the cooked vegetables to the sauce, along with the green onions and the cornstarch slurry. Simmer for 5 minutes, uncovered.

Meanwhile, place all the ingredients for the dressed cucumbers in a small bowl. Add ¼ teaspoon of salt, mix to combine, and set aside.

Cook the pappardelle in salted boiling water until al dente, then divide among four bowls. Ladle the meat sauce over the pasta and top with some of the dressed cucumbers. Finish with the cilantro and sesame seeds and serve, with the remaining cucumbers on the side.

Stroganoff meatballs

1 lb 2 oz/500g dried tagliatelle
(or pappardelle or linguine)
¼ cup/50g unsalted butter
2 tsp poppy seeds

Meatballs
2½ oz/70g day-old white
bread, crusts removed and
bread roughly torn
7 tbsp/100ml milk
1 tbsp olive oil
1 onion, finely chopped
(1¼ cups/180g)
2 garlic cloves, crushed to a paste
1 lb 2 oz/500g ground beef
or pork, at least 15% fat
2 tsp Dijon mustard
1 egg
¼ oz/5g dill, finely chopped
1 tsp finely grated lemon zest
¼ cup/60ml olive oil, for frying
salt and black pepper

Mushroom sauce
3 shallots, thinly sliced
(1¾ cups/200g)
3 garlic cloves, crushed to a paste
¼ cup/50g unsalted butter
14 oz/400g small brown button
mushrooms, quartered
3 tbsp cognac (or brandy)
1½ tsp hot smoked paprika
1½ tbsp tomato paste
1 tbsp Dijon mustard
1 tbsp Worcestershire sauce
2¾ cups/650ml beef stock
⅔ cup/150g sour cream
(or crème fraîche)

To serve
4½ oz/125g dill pickles, roughly
chopped
⅓ oz/10g dill, roughly chopped

We love the richness (and retro-ness!) of beef stroganoff, but beef tenderloin is not always the way to feed a crowd! Here, we've taken the richness of stroganoff but made it into meatballs. This not only makes the meat go further—it almost makes it pure comfort in a bowl. We serve this with pasta but egg noodles work just as well, as does rice, orzo, or mashed potato.

Getting ahead: This dish, except for the pasta, can be made a day in advance.

Serves 6

First make the meatballs. Place the bread in the milk in a large mixing bowl and set aside, for about 5 minutes, to soak.

Put the oil into a small frying pan and place on medium heat. Add the onion and cook for 8–10 minutes, stirring a few times, until soft. Add the garlic, cook for 1 minute, then scrape into a medium bowl. Allow the mix to cool a little, then add it to the bowl of soaked bread, along with all the remaining ingredients for the meatballs, minus the olive oil, plus 1 teaspoon of salt and some pepper. Mix well, then form into 26 balls, 1 oz/30g each. Keep in the fridge, covered, until ready to cook.

Put 2 tablespoons of the oil into a large sauté pan and place on medium-high heat. Once hot, add half the meatballs and cook for 8 minutes, until nicely browned and just cooked through, gently shaking the pan to turn them over. Transfer to a plate and repeat with the remaining batch, adding another 2 tablespoons of oil. Transfer these to the plate of meatballs and set aside.

Next, make the mushroom sauce. Without washing the pan, and keeping the heat on medium-high, add the shallots and cook for 5–7 minutes, stirring a few times, until starting to caramelize. Add the garlic, cook for 1 minute, then scrape the mixture into a medium bowl.

Add half the butter to the same pan and return to medium-high heat. Add half the mushrooms, along with ¼ teaspoon of salt, and cook for 6 minutes, resisting the urge to stir too much, until all the moisture has evaporated and the mushrooms are well browned. Tip them into the bowl of shallots and set aside while you repeat with the remaining butter, mushrooms, and another ¼ teaspoon of salt.

Return the shallots and mushrooms to the pan, still on medium-high heat, and bring the mixture to a simmer. Add the cognac and let it bubble away for a few seconds, then add the paprika, tomato paste, mustard, Worcestershire sauce, and beef stock. Bring to a boil, then lower to a simmer and cook for 15 minutes, until reduced by a third. Add the sour cream, meatballs, ½ teaspoon of salt, and some pepper and simmer for 5 minutes, until the meatballs are cooked through.

Meanwhile, cook the pasta in salted boiling water until al dente. Drain and return it to the pot, then add the butter and poppy seeds. Toss gently until the butter has melted. Divide among six bowls and spoon the meatballs and sauce on top. Top with the chopped pickles and dill to serve.

One-pot chicken with orzo and porcini

3–4 dried cascabel (or ancho) chiles (¾ oz/25g)
4 cinnamon sticks
1 oz/30g dried porcini mushrooms
4⅔ cups/1.1 liters boiling water
1 whole chicken (3⅓ lb/1.5kg)
2 lemons: 1 halved and the other cut into 4 wedges to serve
¼ cup/60ml olive oil
1 lb 2 oz/500g celery, cut at a slight angle into 1½-inch/4cm lengths
2 onions, each peeled and cut into 8 wedges
6 garlic cloves, thinly sliced
8 thyme sprigs
1½ cups/320g dried orzo
¼ oz/5g parsley, roughly chopped, to serve
salt and black pepper

Cooking the chicken the way we do here makes for the tenderest of meat, but our favorite bit, truly, is the orzo pasta, which gets to drink in all the chicken juices. Serve with your favorite savory chile sauce, if you like.

Serves 4, generously

Preheat the oven to 400°F.

Put the chiles and cinnamon into a small dry frying pan on medium-high heat. Cook for 8 minutes, until fragrant and toasted, then transfer to a large bowl with the porcini mushrooms. Add the boiling water, cover with a plate, and let soak for at least 15 minutes.

Meanwhile, pat the chicken dry and sprinkle all over with ½ teaspoon of salt and a good grind of pepper. Stuff one lemon half into the cavity.

Put 2 tablespoons of the oil into a large Dutch oven and place on medium-high heat. Add the chicken and cook on all sides until browned—about 7 minutes in total. Transfer the chicken to a plate, and add the remaining 2 tablespoons of oil to the saucepan, along with the celery and onions. Cook for 6 minutes, until lightly golden. Add the garlic and thyme and cook for 1 minute. Return the chicken to the pan, breast side up, and pour in the soaked mushrooms and their liquid, along with all the aromatics, 2 teaspoons of salt, and a good grind of pepper. Bring to a simmer, cover with a lid, and transfer to the oven for 50 minutes. Remove from the oven and stir in the orzo, pushing some into the chicken cavity. Replace the lid and bake for 20 minutes more, until the orzo is cooked and has absorbed most of the liquid.

Increase the oven temperature to 425°F, remove the lid, and bake for 10 minutes, or until browned on top. Let cool slightly, 10–15 minutes.

Squeeze the other lemon half over the top, sprinkle with the parsley, and serve directly from the pan, with the lemon wedges alongside.

Zucchini and fennel lasagne

6–7 large zucchini, thinly sliced
(3⅓ lb/1.5kg)
3 large fennel bulbs, thinly sliced
(2 lb 2 oz/1kg)
2 bunches of green onions, finely
sliced (2¼ cups/175g)
1 cup plus 2 tbsp/265ml olive oil
4 garlic cloves, crushed to a paste
⅓ cup/45g capers, roughly chopped
1½ tsp fennel seeds, toasted and
roughly crushed
1¾ oz/50g dill, roughly chopped
1 oz/30g parsley, roughly chopped
1 large lemon: finely grate the
zest to get 1 tsp, then juice to
get 3 tbsp
⅔ cup/160ml vegetable stock
(or water)
½ tsp honey
3 tbsp pumpkin seeds, toasted
10½ oz/300g fresh lasagne sheets
salt and black pepper

Ricotta cream
1 cup/250g ricotta
6 oz/175g pecorino romano, finely
grated (1⅔ cups)
4½ oz/125g buffalo
mozzarella, roughly chopped
⅓ cup/80ml heavy cream

Thanks to Verena, we have the veggie lasagne everyone has been waiting for. The veggies get a relatively long time roasting before the dish is assembled, which makes for a hugely rich and concentrated flavor. The white sauce, on the other hand, takes much less time than it normally does. It's a no-cook version, taking seconds to blitz up. *Pictured on page 216.*

Serves 8

Preheat the oven to 500°F.

Combine the zucchini, fennel, and green onions in a large bowl, along with ⅔ cup/160ml of the olive oil, 2¼ teaspoons of salt, and a good grind of pepper. Mix well, then spread out on two parchment-lined rimmed baking sheets. Roast for 40 minutes, rotating the sheets and giving everything a good stir halfway through.

Remove the sheets from the oven and combine the vegetables on one sheet. Add the garlic, capers, fennel seeds, half of the dill, two-thirds of the parsley, and 1 tablespoon of lemon juice and stir to combine. Return the sheet to the oven for 10 minutes.

Turn the oven down to 400°F, add the stock to the vegetables, and cook for 5 minutes. Carefully transfer to a bowl and set aside.

Next, make the pesto. Put the remaining dill, parsley, lemon juice, and the lemon zest into the small bowl of a food processor. Add 7 tbsp/100ml of the olive oil, the honey, toasted pumpkin seeds, and ¼ teaspoon of salt, and blitz to combine. Transfer to a small bowl and set aside.

For the ricotta cream, put the ricotta, 4½ oz/125g (1¼ cups) of the pecorino, and all the mozzarella into the large bowl of the food processor. Add the heavy cream and ⅛ teaspoon of salt and blitz until thoroughly combined.

Spoon a small portion of the vegetables into the bottom of an 8 x 12-inch/20 x 30cm baking dish, just enough to cover the bottom in a thin layer. Arrange a layer of pasta sheets over the top (cut them to fit your dish) and spoon on a third of the remaining vegetables, followed by 6 tablespoons of the ricotta cream (just roughly dotted around is fine) and 1½ tablespoons of the pesto. Sprinkle with about ½ tablespoon of the pecorino and repeat the layering process twice more, until you are left with a bare layer of pasta on top. Spread the remaining ricotta cream over the top and sprinkle with the rest of the pecorino. Drizzle with the remaining 1 tablespoon of olive oil and bake for 40–45 minutes, rotating the dish halfway through, until nicely browned. Let rest for 20–30 minutes before serving with the remaining pesto alongside.

Sausage ragù lasagne for one

1 tbsp olive oil

4 small sausages, casings removed
and discarded (9 oz/250g)

1 small carrot, finely chopped
(⅓ cup/50g)

1–2 shallots, finely chopped
(½ cup/70g)

½ tsp thyme leaves

⅓ oz/10g oregano leaves

3 garlic cloves, crushed to a paste

1 tsp fennel seeds, lightly crushed

½ x 14-oz/400g can of whole,
peeled tomatoes, crushed

¾ cup plus 2 tbsp/200ml boiling
water

3 fresh (or dried) lasagne sheets
(4½ oz/130g)

4½ oz/125g buffalo mozzarella

salt and black pepper

The image we tend to have of lasagne is that it's always served in a great big dish, brought to a heaving table. We wanted to reclaim it for the solo diner, though, which is what our clever test kitchen colleague Chaya Pugh did for a *Guardian* column, themed "eating for one." It has all the delights of pasta and lasagne without all the prep time (or crowds!). And don't worry about missing out on a corner piece (with all their crispy edges)—the folded lasagne sheets are great for creating these crispy bits. To make this vegetarian, swap the sausage for firm tofu or mushrooms. *Pictured on page 216.*

Serves 1, with leftovers

Put the oil into a small ovenproof sauté pan and place on medium-high heat. Once hot, add the sausage meat, carrot, shallots, thyme, and three-quarters of the oregano. Cook for about 15 minutes, stirring frequently, until lightly golden, using the spoon to break up the sausage meat. Add the garlic and fennel seeds and cook for 2 minutes until fragrant. Stir in the tomatoes and cook for 5 minutes, until bubbling. Add the boiling water, a good grind of pepper, and ½ teaspoon of salt. Decrease the heat to medium and simmer for about 10 minutes, until the sauce has thickened and looks glossy.

Preheat the oven broiler to its highest setting.

Fill a medium saucepan with 1 quart/liter of water, add 1 tablespoon of salt, and place on medium-high heat. Once simmering, add the lasagne sheets and cook for 2 minutes (or 6–8 minutes, if using dried). Drain and set aside.

Tear or cut the lasagne sheets in half and stir into the ragù. Simmer for 2 minutes, stirring occasionally, until the pasta has softened and is nicely coated in the sauce. Using a spoon, lift and arrange the sheets so they sit in folds, like handkerchiefs nestling in the sauce. Roughly tear the mozzarella and place it in between the layers and on top of the lasagne.

Place under the broiler for about 6 minutes, until the cheese is bubbling and some of the lasagne sheets have crispy edges.

Remove from the oven and serve, with the remaining oregano on top.

Tomato and eggplant one-pot baked pasta

¼ **cup/60ml olive oil**

2 eggplants, quartered lengthwise and then each quarter cut in half crosswise (1 lb 2 oz/500g)

12¼ oz/350g cherry tomatoes, half sliced and half left whole

1 x 14-oz/400g can of diced tomatoes

1 tsp dried oregano

1 cup/20g basil leaves, roughly torn, plus a few extra leaves to serve

6 garlic cloves, thinly sliced

1 small, hot red chile, sliced in half lengthwise, but stem intact

2 tbsp tomato paste

1 tsp granulated sugar

7 tbsp/100g unsalted butter, cut into ¾-inch/2cm cubes

9 oz/250g dried fusilloni (or other large pasta such as paccheri)

1²⁄₃ cups/400ml boiling water

⅓ oz/10g parsley, roughly chopped

1½ oz/40g parmesan, finely grated (⅓ cup)

salt and black pepper

This is our take on our former colleague Noor Murad's take on the iconic tomato butter sauce of Marcella Hazan. The clue is in the name of Hazan's sauce: it turns out that slow-cooking tomatoes in a lot of butter really *is* the way to make the most comforting and delicious of all sauces. It doesn't actually taste that buttery, strangely—just silky, smooth, and rich. If you have kids who are, like Tara's, as yet unconvinced by the wonder that is the roasted eggplant, this dish also works really well without it.

Serves 4

Preheat the oven to 425°F.

Put the oil into a large ovenproof sauté pan, for which you have a lid, along with the eggplants, 1 teaspoon of salt, and a good grind of pepper. Toss to combine, then arrange the eggplants skin side down. Roast for 30 minutes, until nicely golden and starting to catch in places.

Add all the remaining ingredients to the pan, except the parsley and parmesan, along with ¾ teaspoon of salt and a good grind of pepper. Stir to combine, then bake for 30 minutes, covered, until the tomatoes have cooked down and the pasta is tender. Don't worry if all the pasta is not completely covered with liquid at this stage.

After the pasta has been in the oven for 30 minutes, give everything a good stir and cook for a final 10–15 minutes, uncovered, until the sauce clings to the pasta and is starting to catch in places. Let rest for 10 minutes before serving with the parsley, parmesan, and extra basil leaves sprinkled over the top.

Turkey rags-to-riches

9 oz/250g turkey (or chicken)
  breasts, skinless
1½ tbsp all-purpose (or rice) flour
1½ tbsp olive oil
2 tbsp unsalted butter
10 sage leaves
1 garlic clove, crushed to a paste
7 tbsp/100ml dry white wine
1 bay leaf
2 tbsp capers, roughly chopped
1 lemon: finely grate the zest to get
  1 tsp, then juice to get 1 tbsp
3 tbsp chicken stock (or water)
¼ oz/5g parsley, finely chopped
salt and black pepper

Soft polenta
½ cup/120ml milk
½ cup/90g quick-cook polenta
½ oz/15g parmesan, finely grated
  (2 tbsp)

This is a dish that Helen's sister Lily first cooked for her, and one that Helen always requests when she goes to dinner at her sister's house. Lily, following a Jill Dupleix recipe that uses chicken instead of turkey, serves it with pappardelle or creamy mashed potato. The name of the dish comes from the transformation the turkey goes through, from its raggy start (once pounded and torn into pieces) to its rich finish, once wine and butter have been introduced.

Serves 2

Pound the turkey breasts to flatten them as thinly as possible—placing them between two sheets of parchment paper before bashing with a rolling pin works well—you want them to be around ⅛ inch/3mm thick. Next, tear the meat into little "rags," about 1½ inches/4cm. Put the flour onto a large plate, along with ¼ teaspoon of salt and a good grind of pepper. Add the turkey, tossing well with your hands.

Put the olive oil and half the butter into a large frying pan and place on high heat. When hot, add the sage leaves and fry for 1 minute, until crisp. Transfer to a plate lined with paper towels. Keeping the pan on the heat, add the turkey pieces in one layer. Cook for 2½ minutes, turning halfway through, so that both sides take on a bit of color—they're not quite cooked through at this stage. Transfer to a plate and set aside.

Keeping the pan on the heat, add the garlic and cook for a few seconds. Add the wine, bay leaf, and capers and bring to a simmer on high heat. Cook for 2 minutes, until slightly syrupy. Add the lemon zest and juice, chicken stock, and the remaining 1 tbsp/15g of butter. Bring back to a boil, swirl to combine, heat for 1 minute, then return the turkey pieces to the pan, along with the parsley, a pinch of salt, and some pepper. Toss, turn off the heat but leave in the pan to heat through while the polenta is being cooked.

For the polenta, put the milk into a small saucepan. Add 1 cup/ 240ml of water and place on high heat. Once boiling, stream in the polenta, whisking continuously as you pour, until thickened and smooth, about 5 minutes. Finally, fold in the parmesan, along with ¼ teaspoon of salt and a few grinds of pepper.

Divide the polenta between two shallow bowls and spoon the turkey on top. Roughly crumble the fried sage leaves over the top and serve.

Baked polenta with zucchini and green harissa

1 lb 3 oz/550g zucchini, cut on the diagonal into 1¼–1½-inch/ 3–4cm chunks
3 tbsp olive oil
1 lemon: finely shave the zest to get 8 strips
1¾ cups/450ml chicken stock (or water)
1¼ cups/300ml milk
1 garlic clove, crushed to a paste
scant 1 cup/150g quick-cook polenta
3½ oz/100g parmesan, grated (1 cup)
5 tbsp/75g unsalted butter
4½ oz/125g Taleggio (or Reblochon), roughly torn
¼ oz/5g chives, cut into 1-inch/ 2.5cm lengths, to serve
salt and black pepper

Green harissa
2 green bell peppers (9¾ oz/275g)
3 green onions (1½ oz/40g)
2 small, hot green chiles
3 garlic cloves, peeled and left whole
¾ oz/20g parsley, roughly chopped, plus extra to serve
¾ oz/20g cilantro, roughly chopped
1½ tsp cumin seeds, toasted and roughly crushed
1½ tsp coriander seeds, toasted and roughly crushed
1 lemon: finely grate the zest to get 1 tsp, then juice to get 1½ tbsp
1 tsp maple syrup
6 tbsp/90ml olive oil
¾ tsp salt

This makes the most lovely veggie main, served with a simple leafy salad, and also works as a side to all sorts of things. It's one to earmark if cooking for friends who are gluten-free.

Serves 4

Preheat the oven to 450°F.

Start with the harissa. Heat a griddle pan over high heat until very hot. Add the bell peppers and cook for 20 minutes, until they are well charred and wrinkly. Transfer to a bowl, cover with a plate, and set aside to steam. Repeat with the green onions and green chiles (3 minutes for the green onions, 5 for the chiles) and then, finally, the garlic cloves for a minute or two. Once cool enough to handle, but still warm, peel off (and discard) the bell pepper skins and seeds. Roughly chop the bell pepper and place in the small bowl of a food processor. Roughly chop the green onions and chiles and add them to the food processor, along with the remaining harissa ingredients. Process until smooth, then transfer to a bowl and set aside.

Meanwhile, put the zucchini into a roasting dish, along with the oil, half the lemon strips, ½ teaspoon of salt, and a few grinds of pepper. Roast for 25 minutes, stirring a couple of times throughout, until golden and softly cooked through. Remove from the oven.

To make the polenta, put the stock, milk, garlic, and the remaining lemon strips into a medium saucepan and place on high heat. As soon as it starts to simmer, steadily stream in the polenta, whisking at the same time. Decrease the heat to low and cook for about 3 minutes, whisking constantly, until the polenta has thickened but is still soft. Remove from the heat and stir in the parmesan, butter, ¾ teaspoon of salt, and some pepper. Transfer to a shallow round ovenproof dish, about 9½ inches/24cm wide and spread out evenly. Dot the Taleggio on top of the polenta and place in the oven for 15 minutes, until the cheese is golden and bubbling and the polenta has heated through.

Add half the harissa to the zucchini and stir to combine. Spoon the zucchini on top of the polenta and sprinkle with the extra chopped parsley and the chives. Serve, with the remaining harissa alongside.

Verena's potato salad

1 lb 2 oz/500g Yukon Gold
   (or other waxy) potatoes
⅓ cup/80ml olive oil
1 small onion, finely chopped
   (¾ cup/125g)
1 garlic clove, crushed to a paste
¾ cup/180ml chicken stock
2 tsp Dijon mustard
2 tbsp apple cider vinegar
½ tsp black peppercorns, coarsely
   crushed in a mortar and pestle
½ oz/15g chives: two-thirds finely
   chopped and one-third cut into
   ½-inch/1½cm lengths
2½ oz/75g diced smoked pancetta
1 tsp paprika
¼ cucumber, sliced lengthwise,
   seeded, and cut into ¼-inch/½cm
   dice (¾ cup/100g)
salt

Growing up in Germany, Verena remembers two camps when it came to potato salad: camp mayo and camp oil/broth. This is an oil/broth-based version, more prevalent in the southern parts of Germany, specifically Swabia and Bavaria. It's less heavy and claggy than the mayo variety and gets its creaminess from the starch released by the potatoes as they sit for a couple of hours in the warm broth. We've strayed from tradition and added some pancetta (because, why not . . .) and a welcome freshness from some chopped cucumber.

Serves 4

Put the potatoes into a medium saucepan, for which you have a lid. Add just enough water to cover, salt generously and place on medium-high heat. Bring to a boil, then decrease the heat to medium-low and cook, covered, for 20–25 minutes, until just tender. Drain and, once cool enough to handle, remove the skins from the potatoes and slice into ¼-inch/½cm-thick rounds. Set aside in a medium bowl.

Put 2 tablespoons of the oil into a medium sauté pan and place on medium heat. Add the onion and cook for 12–15 minutes, stirring regularly, until caramelized. Add the garlic and stock, bring to a simmer, then remove from the heat. Add the mustard, vinegar, 1¼ teaspoons of salt, the pepper, and another 2 tablespoons of oil. Whisk to combine, then pour the mixture over the potatoes. Mix gently but thoroughly: it will look wet (and some of the potatoes will break up), but this is normal. Set aside for about 2 hours, for the potatoes to soak up about half the broth, and then stir in the finely chopped chives.

Meanwhile, wipe clean the sauté pan and place on medium-high heat. Add the pancetta, decrease the heat to medium-low, and cook for 10–12 minutes, stirring occasionally, until the pancetta is crispy. Using a slotted spoon, transfer to a plate lined with paper towels—leave about 1 tablespoon of the fat in the pan—and set aside. Once cool, finely chop the pancetta into crumbles.

Add the remaining 1 tablespoon of oil to the fat in the pan, along with the paprika. Stir for 30 seconds or so, until fragrant, then remove from the heat.

When ready to serve, fold the cucumber into the potato salad and transfer to a serving plate. Scatter the pancetta crumbles over the top, along with the cut chives. Spoon on the paprika oil and serve.

Indonesian "home fries"

1 **shallot**, roughly chopped
    (⅓ cup/60g)
6 **garlic cloves**, peeled and left whole
3–4 **stalks of lemongrass**, white
    part only, roughly chopped
    (¼ cup/25g)
1 **bird's-eye chile** (these are hot,
    so leave it out if you prefer)
2 **small, hot red chiles**, seeded
    and roughly chopped
2 **tbsp ketchup**
2 **tbsp lime juice**
7 **tbsp/100ml water**
⅓ **cup/80ml peanut**
    (or sunflower) oil
2 **tbsp roughly chopped palm sugar**
    (or granulated sugar)
½ **cup/100g mayonnaise**
2 **lb 2 oz/1kg roasting potatoes**
    (Yukon Gold or a red-skinned
    kind), unpeeled and cut into
    1¼-inch/3cm wedges
¼ **cup/5g cilantro leaves**, to garnish
salt

When living in Melbourne, there was a popular Indonesian café that Helen used to go to. It sold trays and trays of cubed potatoes to hordes of homesick students. Helen had always assumed the potatoes, sticky and sweet and spicy, were sweet potatoes. It wasn't until she moved to London (homesick herself for the home fries, which were themselves for the homesick) that she got in touch with the chef to find out what was what. It turns out they were regular boiled potatoes, stir-fried in a sticky spice paste. This is our homage to those fries.

Getting ahead: The spice paste can be made a week in advance and kept in the fridge. Once baked, the potatoes are best eaten as close to coming out of the oven as possible.

Serves 4, as a snack

Preheat the oven to 450°F.

Place the first eight ingredients in a blender (or place in a bowl and use an immersion blender). Blitz to form a fine purée.

Put 1 tablespoon of the oil into a small nonstick sauté pan and place on medium heat. Add the spice paste and cook for about 30 minutes, stirring regularly (particularly toward the end), until the paste thickens and darkens. Add the sugar and cook for 2 minutes, to dissolve and caramelize. Remove from the heat and transfer one-third of the paste to a small bowl and set aside to cool, then stir in the mayonnaise. Set aside in the fridge until ready to serve. Keep the remaining paste in the pan.

Meanwhile, put the potato wedges on a parchment-lined rimmed baking sheet. Add the remaining ¼ cup/60ml of oil along with 1 teaspoon of salt. Using your hands, mix well and spread out in a single layer. Cover tightly with foil and roast for 25 minutes. Remove the foil, turn the potatoes over, and continue to roast, uncovered, for another 25 minutes, turning again halfway through, until they are starting to brown. Add the rest of the spice paste, stirring until the potatoes are evenly coated, then return to the oven for 5–10 minutes, until browned.

Transfer the potatoes to a serving dish and scatter the cilantro leaves. Serve, with the spiced mayonnaise alongside for dipping.

Crispy roasted potatoes with rosemary and za'atar

5½ lb/2.5kg russet (or other floury) **potatoes**, peeled and cut into irregular-shaped 1½–2-inch/ 4–5cm chunks

2 tbsp fine salt

3 large rosemary sprigs: 1 left whole and 2 finely chopped

⅔ cup/160ml sunflower oil

2 tbsp rice flour (not the glutinous kind)

1 tsp flaked sea salt

2 tbsp za'atar

Roasted potatoes is a dish that features pretty permanently on people's lists of top 10 all-time comfort foods. Everyone has the secret that makes *their* roasted potatoes the best. Ours is the rice flour (semolina works just as well), which gives the outside layer an extra level of crispiness. To increase the crispiness even more, cut the potatoes into irregular-shaped pieces—the more edges, the better—and blanch well ahead. The drier they are, the crispier they will be!

Serves 6–8, as a side

Put the potatoes into a large saucepan and cover with cold water. Add the fine salt, along with the whole rosemary sprig, and bring to a boil on high heat. Lower the heat to medium-high and cook for 10–15 minutes, or until the potatoes are easily pierced with a sharp knife. Drain well, discard the rosemary, and return them to the dry saucepan. Set aside for at least 15 minutes.

Preheat the oven to 450°F.

Put the oil into a large roasting dish and place in the oven for 10 minutes, to heat up. Add the rice flour to the potatoes and toss gently so that the potatoes are coated and the edges are lightly fluffed. Carefully add the potatoes to the hot oil in the dish, taking care not to splash. Using a spatula, gently spread them out. Roast for 50 minutes, carefully turning halfway through, until deeply golden and crispy. Add the chopped rosemary, gently toss together, and return them to the oven for 3 minutes. Finally, remove the potatoes and stir in the flaked salt and za'atar. Toss to evenly coat and transfer to a large platter to serve.

Garlicky aligot potato with leeks and thyme

4 **large leeks**, cut into ½-inch/1cm
  rounds (5⅓ cups/560g)
4–5 **shallots**, peeled and quartered
  (10½ oz/300g)
1 **head of garlic**, cloves peeled
  and lightly smashed
¼ **cup/60ml olive oil**
2–3 **bunches of green onions**,
  cut crosswise into quarters
  (9 oz/250g)
1½ **tbsp thyme leaves**, chopped
5 **tbsp/75g unsalted butter**
1½ **cups/360ml heavy cream**
7 **tbsp/100ml milk**
3 **rosemary sprigs**
2–3 **thyme sprigs**
2½ **lb/1.2kg russet (or other floury)**
  potatoes, peeled and cut into
  roughly 1¼-inch/3cm chunks
1½ **tbsp Dijon mustard**
9 **oz/250g Comté**, coarsely grated
  (2⅓ cups)
4¼ **oz/120g cheddar**, coarsely
  grated (1 cup)
¼ **oz/5g chives**, finely chopped,
  to garnish
salt and black pepper

Crumb topping
1 **tbsp unsalted butter**, melted
⅓ **cup/20g panko breadcrumbs**

Smooth mashed potato, melted cheese, slow-cooked soft alliums, and woody herbs—in terms of eligibility for a book called *Comfort*, this dish almost feels like cheating.

Serves 8

Preheat the oven to 450°F.

Place the leeks, shallots, and half the garlic cloves on a parchment-lined baking sheet. Pour 3 tablespoons of the oil over the top, and add ¾ teaspoon of salt and some pepper. Stir well, then roast for 20 minutes. Add the green onions, chopped thyme, the remaining 1 tablespoon of oil, and another good grind of pepper. Stir together and roast for 15 minutes, until everything is deeply golden. Set aside.

Make the crumb topping by mixing together the melted butter and panko breadcrumbs in a small bowl. Set aside.

Crush the remaining garlic cloves to a paste and put them into a small saucepan, for which you have a lid, along with the butter, cream, milk, and the rosemary and thyme sprigs. Place on medium heat and, just before it comes to a simmer, switch off the heat, cover, and set aside to infuse.

Put the potatoes into a large saucepan, for which you have a lid, and fill with just enough water to cover them. Place on medium-high heat, add 2 teaspoons of salt, and bring to a boil. Cook for 20–25 minutes, partially covered, until tender. Drain, return the potatoes to the pan, and mash well until no lumps remain.

Return the garlic-infused cream to the heat to warm through—the herbs can be discarded. Place the potatoes on low heat and, a third at a time, add the cream to the potatoes. Beat with a wooden spoon, until the cream is fully absorbed, and then add the mustard. Add the cheese, a handful at a time, and beat quite thoroughly until the potatoes become shiny, silky, and elastic. Add ¼ teaspoon of salt and a good grind of pepper, and spoon the potatoes into a large ovenproof dish.

Preheat the broiler to medium-high and arrange the leek mixture over the potatoes. Scatter the crumb topping and place under the broiler for 5 minutes, until starting to brown. Sprinkle with the chives and serve.

Potato, fennel, and smoked salmon bake

¾ cup plus 2 tbsp/200ml milk

1¾ cups/425ml heavy cream

2 anchovies, finely chopped

3 garlic cloves, lightly smashed
  in their peels

1 lemon: finely shave the zest
  into strips

2 tsp fennel seeds, finely ground

1 lb 14 oz/850g Yukon Gold
  potatoes (or red potatoes), peeled
  and sliced ¼ inch/½cm thick

1–2 large fennel bulbs, thinly
  sliced (3½ cups/300g)

4 egg yolks

½ cup/10g dill fronds, roughly
  chopped

¾ oz/20g chives, finely chopped

1 cup/20g parsley leaves, finely
  chopped

1½ tbsp unsalted butter, softened

7 oz/200g smoked salmon slices,
  roughly torn

salt and black pepper

Lemon butter sauce

2 tbsp lemon juice

2 tsp capers, roughly chopped

3 tbsp unsalted butter, fridge cold
  and roughly cubed

This dish evolved from a recipe for lax pudding that Yotam published a while back in the *Guardian*. Lax pudding is Swedish comfort food 101, with purists spooning on lots of melted butter as they eat it with crisp bread, a leafy salad, and a glass of beer. Adding the fennel makes the texture slightly scrambled, which we like. It lightens the load at the same time as taking nothing from its comfort food credentials. Eat it as a main course. Green salad is a must. The crisp bread and beer are up to you.

Serves 4

Preheat the oven to 375°F.

Put the milk, cream, anchovies, garlic, lemon strips, and ground fennel seeds into a small pan. Cook on very low heat for 10 minutes, stirring occasionally and pressing on the solids to release their flavor, taking care that it does not come to a boil. Remove from the heat.

Place the sliced potatoes and fennel in a medium saucepan and cover with cold, salted water. Bring to a boil and cook for 6–7 minutes, until just tender. Drain and set aside.

In a large bowl, whisk the egg yolks together with ¾ teaspoon of salt and a good grind of pepper. Strain the infused milk mixture into the eggs, pressing the solids against the sieve. Whisk to combine.

Combine all the herbs in a small bowl. Measure out 2 tablespoons into a separate small bowl for the butter sauce and set both aside.

Grease an ovenproof dish—about 10 inches/25cm wide—with ½ tablespoon of the butter. Spoon a third of the potato and fennel all over the bottom and grind in some pepper. Sprinkle with half the herbs and drape half the smoked salmon on top. Repeat with half the remaining potatoes and fennel (plus the pepper), all the remaining salmon, and the other half of the herbs. Arrange the final layer of potatoes and fennel on top and carefully pour in the egg mix. Grind some more pepper and dot with the remaining 1 tablespoon of butter. Bake for 45 minutes, until the custard is just set and golden. Remove from the oven and let rest for 10 minutes.

Meanwhile, put the lemon juice into a small pan on medium-high heat and bring to a bubble. Let it bubble for 1 minute and then add the capers and butter, a few pieces at a time. Whisk until smooth and creamy, take off the heat, and stir in the reserved herbs, along with some pepper. Spoon over the bake and serve warm.

Baked potatoes with eggplant and green tahini

4 large russet potatoes, pricked
a few times with a fork
1½ tsp olive oil
mango chutney (or amba sauce),
to serve
salt and black pepper

Quick-pickled red cabbage
1 tbsp granulated sugar
½ tsp whole black peppercorns
½ cup/120ml water
½ cup/120ml white wine vinegar
7 oz/200g red cabbage, thinly
sliced (2¼ cups)

Eggplants
1 lb 14 oz/850g eggplants
(2–4, depending on size)
¼ cup/60ml olive oil
1 tsp ground cumin
½ tsp ground turmeric

Green tahini sauce
¾ cup/15g mint leaves, plus a few
extra to serve
1¼ cups/25g parsley leaves
2 garlic cloves, peeled and left whole
1 tsp ground cumin
1 small, hot green chile, seeded
3 tbsp lemon juice
rounded ½ cup/150g tahini
7 tbsp/100ml cold water

We set ourselves a challenge with this recipe. Could we make it as rich and comforting as baked potatoes tend to be—largely due to the amount of grated cheddar and butter they have in them—at the same time as keeping it vegan? Thanks to tahini, we could! It's such a naturally creamy sauce, a real friend to those who want a rich addition to vegan food. There is something of a *sabih* about this—the pita sandwich filled with roasted cubes of eggplant that Yotam grew up on—which doubles down on the comfort.

Serves 4

First pickle the cabbage. Put the sugar, peppercorns, and water into a small saucepan along with 2 teaspoons of salt. Bring to a simmer on medium-low heat and simmer for 1 minute, stirring. Remove from the heat and set aside for 10 minutes. Strain into a medium bowl (the peppercorns can be discarded) and add the vinegar. Add the cabbage, submerge, then cover and keep in the fridge. This can be made up to 3 days ahead.

Preheat the oven to 425°F.

Place the potatoes on a lined baking sheet and dribble the oil over top, sprinkle with salt and pepper, and place on a low shelf in the oven. Bake for 1–1¼ hours, until the potatoes are cooked through and their skin is nicely wrinkled.

In the meantime, using a vegetable peeler, peel the eggplants from top to bottom, in alternate strips, so that they look like a zebra. Cut into roughly 1¼-inch/3cm cubes and place in a large bowl, along with the oil, cumin, turmeric, 1 teaspoon of salt, and some pepper. Toss, then spread out on a parchment-lined sheet. Place on the top shelf of the oven and roast for 40 minutes, stirring once or twice, until golden brown.

To make the green tahini sauce, put all the ingredients into a blender, along with 1 teaspoon of salt and some pepper. Blend until smooth and transfer to a bowl.

When the potatoes are cooked, cut a large X in the middle of each one. Using a clean tea towel, squeeze the potato from the bottom to open up the cross. Spoon a large dollop of the tahini sauce in the middle, followed by the eggplant. Drain the red cabbage and place a heaped tangle on top. Finish with some mint leaves, roughly torn, and serve with the mango chutney and extra tahini sauce alongside.

Pies, pastry, bread

Breakfast boureka with spinach

3 tbsp olive oil
¼ cup/50g unsalted butter, melted
7 sheets of good-quality filo
    pastry (9½ oz/270g)
1 tsp sesame seeds
1 tsp nigella seeds (or black
    sesame seeds)

Filling
1 tbsp olive oil
1 tbsp unsalted butter
1 onion, finely chopped (1 cup/150g)
1 garlic clove, crushed to a paste
1 lb 2 oz/500g frozen spinach,
    defrosted and squeezed well
    (7 oz/200g)
3 green onions, finely
    sliced (⅓ cup/30g)
¾ oz/20g dill, chopped
1 tsp dried mint
¼ cup/30g pine nuts, toasted
    and roughly chopped
1 egg, lightly beaten
4½ oz/125g feta, crumbled
½ cup/125g ricotta
salt and black pepper

Tahini sauce
rounded ¼ cup/80g tahini
4–5 tbsp/60–75ml water
1 tbsp lemon juice
1 garlic clove, crushed to a paste
⅛ tsp ground cumin

Tomato and harissa sauce
2–3 tomatoes, chopped
    (mounded 1 cup/200g)
2 tbsp rose harissa paste
1 tbsp olive oil

To serve (any or all of the following)
hard-boiled eggs
sliced cucumber
green olives

Bourekas are something Yotam grew up eating, in all sorts of shapes and sizes, with all sorts of fillings. They were a staple at every large gathering, appearing on the table to be eaten by hand. They're also a fantastic option for breakfast or brunch, served with a selection of extras: hard-boiled eggs, sliced cucumber, green olives, chunks of feta. We've given a couple of our favorite sauces—a creamy tahini one and a fresh tomato one—but feel free to play around. *Pictured on page 241.*

Getting ahead: The boureka can be assembled the day before baking and kept in the fridge, all ready to bake.

Serves 6

Put the oil and butter for the filling into a medium frying pan and place on medium heat. When hot, add the onion and cook for 10 minutes, stirring from time to time, until softened and beginning to color. Add the garlic, cook for 2 minutes, then transfer to a large bowl. Add the spinach and then set aside to cool before adding all the remaining filling ingredients, ¾ teaspoon of salt, and some pepper. Mix well and set aside.

Preheat the oven to 400°F.

Have ready a 15 x 10-inch/38 x 25cm baking dish and a piece of parchment paper cut to fit.

When ready to assemble, combine the 3 tbsp oil and the melted butter in a small bowl. You'll need to work quickly, so the filo doesn't dry out.

Lay one piece of filo out on a large, clean work surface with the short end facing you. Dip a pastry brush in the melted butter/oil mix and brush a 2-inch/5cm strip along the right-hand side. Place another sheet so that it overlaps the buttered strip and the left side of the second sheet is stuck to the right side of the first sheet. Continue in the same way with a third sheet. Once you have your three sheets of filo stuck together—see image on page 240—brush the whole sheet with the oil/butter mix.

Leaving a 2-inch/5cm border clear at the bottom and sides of the filo, spoon half the spinach mix into a long, thin log along the bottom of the sheet. Carefully roll up the filo over the filling to form a long sausage, folding in the sides of the filo about a quarter of the way up to seal the ends. Repeat the whole process again with three more sheets of filo and the remaining spinach mix.

Starting with one sausage, carefully roll it into a coil to make a snake shape (don't worry if it begins to break up when you start rolling: you can patch it up later). Place the end of the second sausage adjacent to the end of the coil and continue to coil it around to make one large snake. Slide the snake onto the piece of parchment paper, then carefully lift or slide it onto the baking sheet. Use the remaining sheet of filo to patch up any tears or holes, if needed, then brush the whole thing liberally with the remaining butter/oil mix. Sprinkle with the sesame and nigella seeds and bake for 50–60 minutes, until deeply golden brown. Carefully slide the parchment onto a wire rack and set aside to cool for 20 minutes.

Meanwhile, make both sauces (and prepare any other accompaniments). Combine all the ingredients for the tahini sauce in a small bowl, along with ¼ teaspoon of salt, and whisk until smooth, adding a little more water if needed until it is the consistency of heavy cream. Place all the ingredients for the tomato sauce in the small bowl of a food processor, along with ¼ teaspoon of salt. Blitz until smooth.

Serve the boureka, sauces, and accompaniments all together.

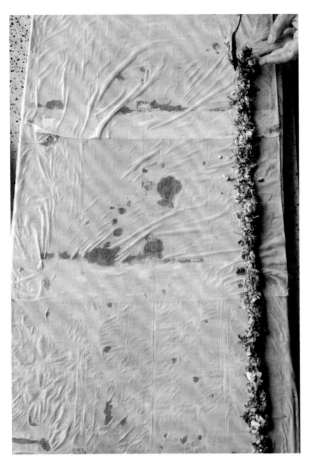 

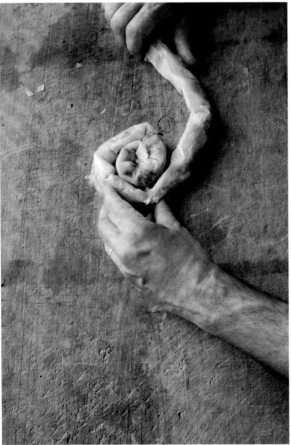 

German-style sausage rolls with honey mustard

¼ tsp white peppercorns

¼ tsp black peppercorns

1 tsp coriander seeds

2 tsp caraway seeds

1¼ tsp dried marjoram (or thyme)

¾ tsp ground ginger

1 tsp ground mace (or nutmeg)

½ tsp English mustard powder

1¾ oz/50g salted pretzels, roughly crushed

¼ cup/60ml milk

1 egg, beaten, ½ tablespoon reserved for brushing

1 tbsp olive oil

2 tbsp unsalted butter

2 onions, chopped into roughly ½-inch/1cm dice (2¼ cups/325g)

2 tsp dark brown sugar

12¼ oz/350g good-quality pork sausage meat (or start with pork sausages, and remove the casing)

½ oz/15g chives, finely chopped

1 package of pre-rolled all-butter puff pastry (11¼ oz/320g)

flour, for dusting

salt

Honey mustard dipping sauce

3 tbsp yellow mustard (we like French's)

1½ tbsp mayonnaise

1 tbsp honey

½ oz/15g chives, finely chopped

If you want to spot a "Verena recipe," the inclusion of butter and pastry are often clues, as is the use of mustard. These are no exception: inspired by everything she associates with German sausages—the spices in bratwurst, for example, the mustard dipping sauce, the pretzels—and a celebration of all the wonderful things that can be wrapped up in all-butter puff pastry.

Getting ahead: These can be made a day ahead of baking and kept in the fridge (or further ahead, if baking from frozen).

Serves 6

Put the peppercorns, coriander seeds, and 1 teaspoon of the caraway seeds into a medium sauté pan and place on medium-high heat. Cook for 1 minute, until fragrant, then transfer to a spice grinder (or a mortar and pestle). Blitz to form a semi-fine powder, then add the remaining spices, along with the mustard powder and ¾ teaspoon of salt. Set aside.

Combine the pretzels, milk, and egg in a bowl and set aside to soften.

Add the oil and butter to the same sauté pan and place on medium-high heat. Add the onions, along with ¼ teaspoon of salt, and cook for 15 minutes, stirring often, until softened and starting to caramelize. Add the sugar and cook for 5 minutes, stirring a few times, until fully caramelized. Set aside to cool.

Add the sausage meat to the bowl containing the pretzel mixture, along with the chives, spices, and cooked onions. Mix well to combine.

Mix together all the ingredients for the dipping sauce and set aside. Preheat the oven to 425°F.

Unroll the puff pastry and place on a lightly floured work surface. Slice it in half, lengthwise, to form two long, wide strips, about 4½ x 15 inches/11½ x 38cm. Arrange half the sausage meat in a long log shape down the middle of one of the pastry strips, then lift one edge of the pastry over the meat. Brush the remaining free edge with some of the reserved egg, then lift and slightly pull it up and over the pastry, overlapping a little to ensure that it sticks. Repeat with the remaining pastry and sausage meat, then roll each log over so that the seams are both underneath. Brush all over with egg wash, sprinkle with the remaining 1 teaspoon of caraway seeds, then lightly score the top of each log, each cut about ¾ inch/2cm apart. Arrange the logs on a large parchment-lined baking sheet and bake for 32–35 minutes, rotating the sheet halfway through, until golden brown.

Remove from the oven and let cool for 15 minutes before cutting into 12 portions. Serve warm, or at room temperature, with the dipping sauce alongside.

Potato, cheese, and chermoula hand pies

1 lb 2 oz/500g russet (or other floury) potatoes, peeled and cut into ½-inch/1cm dice
3 onions, roughly diced (3⅓ cups/500g)
2 garlic cloves, unpeeled
2 tsp ground cumin
1½ tsp olive oil
3 tbsp unsalted butter, diced
½ cup/75g pitted green olives, roughly chopped
4½ tbsp store-bought chermoula
7 oz/200g sharp cheddar, grated (1¾ cups)
¾ oz/20g cilantro, roughly chopped
3 green onions, finely sliced (⅓ cup/30g)
¼ cup/60g crème fraîche
2½ batches of cream cheese pastry (see page 254) (or 3 x 11¼ oz/320g packages of pre-rolled all-butter puff pastry)
flour, for dusting
1 egg
1½ tsp nigella seeds (or black sesame seeds), for sprinkling
salt and black pepper

These pies are our take on a cheesy potato and onion pie, dialed up in flavor with the chermoula. Chermoula is a powerful North African paste we love to use. It's good to have around, ready to be brushed on things like sliced eggplant or squash before they're roasted.

Make all of the pies, even if you are only going to have a few for the first round. They can be made in full, frozen, and baked straight from frozen when you want one. If you do this, just add an extra 5 minutes or so to the baking time.

Makes 12

Preheat the oven to 400°F.

Add the potatoes, onions, garlic, cumin, oil, and butter to a parchment-lined rimmed baking sheet. Add 1½ teaspoons of salt and a good grind of pepper and mix to combine. Roast for 35–40 minutes, stirring once or twice, until cooked through and nicely golden. Let cool, then transfer to a bowl. Add the olives, chermoula, cheddar, cilantro, green onions, and crème fraîche. Mix to combine and set aside.

Cut the pastry in half and, working with one half at a time (keep the other half in the fridge) on a well-floured work surface, roll it out to form a roughly 20 x 12-inch/50 x 30cm rectangle, ¹⁄₁₆–⅛ inch/2–3mm thick. Using a 7-inch/18cm-wide pastry ring or plate, cut out four circles and place them on a parchment-lined baking sheet. Place in the fridge while you repeat the process with the second half of the pastry. Save and re-roll the pastry offcuts—you should be able to make four more circles from these.

Whisk the egg in a small bowl. Take the first four pastry circles and spoon just under 3½ oz/100g of filling into the center of each circle. Brush half of the pastry edge with egg and fold this side over to cover the filling and meet the opposite edge. Firmly crimp/twist the edges together decoratively (or use the tines of a fork), brush the surface with the egg wash, and sprinkle nigella seeds on top. Using a small knife, make three ½-inch/1cm-wide cuts in the middle of each pie to allow steam to escape. Set aside in the fridge while you repeat the process with the remaining circles.

Arrange a maximum of six pies per sheet on parchment-lined baking sheets and bake for 30–35 minutes, rotating the sheets halfway through, until golden brown. Set aside to cool on the sheets for a few minutes before transferring to a wire rack to cool further. Serve the pies warm or at room temperature.

Beef, black garlic, and baharat pie

3 tbsp olive oil

1 tbsp unsalted butter, plus 2 tsp for greasing the cake pan

2 onions, cut into ½-inch/1cm dice (1⅔ cup/250g)

2 celery stalks, cut into ½-inch/1cm dice (1⅓ cups/140g)

1 large carrot, peeled and cut into ½-inch/1½cm dice (⅔ cup/100g)

2 garlic cloves, crushed to a paste

2 russet (or other floury) potatoes, peeled and cut into ½-inch/1½cm dice (scant 1 cup/200g)

7 oz/200g turnips (or ¼ rutabaga), peeled and cut into ½-inch/1½cm dice

1¾ lb/800g ground beef, 10–12% fat

1½ tbsp baharat

1–2 tomatoes, chopped (mounded 1 cup/200g)

1 tbsp tomato paste

1¾ oz/50g black garlic, roughly chopped

2 bay leaves

1 tbsp red wine vinegar

2½ tbsp all-purpose flour, plus extra for dusting

2½ cups/600ml beef stock

½ cup/75g pitted green olives

1 package of pre-rolled pie crust dough (11¼oz/320g)

1 package of pre-rolled all-butter puff pastry (11¼oz/320g)

1 egg, lightly beaten

salt and black pepper

An Aussie meat pie (specifically, a "Four'n Twenty" pie) is one of the first things Helen seeks out when she lands in Australia for her annual trip back to see her family. She's not the only fan—according to Wikipedia, 21,000 of these pies are produced every hour, 24 hours a day! There's clearly more going on than just nostalgia. This is our homage to the Four'n Twenty, with the addition of baharat and black garlic.

Getting ahead: The beef mix can be made a day or two ahead and kept in the fridge. Just bring it back to room temperature before it goes into the pie. Once it is assembled and baked, the pie is best eaten on the day of baking.

Serves 6–8

Put 2 tablespoons of the oil and the butter into a medium heavy-bottomed saucepan, for which you have a lid, and place on medium-high heat. Add the onions, celery, and carrot and cook for 10–12 minutes, stirring from time to time, until softened and taking on a little bit of color. Add the garlic, potatoes, and turnips, cook for 5 minutes, then tip everything out into a bowl.

Increase the heat to high and add the remaining 1 tablespoon of oil. Add the beef and cook for 10 minutes, breaking it up with a wooden spoon and stirring a few times, until browned. Add the baharat, tomatoes, tomato paste, black garlic, and bay leaves, along with 1½ teaspoons of salt and a little black pepper, and cook for 2–3 minutes, stirring regularly. Add the red wine vinegar and let it bubble away for a few seconds, then stir in the flour. Return the vegetables to the pan and give everything a good stir. Pour in the stock, bring to a boil, decrease the heat to medium-low, and simmer, covered, for 30 minutes and then, partially covered, for another 30 minutes, stirring regularly, until the sauce is thick and glossy. Remove from the heat and stir in the olives. Set aside to cool, then refrigerate until cold.

When ready to make the pie, preheat the oven to 400°F. Brush the bottom and sides of a 9-inch/23cm springform cake pan with butter. Place a large baking sheet in the center of the oven to heat up.

On a lightly floured work surface, roll out the pie crust dough so that it is 1 inch/2.5cm wider than the cake pan. Using a rolling pin to help you, transfer the pastry to the cake pan and press evenly into the bottom and corners and all the way up the sides of the pan (you may need to trim some of the dough and patch it on to other parts to make it fit evenly around the sides). Spoon the beef filling into the center of the pan, mounding it slightly in the middle so that there is room around the edges for the pie lid.

Lightly flour your work surface once again and gently roll out the puff pastry so that it is large enough to cover the whole pie. Drape the pastry over the filling, pressing it against the sides of the pan to seal the puff pastry and pie crust dough edges together. Trim away the majority of the excess pastry, leaving about ¾ inch/2cm all around. Roll or fold the excess pastry inward, then use a lightly floured fork to press against the sides and create a decorative edge.

Brush the pie with the egg wash, add a good grind of pepper and then, using a sharp knife, make a few small slits in the middle of the pie to act as vents. Place the pie on the hot baking sheet and bake for 1–1¼ hours, until the pastry is golden brown and crisp and the filling is starting to bubble up through the vents. You might need to cover the pie with foil toward the end if it is taking on too much color. Remove the pie from the oven and allow to cool for 15 minutes before removing from the pan and serving.

Leek, cheese, and za'atar rugelach

Cream cheese pastry
1⅓ cups/160g all-purpose flour, plus extra for dusting
¼ tsp baking powder
1½ oz/40g parmesan, finely grated (⅓ cup)
½ cup plus 1 tbsp/125g unsalted butter, fridge-cold, cut into roughly 1¼-inch/3cm cubes
4½ oz/125g cream cheese, fridge-cold
1 egg, lightly beaten with a pinch of salt, for brushing
salt and black pepper

Filling
1 tbsp olive oil
2 small leeks, thinly sliced (3 cups/300g)
1 tsp finely grated lemon zest
2½ oz/70g feta, crumbled
1 tbsp cream cheese
2 tsp za'atar, plus 1 tbsp extra for sprinkling
3½ oz/100g cheddar, finely grated (1 cup), plus about ¼ cup/30g extra for sprinkling on top

This is a savory version of the typically sweet rugelach. The cream cheese in the pastry makes them every bit as irresistible. Play around with the filling: cooked spinach, dill, and crumbled feta work really well.

Getting ahead: Both the pastry and filling can be made ahead: 2 days for the filling, 3 days for the pastry. Once baked, the rugelach are best eaten on the same day. They can also be prepared ahead in full, frozen, and baked straight from the freezer. If doing this, they'll just need an extra minute in the oven.

Makes 16

First make the pastry. Place the flour, baking powder, half of the parmesan, ¼ teaspoon of salt, and some pepper in a food processor. Blitz for 15 seconds, to combine, then add the butter. Process for a few more seconds, until the mixture has the texture of breadcrumbs, and then add the cream cheese. Process just until the dough begins to come together—take care not to over-process here. Tip the dough onto a lightly floured work surface and knead for a few seconds, just to bring it together. Divide into two equal pieces, wrap each loosely in reusable plastic wrap, then press to flatten. Chill in the fridge for at least 1 hour.

Next, make the filling. Put the oil into a frying pan and place on medium heat. Add the leeks and ½ teaspoon of salt and cook for 15–18 minutes, until softened but having not taken on any color. Stir in the lemon zest and some pepper, then remove from the heat and set aside to cool. Smoosh together the feta and cream cheese and add this to the leeks, along with the za'atar and cheddar. Mix and set aside.

When ready to assemble, preheat the oven to 400°F.

On a lightly floured work surface, roll out one of the dough halves into a circle, roughly 11 inches/28cm wide and about ¹⁄₁₆ inch/2mm thick. Spoon half the leek mixture on top and spread it out evenly over the surface. Then, using a sharp knife, cut the circle as though you are slicing a round cake or pizza into eight equal slices.

One at a time—starting from the bottom of the triangle—roll each wedge quite tightly from the outer edge toward the tip so that the filling is enclosed. Place them on two parchment-lined baking sheets, seam side down. Repeat with the remaining dough and filling. Lightly brush the tops of each crescent with the egg wash and sprinkle with the remaining parmesan, cheddar, and za'atar. Bake for 23–25 minutes, rotating the sheets halfway through, until the rugelach are golden brown all over. Let cool for 5–10 minutes before serving.

Tomato galette with cheese and Marmite

1 large head of garlic
6 oz/175g cream cheese
2½ tsp Marmite
1 tbsp maple syrup
4½ oz/125g Robiola (or Brie),
   roughly torn
1 egg, beaten
salt and black pepper

Pastry
1⅓ cups plus 1 tbsp/175g
   all-purpose flour, plus extra
   for dusting
⅔ cup/70g whole wheat flour
½ cup plus 2 tbsp/150g unsalted
   butter, fridge-cold, cut into
   1¼–1½-inch/3–4cm cubes
2 tbsp ice-cold water
2 tbsp milk, fridge-cold
1 tsp white wine (or cider) vinegar

Slow-roasted tomatoes
1¾ lb/800g mixed tomatoes, sliced
   into ½-inch/1cm-thick rounds
3 red onions, cut into ½-inch/
   1cm-thick rounds (12¾ oz/360g)
1 tbsp thyme leaves, chopped, plus
   ½ tsp extra leaves to garnish
1¼ tsp caraway seeds, roughly
   crushed
⅓ cup/80ml olive oil

Marmite: "*you either love it or hate it*" (according to the 90s advertisement), but here we are hoping to have our galette *and* eat it. If you love it, you will love what it does here in the Marmite cream and glaze, but even if you hate it, you'll be taken by the salty-umami note that it brings to proceedings. *Pictured on page 259.*

Getting ahead: The dough for the pastry can be made up to 3 days ahead (or 1 month, if freezing) and kept in the fridge. Once assembled and baked, the galette is best eaten warm on the day.

Serves 8

First make the pastry. Place both flours in a food processor, along with ½ teaspoon of salt and a little pepper. Pulse a few times, then add the butter. Process until it has the consistency of breadcrumbs, then add the water, milk, and vinegar. Pulse a few times, just until the dough starts to come together, then tip out onto a clean work surface. Knead gently and briefly, just to bring it together into a ball, then wrap loosely in reusable plastic wrap. Press lightly to flatten, then refrigerate for at least 1 hour.

Preheat the oven to 400°F.

Cut off (and discard) the top of the garlic head, so that the cloves are exposed, then wrap in foil. Place in the bottom of the oven.

Put the tomatoes, onions, chopped thyme, caraway seeds, and olive oil on a parchment-lined rimmed baking sheet, along with ½ teaspoon of salt and some pepper. Using your hands, carefully combine, then arrange them in an even layer. Roast for 50 minutes, rotating the sheet halfway through, until the tomatoes have taken on a bit of color and have lost most of their moisture. Remove from the oven and set aside to cool.

Remove the garlic head from the oven at the same time and take off the foil. Once cool, squeeze the cloves out of their peels into a small bowl (the peels can be discarded). Add the cream cheese and 1½ teaspoons of the Marmite. Mix to combine.

In a separate bowl, mix together the remaining 1 teaspoon of Marmite with the maple syrup. Set aside.

Line a rimmed baking sheet with parchment paper.

Five or 10 minutes before you are going to roll the pastry, take it out of the fridge. On a lightly floured surface, roll out the pastry to form a rough circle, 15 inches/38cm wide and about ⅛ inch/3mm thick. Using a rolling pin, transfer the pastry to the lined baking sheet and spread the cream cheese mix evenly on top, leaving a clear 2½-inch/6cm border all the way around. Scatter two-thirds of the Robiola and arrange the roasted tomato and onion slices on top, so that the cheese is covered. Scatter the rest of the cheese on top, then, working your way around the galette, fold the border up and over the filling. Brush with the egg wash and place in the fridge for 15 minutes to firm up.

Cut out a rough circle of parchment paper, big enough to cover the exposed filling, and place it on top of the galette. Bake for 35 minutes. Remove the parchment, rotate the sheet and continue to bake for 15–20 minutes, until the pastry is deeply golden and cooked through. Brush the pastry edges with half the Marmite and maple glaze, then set aside (keeping the galette on the sheet) to rest for 15 minutes. Drizzle with the rest of the glaze and garnish with the extra thyme leaves. Cut into wedges and serve.

Bohemian fish pie

¼ cup/60ml olive oil
2 small onions, diced
   (1⅓ cups/200g)
1 large fennel bulb, sliced ½ inch/
   1cm thick (2⅓ cups/200g)
10½ oz/300g cherry tomatoes,
   halved
1½ tbsp tomato paste
3 garlic cloves, crushed to a paste
1 tbsp coriander seeds, lightly
   toasted and finely crushed
1 tsp paprika
1½ tbsp thyme leaves
2 strips of orange peel
7 tbsp/100ml dry white wine
1 cup/240ml fish (or chicken) stock
1 tsp Tabasco sauce
1½ tsp cornstarch
1 lb 5 oz/600g bag of fresh or
   frozen (and then defrosted)
   mixed seafood
parsley leaves, roughly chopped,
   to garnish (optional)

Celery root and cannellini mash
1 large celery root, peeled and
   cut into 1-inch/2.5cm chunks
   (scant 5 cups/750g)
3 garlic cloves, peeled and smashed
1 x 15-oz/425g can of cannellini
   beans, drained and rinsed
3 tbsp unsalted butter, cubed
¼ cup/60ml heavy cream
salt and black pepper

This is fish pie without all the cream and potato mash it often includes. The result has all the comfort, without all the heavy. It's inspired by a dish made by friends of Helen's—Alice and James—who called it their renegade or "bohemian" version. We loved the name, so it stuck.

Getting ahead: If you're getting this together ahead of time—a few hours before eating—just make sure the sauce has fully cooled down before the raw seafood is added. The mash should also be cooled before spooning it on top. When baking from chilled, cook for an extra 10 minutes.

Serves 4–6

To make the mash, place the celery root and garlic in a medium saucepan, for which you have a lid. Add enough cold water to just cover the celery root, along with 2 teaspoons of salt. Bring to a boil, then cook on medium heat, partially covered, for 25–30 minutes, until the celery root is tender. Drain, then return to the pan and cook for 3–5 minutes, on low heat, stirring occasionally, to evaporate some of the excess water. Add the cannellini beans, butter, and cream, along with ½ teaspoon of salt and some pepper. Using a hand-held masher (or an immersion blender), mash until smooth.

Preheat the oven to 450°F.

Put 3 tablespoons of the oil into a large ovenproof sauté pan, for which you have a lid, and place on medium-high heat. Add the onions and fennel and cook for 10–12 minutes, stirring a few times, until starting to caramelize. Add the tomatoes, tomato paste, garlic, coriander seeds, paprika, thyme, orange peel, 1¼ teaspoons of salt, and a little pepper. Cook for 3 minutes, then add the wine. Let it bubble away for 2–3 minutes, then add the stock and Tabasco sauce. Bring to a simmer, then decrease the heat to medium-low and cook, covered, for 12 minutes, until the tomatoes have collapsed. Remove the lid and cook for 10–12 minutes, until slightly reduced.

Mix the cornstarch in a small bowl with 2 teaspoons of water to form a slurry, and stir this into the sauce. Cook for 1 minute or so, to thicken, then stir in the seafood. Remove from the heat and spoon the mash on top of the fish mixture, creating some swoops and swirls as you do so. Drizzle with the remaining 1 tablespoon of oil and bake for 25–30 minutes, until golden on top. Remove from the oven and allow the pie to rest for 10–15 minutes before serving, with a sprinkle of parsley, if using.

Spinach and asparagus loaf

6 tbsp/90ml olive oil

1 tbsp unsalted butter, plus 1 tbsp
extra, softened, for greasing
the pan

1 leek, thinly sliced (1⅓ cups/135g)

2⅓ oz/65g watercress, roughly
chopped

5 oz/200g asparagus, woody
ends trimmed and sliced into
½-inch/1cm lengths (5 oz/135g)

1 large garlic clove, crushed to
a paste

2 tsp thyme leaves, chopped

9¾ oz/275g frozen spinach,
defrosted, squeezed out, and
finely chopped (5 oz/135g)

2½ oz/70g parmesan, finely grated
(9 tbsp)

2 tbsp walnuts, finely chopped

1⅓ cups plus 2 tbsp/180g
all-purpose flour

1¼ tsp baking powder

½ tsp baking soda

2 eggs

½ cup/100g sour cream

2 tbsp za'atar

salted butter, at room temperature,
to serve

salt and black pepper

Every year, when asparagus season comes around, we wonder if *this* is going to be the year when, finally, we run out of brand-new ideas for cooking and eating it. It just feels like one of those vegetables where there are only so many ways to do something to make it more interesting. Every year, though, we surprise ourselves with one new recipe to add to the asparagus repertoire. Asparagus spears are baked here into the sort of bread whose texture is wonderfully soft and sweet—almost cakey. It's lovely to have with soup or as it is, smeared with butter for brunch or a picnic.

Storing notes: Have it as it is, or warm through under the broiler (or in a dry pan) for 1 minute or so on each side.

Serves 8–10

Put 1 tbsp of the oil and the butter into a large sauté pan and place on medium heat. Add the leeks, ½ teaspoon of salt, and some pepper, and sauté for 10 minutes, stirring from time to time, until the leeks have softened. Add the watercress, asparagus, garlic, and thyme and cook for 5–7 minutes, until the watercress has lost all its moisture. In the last 2 minutes, stir in the spinach, remove from the heat, and set aside to cool.

Preheat the oven to 375°F.

Brush the inside of an 8½ x 4½-inch/22 x 11 cm loaf pan with the extra softened butter. Mix together 3 tbsp/20g of the parmesan and all the walnuts in a small bowl. Tip the mixture into the pan, then shake and tap the pan, so that the bottom and sides are coated. Tip the excess back into the small bowl. Place the pan in the fridge.

Sift the flour, baking powder, baking soda, and ½ teaspoon of salt into a medium bowl.

Place the eggs, sour cream, and the remaining 5 tbsp/75ml olive oil in a separate large bowl and whisk well. Add the cooled vegetable mixture, the remaining 6 tbsp/50g of parmesan, the za'atar, and the sifted flour mixture. Using a spatula, stir and fold until just combined—there should be no floury streaks, but be careful not to over-mix (as this will produce a rubbery texture).

Scrape the batter into the prepared pan and smooth the surface. Scatter the reserved walnut and parmesan crumbs on top and bake for 50–55 minutes, rotating the pan halfway through, until a skewer inserted into the middle of the loaf comes out clean.

Remove from the oven and allow to cool for 10 minutes before loosening the edges with a knife. Turn out onto a wire rack and let cool completely before serving with salted butter.

Carrot and vadouvan quick-bread

2¼ cups/275g all-purpose flour
2 tsp baking powder
½ tsp baking soda
1 tbsp granulated sugar
2½ tbsp vadouvan (or Madras curry powder)
2 tsp cumin seeds, toasted and lightly crushed
2 tsp coriander seeds, toasted and lightly crushed
3 eggs
½ cup/150g Greek yogurt
7 tbsp/100ml olive oil
1–2 carrots, peeled and coarsely grated (1⅓ cups/150g)
4 green onions, finely chopped (½ cup/40g)
1 garlic clove, crushed to a paste
⅓ oz/10g ginger, peeled and grated
salted butter, at room temperature, to serve, plus extra for greasing
salt

Helen was inspired to create this after eating a bowl of carrot and vadouvan soup in a café near her son's school when she was waiting to pick him up. It was so delicious and distinct that Helen did some of her own school homework while she was waiting. The distinct flavor was from vadouvan, a wonderfully complex French curry powder. It's a sweeter, shallot-based version of masala curry—mellow, smoky and, indeed, distinct. Sliced and spread with salted butter, this is wonderful for lunch with either soup or cheese.

Ingredients note: Vadouvan is increasingly available as a pre-mixed blend, but if you can't find it, a mild Madras curry powder works really well as an alternative. In the photo, we flavored our butter with some more of the vadouvan, but plain salted butter is just as good!

Storing notes: This is at its best eaten the day it is baked but keeps for up to 2 days.

Serves 6–8

Preheat the oven to 400°F. Grease an 8½ x 4½-inch/22 x 11cm loaf pan with butter and line with parchment paper.

Sift the flour, baking powder, baking soda, sugar, and 1 teaspoon of salt into a large bowl. Add the vadouvan, cumin, and coriander seeds and mix to combine.

Put the eggs into a large bowl, along with the yogurt and oil. Whisk to combine, then stir in the carrots, green onions, garlic, and ginger. Pour this wet mix into the dry ingredients and gently fold together until just combined—do not overmix. The batter will seem fairly stiff, but this is how it should be.

Scrape the batter into the prepared loaf pan, smooth over the surface, and bake for 50–55 minutes, or until a skewer inserted into the center comes out clean. Remove from the oven and cool on a wire rack for 10 minutes, then turn out to cool completely. Slice and serve, with plenty of salted butter.

Bread rolls

1 small russet (or other floury) potato, peeled and cut into 1¼-inch/3cm chunks (scant 1 cup/200g)

3 cups/375g bread flour

1 packet of fast-acting dried yeast (2¼ tsp/7g)

3 tbsp granulated sugar

1½ tsp salt

2 eggs

¼ cup/50g sour cream

5 tbsp/70g unsalted butter, at room temperature and cut into ½-inch/1cm cubes

flaked sea salt, for sprinkling

For all the elaborate things made in the kitchen, there's something *particularly* satisfying about the smell and the squish of a freshly baked roll. In terms of squish factor, we have a secret weapon: potato! You wouldn't know it's there, but once you do, the soft and pillowy nature of these rolls makes perfect sense.

If making rolls is one of the most satisfying things to do, thinking of all the things that can go in them is a close second. Everyone has their favorite filling: butter and mortadella for Helen; egg and watercress for Verena (see page 25); chicken, avocado, olives, and feta for Tara; butter, cheddar, and pickles for Yotam. So very many options. *Also pictured on page 268.*

Getting ahead: These are best eaten the day they are made, but with the moisture from the potatoes and if wrapped up well, they are fine the next day. They won't be quite as fluffy but can be warmed through in the oven for a few minutes to bring them back to life.

Makes 16

Place the potato in a small saucepan and add enough water to just barely cover. Bring to a boil, decrease the heat to medium, and cook for 15–20 minutes, partially covered, until the potatoes are tender. Drain in a sieve set over a bowl and return the potatoes to the saucepan. Place on low heat and allow to dry out for 2–3 minutes. Mash really well (use a potato ricer if you have one) so that no lumps remain. Transfer ½ cup/130g to a plate and set aside to cool.

Whisk together the flour, yeast, sugar, and salt in a medium bowl and set aside.

Measure ⅓ cup/80ml of the reserved potato cooking water (or tap water, if you've forgotten to reserve the potato water!) into the bowl of a stand mixer with the dough hook attached. Add one of the eggs, along with the sour cream, the flour mixture, the butter, and the ½ cup/130g of cooled mashed potato. Mix on low speed for about 2 minutes, until just combined. Then increase the speed to medium-high and mix for 8–10 minutes, until the dough is smooth, silky, and elastic.

Transfer the dough to a lightly oiled work surface and shape it into a ball. Return it to the bowl, cover with a clean tea towel, and put it somewhere warm to rise, for 1–1½ hours (or until doubled in size).

Line a 9-inch/23cm square pan (about 1½ inches/4cm deep) with a long strip of parchment paper that rises ¾ inch/2cm above the sides of the pan.

Turn the risen dough out onto a lightly oiled work surface once again and divide the dough into 16 pieces, each weighing just under 1¾ oz/50g. Roll each piece into a ball—pulling in all the edges and then sitting them on those pulled-in bits so that the top looks perfect—and arrange in four rows of four in the pan (there will be a slight gap between each roll and the next, which will close as they rise).

Cover and let rise for 1½ hours, or until doubled in size.

Preheat the oven to 400°F.

Beat the remaining egg and use this to brush all over the risen rolls. Sprinkle with a couple of pinches of flaked sea salt and bake for 15 minutes. Rotate the pan and bake for 10 minutes, until well risen and deeply golden. Carefully lift the rolls out of the pan, using the parchment paper to help you, and transfer to a wire rack to cool completely.

Sweet things

Cinnamon baked oatmeal with bananas and strawberries

⅔ cup/130g steel-cut oats
1 cup/80g rolled oats
¼ cup/30g sliced almonds, lightly toasted
1 tsp baking powder
1½ tsp ground cinnamon
½ tsp salt
1 large, just-ripe banana, thinly sliced (scant 1 cup/125g)
4–5 strawberries, thinly sliced (⅔ cup/100g)
1 egg
¼ cup/60ml maple syrup, plus extra to serve
2 tbsp unsalted butter, melted and set aside to cool slightly
2 cups/480ml almond (or any other) milk
2 tsp vanilla extract
powdered sugar, for dusting
heavy cream, to serve (optional)

This is one of Helen's go-to family comfort dishes. Usually served for a leisurely weekend breakfast, it's also been known to "do" for supper when the day needs a smooth end. It's adapted from Heidi Swanson's baked oatmeal in her book *Super Natural Every Day*. We've made it our own—we love the addition of steel-cut oats, for example, for the chew they bring, but if you don't have steel-cut, use a total of 2⅓ cups/210g rolled oats instead. Serve it hot, with a little bit of cold cream poured over, or cold, for breakfast or dessert, with a little bit of extra maple syrup.

Getting ahead: If you want to wake up and be able to put this in the oven straight away, everything except the fruit can be combined and kept in the fridge, ready to go (once the fruit is added). If you do this, much of the liquid will have been absorbed overnight and the cooking time goes down to 30 minutes.

Serves 4–6

Preheat the oven to 375°F.

Place all the oats, almonds, baking powder, cinnamon, and salt in a medium bowl and toss gently to combine. Transfer to an ovenproof dish (about 10¼ inches/26cm wide), scatter the banana and strawberry slices on top, and set aside.

Whisk the egg in a large bowl and add the maple syrup and butter. Whisk well to combine, then add the milk and vanilla extract. Carefully pour the mix into the dish and gently shake so that the fruit is evenly scattered on top. Don't worry if it isn't neat—the fruit will bob up as it bakes.

Bake for 40–45 minutes, or until the top is golden brown and the oats have set. Remove from the oven and allow to cool for a few minutes before serving, dusted with powdered sugar and with the cream or extra maple syrup on the side.

GF caramelized white chocolate and macadamia cookies

1⅓ cups/300g softened unsalted butter, cut into ¾-inch/2cm cubes
packed 1⅓ cups plus 1 tbsp/300g dark brown sugar
6 tbsp/75g granulated sugar
1 tbsp/20g vanilla bean paste
1 whole egg and 2 yolks
1⅓ cups plus 1 tbsp/175g cassava (or all-purpose) flour
1⅔ cups/150g rolled oats, blitzed to a very fine powder
¾ tsp baking soda
¾ tsp fine salt
1 tsp flaked sea salt
¾ cup/100g macadamia nuts, toasted and roughly chopped
7 oz/200g caramelized (or plain) white chocolate, roughly chopped (we like Valrhona Dulcey 32%)

These are inspired by memories Verena has of hanging out at the mall as a teenager, feeling as though she was in a movie, when her parents were working in Washington DC for a couple of years. Verena was always drawn to the Mrs Fields cookie stand and their white chocolate chip macadamia cookies. The crispy edges; the soft and chewy middle!

Ingredients note: Caramelized white chocolate is an amazing ingredient—think buttered toast in chocolate form. It's increasingly available, but as an alternative, plain white chocolate works just fine. We've used cassava flour here to make these gluten-free, but if that's not a concern, regular all-purpose flour can be used instead.

Getting ahead: The raw cookie dough can be made up to 3 days in advance and kept, rolled into balls, in the fridge in an airtight container (where they will improve with age!), ready to be baked whenever needed.

Makes 25

Weigh out half the butter into a small saucepan and place on medium-high heat. Cook for about 5 minutes, whisking often, until the butter has turned amber in color and smells nutty. Meanwhile, put the remaining butter, both sugars, and the vanilla bean paste into a large bowl. Pour in the hot butter and stir to combine. Set aside for 5 minutes or so, until the rest of the butter has completely melted. Add the egg and yolks and mix for about 30 seconds, until well combined and emulsified. Add the rest of the ingredients and mix until there are no more traces of flour. Cover and let rest in the fridge for at least 2 hours, until firm.

Preheat the oven to 400°F.

Using a spoon, scoop out 1¾–2 oz/50–55g of the cookie dough at a time, roll each scoop into a ball, and arrange, spaced well apart, on a parchment-lined rimmed baking sheet—you should be able to get 8 cookies per sheet. Bake for 7 minutes, then rotate the sheet and bake for 3 minutes, until the cookie edges are lightly golden and the centers are puffy and pale. Let cool on the sheet for 10 minutes before eating.

Baked custard affogato

Baked custard
**¾ cup plus 2 tbsp/200ml heavy
 cream**
¾ cup plus 2 tbsp/200ml milk
**packed ⅓ cup/75g light brown
 sugar**
scraped seeds of 1 vanilla pod
4 egg yolks (reserve 2 of the whites
 for the brittle)
⅛ tsp salt

Meringue brittle
2 egg whites
⅛ tsp salt
¾ cup/150g granulated sugar
**⅓ cup/50g blanched
 hazelnuts**, toasted: half blitzed
 to form a fine powder and half
 roughly chopped
1 tsp cornstarch
1 tsp apple cider vinegar
**½ cup/40g unsweetened dried
 shredded coconut**

To serve
4 espresso shots, hot (optional)

This is somewhere between an affogato, a crème brûlée, and a nutty meringue. It works just as well without the shot of espresso, so it's great for the whole family. *Also pictured on page 278.*

Getting ahead: Both the cream and the meringue can be made in advance (the cream a day before, the meringue up to 1 week ahead), ready to be put together just before serving.

Serves 4

Preheat the oven to 475°F.

Combine the ingredients for the baked custard in a small saucepan and place on medium heat. Cook, whisking often, for 10–12 minutes, until the mixture has the consistency of a thin custard. Strain into a 12 x 8-inch/30 x 20cm baking dish and bake for 15–20 minutes. The top will have blackened in patches and the custard will look completely curdled—this is just as it should be!

Transfer to a small bowl, making sure to include all the browned bits from the sides, then, using an immersion blender, blitz for about 30 seconds until really smooth, shiny, and glossy, scraping down the sides of the bowl. Refrigerate for at least 4 hours (or overnight).

Lower the oven temperature to 350°F and line a rimmed baking sheet with parchment paper.

Next make the meringue brittle. Place the egg whites and salt in the bowl of a stand mixer. Whisk on medium-high speed for 1-2 minutes, until starting to stiffen. Pour in the sugar, bit by bit, and whisk for 3–5 minutes, until the meringue is thick and shiny. Using a spatula, fold in the blitzed hazelnuts, cornstarch, apple cider vinegar, and coconut. Dot a tiny amount of meringue underneath each corner of the parchment paper to make it stick to the baking sheet. Spread the meringue thinly on the prepared sheet, making sure to cover the entire surface, and sprinkle with the chopped hazelnuts. Bake for 30 minutes. Let cool, then break into rough shards.

When ready to serve, gently stir the custard to loosen it up—it should have a soft pudding-like consistency. Spoon into four small glasses and top with the meringue shards. Serve the espresso shots alongside, if using, pouring as much or as little as you'd like.

Lemon and blueberry meringue kataifi mess

1¾ oz/50g kataifi pastry
3 tbsp powdered sugar
½ tsp ground cinnamon
¼ tsp salt
2 tbsp unsalted butter, melted
⅔ cup/100g fresh blueberries
1¾ oz/50g store-bought
  meringues, roughly broken up

Lemon syrup
⅔ cup/160ml lemon juice
  (from about 4 lemons)
6 thinly shaved lemon peel strips
½ cup plus 2 tbsp/125g granulated
  sugar
1 chamomile tea bag (optional: only
  if you have some already)
1 cinnamon stick
1 scraped-out vanilla pod (the seeds
  are set aside for the cream)

Yogurt cream
¾ cup plus 2 tbsp/200ml heavy
  cream
⅔ cup/200g Greek yogurt
scraped seeds of 1 vanilla pod
  (see above)
6 tbsp/50g powdered sugar

We can't have a yogurty-creamy "mess"-type kataifi dessert and *not* reference the incarnation of the dish created by our great friends Itamar Srulovich and Sarit Packer—the honeys—of Honey and Co. It's a staple of their restaurant and café menus and the stuff of dreams. In our version, we've dialed up the lemon flavor and introduced the store-bought meringue. Make the various elements in advance and then it's a really easy and quick one to throw together.

Getting ahead: The kataifi pastry can be baked well ahead. It keeps in a sealed container for up to 5 days and is wonderful sprinkled over all sorts of yogurty, creamy dishes. The lemon syrup also keeps well for the same amount of time. The yogurt cream is best whipped just before serving.

Serves 4 (but easily scalable if feeding a crowd)

Preheat the oven to 350°F and line a rimmed baking sheet with parchment paper.

Put the kataifi, powdered sugar, cinnamon, and salt into a medium bowl and, using your hands, mix to combine. Add the melted butter and mix together again, so that the strands of kataifi are evenly coated. Transfer to the prepared baking sheet and spread the mixture out in a thin layer. Place another sheet of paper on top and press down with a rolling pin—it should be about ¼ inch/½cm thick. Remove the top sheet of paper and bake for 18–20 minutes, or until deeply golden. Once cool, break into shards.

Meanwhile, put all the ingredients for the lemon syrup into a small saucepan and place on medium-high heat. Bring to a boil, then decrease the heat to medium-low and simmer for 10–12 minutes, stirring every now and again, until slightly thickened and reduced (it will thicken further as it cools). Transfer to a bowl and set aside in the fridge to cool completely.

When ready to serve, whip the heavy cream, yogurt, vanilla seeds, and powdered sugar to form soft peaks. Transfer to a serving plate, using a spoon to make swoops and swirls, and scatter the blueberries and pieces of meringue. Tuck the kataifi in among the "mess" and spoon some of the lemon syrup over the top, including the strips of lemon peel. Serve with more of the syrup and kataifi alongside.

Chocolate ripple fridge cake

3 tbsp milk (or 7 tbsp/105ml if not
  using the Grand Marnier)
¼ cup/60ml Grand Marnier
  (if using)
1 espresso shot, regular or decaf
  (2 tbsp/30ml)
2¾ cups/650ml heavy cream
1⅓ cups/325g crème fraîche
6 tbsp/50g powdered sugar
1½ tsp vanilla extract
1½ tsp ground cinnamon

Cookies
1¾ cups plus 1 tbsp/225g
  all-purpose flour
⅔ cup/50g cocoa powder
¾ tsp baking powder
½ tsp baking soda
¼ tsp salt
7 tbsp/100g unsalted butter,
  at room temperature
1 cup/200g granulated sugar
3 tbsp vegetable oil
2½ tbsp golden syrup (or light
  corn syrup)
1 egg

Macerated strawberries
1 lb 5 oz/600g strawberries, hulled
  and quartered
1½ tbsp granulated sugar
1 tsp finely shaved orange zest
2 tbsp Grand Marnier
  (or orange juice)
2 strips of orange zest, julienned

As anyone who's ever been to an Australian barbecue will know, chocolate ripple cake is a ubiquitous, no-bake dessert. In Australia, it's made with store-bought chocolate cookies, which are then sandwiched together with cream. The recipe is so simple that it's printed on the back of the cookie box! On a recent family trip back to Melbourne, Helen's kids were so taken by the cake that they begged her to make it back in London. Not being able to find the right cookies—Arnott's Choc Ripple (though they are now available online)—Helen made them from scratch. They're so quick and simple to bake that Helen now not only bakes them to make the cake but also makes extra cookies to have around. No birthday party (or barbecue!) is complete without them. Pictured on page 284.

Getting ahead: The cookies can be made and baked up to 7 days in advance, kept in an airtight container. The cake needs to be made up to 6 hours before serving, to allow it to soften and meld together, but can be made up to 2 days in advance, left to sit and wait in the fridge.

Playing around: The strawberries work really well here, but as an alternative, just crumble another cookie or a chocolate flake over the top.

Serves 8–10

First make the cookies. Sift the flour, cocoa powder, baking powder, baking soda, and salt into a medium bowl.

Place the butter, sugar, oil, and golden syrup in the bowl of a stand mixer with the paddle attachment in place. Beat on medium speed for 2 minutes, until light and creamy. Scrape the sides of the bowl, then add the egg and beat again until combined. Decrease the speed to low, add the dry ingredients, and mix until the dough comes together. Wrap and chill in the fridge for at least 2 hours.

When ready to bake, preheat the oven to 375°F.

Pinch off 1-oz/30g pieces of dough and roll them into balls, then place them, spaced about 2 inches/5cm apart, on two parchment-lined rimmed baking sheets. You should make about 23 balls. Flatten them with your hand—they should be about 2 inches/5cm wide—then bake for 12-15 minutes, until firm and the tops are cracked or "rippled." Remove from the oven and allow to cool for 5 minutes before transferring to a wire rack to cool completely.

When ready to assemble the cake, combine the milk, Grand Marnier (if using), and espresso and set aside.

Place the cream, crème fraîche, powdered sugar, vanilla extract, and cinnamon in the bowl of the stand mixer with the whisk attachment in place. Whisk on medium-high speed until soft peaks form—be careful not to over-whip, as the cream will thicken as you spread it. Transfer 2 cups/200g of the mixture to a small bowl and refrigerate—this will be used to finish the cake. Pipe or dollop a roughly 12-inch/30cm-long line (about ¾ inch/2cm wide) of the remaining cream mixture down the center of a long cake plate or board—this is to help position the cookies for assembly.

Take 20 of the cookies and, working with one cookie at a time, lightly brush both sides with the milk mixture—you want to just moisten the entire cookie without drenching it. Then, using a small spatula or knife, spread 2 tablespoons of the cream on one side of the cookie. Standing the cookie upright, press it down onto one end of the strip of cream. Repeat with another cookie, then place alongside the first cookie, pressing to sandwich them together. Continue with the remaining cookies to form a long log cake. Spread the remaining cream mixture over the top and sides of the log—don't worry if it only barely covers the cake, as it will be topped up with the reserved cream the following day. Cover loosely and refrigerate for at least 6 hours or overnight.

About 15 minutes before you're ready to serve, combine the strawberries in a bowl with the sugar, finely shaved orange zest, and Grand Marnier. Allow to macerate for 10–15 minutes.

Meanwhile, spread the reserved cream over the top and sides of the log.

When ready to serve, tumble about half the strawberries along the top of the cake, pressing them on slightly to help them stick. Drizzle any syrup over and around the plate. Finish with the orange zest strips on top. When serving, slice on the diagonal—warming the blade of the knife with hot water helps with the cleanness of the slice—to reveal the stripes.

Chocolate mousse with orange caramel

12¾ oz/360g **dark chocolate**
 (around 64% cocoa solids),
 roughly chopped
6 eggs, yolks and whites separated
¼ cup plus 1 tbsp/60g **granulated
 sugar**
1½ cups plus 7 tbsp/460ml **heavy
 cream**
½ cup/100g **sour cream**
⅓ cup/50g **blanched hazelnuts**,
 toasted and roughly chopped, to
 serve
flaked sea salt

Orange caramel (optional)
½ cup/100g **granulated sugar**
2–3 large **oranges**: 4 strips
 of peel julienned to garnish,
 then juice to get ½ cup/120ml

The orange caramel gives this a lovely citrus twist, but the mousse works just as well without it. Don't skimp on the cream and nuts, though—they both do something special here.

Storing notes: The mousse keeps well in the fridge for up to 3 days.

Serves 8

Melt the chocolate by placing it in a heatproof bowl set over a pot of simmering water, making sure that the bottom of the bowl is not touching the water. Stir from time to time, until melted, then remove from the heat and set aside to cool slightly—it can be just warm, but not hot.

Put the egg yolks into a medium mixing bowl and, using electric beaters, beat for 1 minute or so until lightened. Add the cooled melted chocolate and stir gently to combine.

Whisk the whites in a stand mixer on medium-high speed for 2 minutes, until frothy. Slowly stream in the sugar and continue to whisk for 2–3 minutes, until shiny and stiff peaks form. In batches of three, add the whisked egg white mixture to the chocolate mix, folding gently to combine and taking care not to overwork it—it should remain looking streaky.

Without washing the mixer bowl, add 1½ cups/360ml of the cream and whisk on medium speed for 3 minutes, until soft peaks form—keep a close eye here, as it can over-whip. Fold gently, but thoroughly, into the chocolate mixture, along with ½ teaspoon of flaked sea salt, then scrape the mix into a serving bowl or into eight individual glasses. Refrigerate for 3 hours (or overnight—though it's fine for up to 3 days), until cold.

If making the orange caramel, place a small saucepan on medium-high heat and sprinkle with half the sugar. Stir to melt, then add the rest of the sugar and cook for about 3 minutes, stirring from time to time, until a deep amber caramel is formed. Remove from the heat and carefully pour in the orange juice—it will splutter quite a bit. Return to the heat, stirring so that any unmelted bits of sugar dissolve. Stir in ¼ teaspoon of flaked sea salt and set aside to cool.

Put the remaining 7 tbsp/100ml of heavy cream into a small bowl and add the sour cream. Whisk for about 1 minute, until starting to thicken.

About 15 minutes before serving, remove the mousse from the fridge. Dollop the cream topping over the mousse, drizzle some of the caramel, and finish with a sprinkle of the hazelnuts and orange peel.

Apple, blackberry, and ginger crumble cake

1⅓ cups plus 2 tbsp/180g
  all-purpose flour
1½ tsp baking powder
¼ tsp salt
4 small Granny Smith apples,
  peeled, cored, and thinly
  sliced (3⅔ cups/360g)
1¼ oz/35g fresh ginger, peeled and
  finely grated
1 lemon: finely grate the zest to get
  1 tsp, then juice to get 1½ tsp
¾ cup/180g unsalted butter, diced,
  at room temperature, plus about
  2 tsp extra for greasing
½ cup plus 2 tbsp/130g granulated
  sugar
3 eggs and 1 egg white
1 tsp vanilla extract
2 cups/300g blackberries
very softly whipped cream, to serve

Crumble topping
¾ cup/90g all-purpose flour
6 tbsp/80g demerara sugar
1 tsp ground ginger
1 tsp ground cinnamon
mounded ½ cup/60g sliced
  almonds
¼ tsp salt
5 tbsp/75g unsalted butter, melted
  and then slightly cooled

Baked in an ovenproof dish and brought directly to the table while still warm, this is a gorgeously cozy cake. It works in all seasons, as well, if you play around with the fruit. Peaches with raspberries in the summer, for example, apples with plums when it's autumn.

Getting ahead/storing notes: This is best eaten warm but is great, also, the next day at room temperature, cut into pieces. The amount of fruit—it's a lot!—means that any longer than a day later and the cake will be a bit soggy. The crumble can be made up to 4 days ahead and kept, refrigerated, in an airtight container or frozen for up to 1 month. It can also be used as a topping for muffins.

Serves 6–8

First make the crumble topping. Put the flour, sugar, ginger, cinnamon, almonds, and salt into a medium bowl. Stir to combine, then add the butter and, using a fork, mix together until combined and clumps form. Set aside in the fridge.

Preheat the oven to 375°F. Grease a large, deep ovenproof dish—about 10¼ inches/26cm wide—with butter and set aside. Sift the flour, baking powder, and salt into a small bowl and set aside.

Combine the apples, ginger, and lemon juice in a separate small bowl and allow to macerate while you make the batter.

Place the butter, sugar, and lemon zest in the bowl of a stand mixer. Use the paddle attachment to beat on medium-high speed for 3 minutes, until light and creamy. Whisk the eggs, egg white, and vanilla extract in a small bowl and, with the machine on, stream into the creamed butter mixture, in 4–5 additions, scraping down the sides of the bowl, until combined. The mixture will appear curdled, but don't worry—it will come together again. Decrease the speed to low, add the sifted dry ingredients, and mix until just combined. Remove the bowl from the stand mixer. Reserving ¾ cup/100g each of the macerated apples and the blackberries, gently fold the rest into the cake batter.

Scrape the mixture into the greased dish and smooth over the top. Scatter the reserved apples and blackberries on top, followed by the crumble topping—break the crumble into uneven clumps for texture, and make sure some of the fruit is poking out in places.

Bake for about 50 minutes, or until a skewer comes out clean. Set aside to cool for about 30 minutes before serving warm, with the whipped cream.

Dutch apple cake

Pastry
1¼ cups/280g unsalted butter,
at room temperature
packed ⅓ cup/75g light brown
sugar
1¼ cups/255g granulated sugar,
plus 1 tsp extra for sprinkling
1 tsp lemon zest
scraped seeds of 1 vanilla pod
1 egg and 2 yolks
2½ cups/310g all-purpose flour,
plus extra for dusting
⅔ cup/65g almond flour
1¼ tsp mahleb (leave this out if you
don't have it)
1½ tsp baking powder
¾ tsp salt

Filling
⅓ cup/40g sliced almonds,
toasted and roughly crushed
⅓ cup/50g raisins
3 tbsp dark rum (or apple juice)
2 tbsp unsalted butter, melted
4 Granny Smith apples, peeled,
cored, and cut into 1-inch/2.5cm
chunks (5⅔ cups/560g)
2 Pink Lady apples, peeled, cored,
and cut into 1-inch/2.5cm
chunks (3¼ cups/320g)
1 tbsp lemon juice
3 tbsp light brown sugar
1 tbsp molasses
⅛ tsp salt
¾ tsp ground cinnamon
¾ tsp mahleb (leave this out if you
don't have it)
½ tsp freshly grated nutmeg
⅓ cup/20g panko breadcrumbs

To serve
whipped cream

This cake is the result of two sets of memories. First Yotam's of living and studying in Amsterdam, where he'd stop by a café called Villa Zeezicht, now sadly closed, for a slice of their famous apple cake. The second set of memories are Verena's, of the German cake she grew up on—*gedeckter apfelkuchen* (covered apple cake)—raisin-filled and covered with a thin layer of lemon icing. Verena was also inspired by another Dutch sweet staple, *boterkoek* (literally "butter cake"), sweet, egg-rich, and very buttery, which pairs beautifully with the spiced apple filling. Either way, this cake is always served with whipped cream. *Pictured on page 293.*

Ingredients note: Mahleb is an aromatic ground spice made from the pit of the St Lucie cherry. It's wonderfully distinct—bitter and almond-like—but if you don't have any, just leave it out.

Serves 8–10

First make the pastry. Put the butter into the bowl of a stand mixer, with the paddle attachment in place. Add both sugars, the lemon zest, and vanilla seeds and mix on medium speed for 2 minutes, until lightened in color and creamy (but not super fluffy and airy). Whisk together the egg and yolks and set aside a small spoonful of it to use for brushing later. Add the remaining egg to the mixer bowl and continue to mix, until just combined. Decrease the speed to low, add the dry ingredients, and mix just until a dough forms. Transfer the dough to a piece of parchment paper and form it into a rectangle. Wrap it in parchment and chill in the fridge for at least 1½ hours (or overnight).

Preheat the oven to 375°F and place a parchment-lined baking sheet inside.

Butter the bottom and sides of a 9-inch/23cm springform cake pan, line the bottom with parchment paper, and set aside.

Divide the pastry equally into thirds. Take one piece of the pastry (keeping the rest in the fridge) and transfer it to a well-floured work surface. Using a floured rolling pin, roll the dough out into a circle, about 8½ inches/22cm wide. Use this to line the bottom of the cake pan, using your fingers to push it into the corners of the pan—don't worry if your dough breaks up or tears a little—just patch it up as you go.

Take a second piece of pastry and roll it out into a 5½ x 11½-inch/ 14 x 29cm rectangle. Cut it in half lengthwise (so you have two strips) and use it to line the sides of the pan. Again, use your fingers to push it into the sides and corners as needed. Set aside in the fridge. Roll out the remaining piece of dough into an 8½-inch/22cm-wide circle and set aside on a parchment-lined plate in the fridge.

Combine all the ingredients for the filling in a large bowl and mix together until well combined. Remove the pastry-lined cake pan from the fridge and spoon the filling into it. It will seem like a lot, but it will cook down. Remove the pastry circle from the fridge and place on top of the filling. Seal the top by pinching it together with the pastry sides. Brush the surface with the reserved egg mixture and sprinkle with the extra granulated sugar. Place on the prepared baking sheet and bake for about 1 hour, rotating the pan halfway through, until deeply golden.

Remove the cake from the oven and allow it to cool on a wire rack for at least 2 hours. Carefully run a small knife between the cake and the sides of the pan before releasing the spring lock. Cut into thick wedges and serve with the whipped cream alongside.

Verena's back-to-childhood marble cake

Vanilla cake batter

1 cup plus 2 tbsp/250g unsalted butter, softened, plus extra for greasing the pan

2¼ cups/275g all-purpose flour, plus extra for dusting the pan

1¼ cups plus 3 tbsp/285g granulated sugar

scraped seeds of 2 vanilla pods (or 1 tbsp vanilla bean paste)

1 tsp baking powder

½ tsp baking soda

¾ tsp salt

2 eggs and 2 yolks, at room temperature, whisked together

¾ cup/180ml kefir (or buttermilk), at room temperature

¼ cup/60ml advocaat liqueur (optional)

Chocolate cake batter

2½ oz/70g dark chocolate (70% cocoa solids), melted and cooled

2 tsp cocoa powder

Chocolate ganache glaze (optional—a dusting of powdered sugar also works)

4½ oz/125g good-quality milk (or dark) chocolate, melted and cooled

⅛ tsp flaked sea salt

7 tbsp/100ml heavy cream

multicolored sprinkles, to decorate (optional)

This is Verena's "madeleine moment" cake. No birthday celebration or family get-together was complete without a marble cake. Them were the rules! Other rules were relaxed, however, with Verena being allowed to have a tiny sip of her mum's advocaat, the rich and creamy Dutch tipple, of which they always had a bottle open. It's an old-school drink but worth seeking out and trying, for either nostalgia or novelty's sake. It's fine to leave it out, though, if you prefer.

Getting ahead/storing notes: Once baked and glazed, this keeps well in an airtight container, or well wrapped, for up to 3 days.

Serves 10–12

Preheat the oven to 375°F. Generously butter a 10-inch/25cm or 10¼-inch/26cm kugelhopf pan and dust the inside with flour. Invert the pan, give it a couple of bangs against the counter to remove any excess flour, and set aside.

Combine the butter, sugar, and vanilla seeds in the bowl of a stand mixer with the paddle attached. Cream on medium-high speed for 5 minutes, until light and fluffy, scraping down the bowl a couple of times. Meanwhile, sift together the dry ingredients and set aside. In a liquid measuring cup, whisk together the kefir and advocaat (if using) and set aside.

Decrease the mixer speed to medium-low and add the egg mixture, in 3–4 additions, scraping down the sides of the bowl in between. Decrease the speed to low and add—in three alternate batches—the flour mix and kefir mix, mixing until just combined before the next addition. Once combined, remove the bowl and give the batter a couple of stirs with a rubber spatula.

Weigh out 15 oz/430g of the batter into a separate bowl. Mix together the melted chocolate and cocoa powder, add to the weighed-out batter and mix to combine. Dollop large spoonfuls of the vanilla batter into the prepared pan, leaving some gaps in between. Then dollop spoonfuls of the chocolate batter into the gaps. Continue in this way, until both batters are used up. Take a skewer and gently swirl the batter in a figure-eight motion to create a marble effect. Smooth the surface and bake for 30 minutes. Carefully rotate the pan. Bake for 10–15 minutes, until a skewer inserted into the cake comes out clean. Let rest in the pan for 15 minutes before carefully inverting the cake onto a wire rack to finish cooling—this should take about 1½ hours.

To make the glaze, place the chocolate and salt in a small heatproof bowl. Heat the cream until it just starts to come to a simmer, then pour it over the chocolate. Allow to sit for 1 minute before gently whisking to form a smooth and shiny ganache. Drizzle over the cake and decorate with sprinkles, if you like, then set aside to firm up before slicing and serving.

Bottomless cheesecake with plum compote

¾ cup/175g unsalted
   butter, softened
1¼ cups plus 2 tbsp/275g
   granulated sugar
scraped seeds of 2 vanilla pods
   (pods reserved for another use)
2 lemons, zested to get 2 tsp
4 eggs and 2 yolks (at room
   temperature)
2 tsp vanilla extract
⅔ cup/100g **fine semolina**
   (or fine polenta if going GF)
2 tbsp custard powder
   (or cornstarch)
¼ tsp salt
1 tsp baking powder
1¾ cups plus 2 tbsp/450g
   Greek yogurt, 5% fat (at room
   temperature)
2½ cups/600ml **heavy cream**
   (at room temperature)
1 tbsp lemon juice

Plum compote (optional)
1 lb 2 oz/500g red plums, pits
   removed, sliced ¼ inch/½cm thick
¼ cup plus 1 tbsp/65g **granulated**
   sugar
1 tbsp lemon juice
1 orange: shave the zest with a
   vegetable peeler to get 3 strips,
   then juice to get 1 tbsp
1 whole star anise

Verena grew up eating this sort of cheesecake in Germany. Traditionally, lower-fat cheese, often quark, is used, along with fine semolina to bind. We have upped the creaminess here and given the option of using polenta instead of semolina, for those who want it gluten-free. The name comes from its having no bottom. It's a great way to feed a crowd but also keeps in the fridge (for up to 4 days), so it's great to return to once the crowds have gone.

Getting ahead: Unless you start baking very early in the morning, the cake needs to be made the day before serving, so that it can chill in the fridge overnight. The plum compote will keep for 1 week in the fridge.

Serves 8–10

Preheat the oven to 475°F. Lightly grease a 9-inch/23cm cake pan (with a removable bottom) and line with a circle of parchment about 16 inches/40cm wide—it will seem too large, but you want the paper to have ruffled edges.

Put the butter, sugar, vanilla seeds, and lemon zest into the bowl of a stand mixer with the paddle attachment and beat on medium speed for 5 minutes, until light and fluffy.

In a small bowl, whisk together the eggs, yolks, and vanilla extract and—in about three additions—stream into the creamed mixture (scraping down the sides of the bowl well).

In a small bowl, whisk together the semolina, custard powder, salt, and baking powder and add to the creamed butter/egg mixture. Mix on low speed until combined, scraping the sides of the bowl. Add the yogurt and mix until just combined, then stream in the heavy cream and lemon juice, scraping the bottom and sides of the bowl as necessary, until the mixture is smooth.

Pour the mixture into the prepared cake pan and give the pan a couple of good bangs on the worktop (to get rid of any major air bubbles). Bake for 20 minutes, then decrease the oven temperature to 350°F and bake for 20 minutes, until the cake has puffed up, is really well browned on top, and jiggles in the middle (it will collapse as it cools). Switch the oven off, but leave the cheesecake inside for 2 hours (30 minutes with the door still closed and the remaining time with the door slightly ajar). Transfer to a wire rack and let it cool completely—about 4 hours. Once cool, transfer to the fridge to set for at least another 4 hours, but ideally overnight.

For the compote, if making, combine all the ingredients in a medium saucepan, for which you have a lid, and place on medium heat. Simmer for 10–15 minutes, partially covered with the lid, until the plums are cooked through and very soft, but still retaining some of their shape. Transfer to a medium bowl and set aside to cool completely. Spoon on top of, or serve alongside, the cake.

Vegan Texas sheet cake

1¼ cups/300ml soy milk
1 tbsp apple cider vinegar
½ cup/100g granulated sugar
packed ½ cup/100g dark brown
   sugar
2 cups/250g all-purpose flour
¾ cup/75g cocoa powder
1½ tsp instant espresso powder
1½ tsp baking soda
1½ tsp baking powder
½ tsp salt
7 tbsp/100ml vegetable oil
3 tbsp maple syrup
¾ cup/180ml hot water,
   just off the boil
vegan whipped cream, to serve

Chocolate icing
¼ cup plus 3 tbsp/110ml soy milk
5 tbsp/65g refined coconut oil
1½ tbsp cocoa powder
⅛ tsp salt
6 oz/175g dark vegan chocolate
   (70% cocoa solids), roughly
   chopped
1⅓ cups/175g powdered sugar
¼ tsp flaked sea salt, for sprinkling

Everyone needs a plain and simple chocolate cake in their repertoire to suit any kind of gathering or celebration (one, like this, that is super portable too, as you just store it in the pan it's baked in). This is a vegan version of a Texas sheet cake—essentially a moist and fudgy chocolate cake that has chocolate icing poured over it as soon as it comes out of the oven.

Storing notes: This keeps well at room temperature, covered, for up to 3 days.

Serves 8–10

Preheat the oven to 375°F. Lightly grease the bottom and sides of a 9 x 13-inch/23 x 33cm baking pan (with 1¼–2-inch/3–5cm-high sides) and line with parchment paper.

In a small liquid measuring cup, stir together the soy milk and apple cider vinegar and set aside to thicken.

Put both sugars into a food processor, along with the flour, cocoa powder, espresso powder, baking soda, baking powder, and salt. Blitz briefly, to combine.

Add the vegetable oil and maple syrup to the now thickened soy milk and pour this into the dry ingredients. Blitz until smooth, scraping the sides of the bowl. Pour in the hot water and blitz again until smooth and fully combined, scraping the sides of the bowl as necessary—it will be very runny! Pour into the prepared pan and bake for 20–25 minutes, or until a toothpick inserted in the center comes out clean.

Meanwhile, make the icing. Put ¼ cup/65ml of the soy milk into a medium saucepan, along with the coconut oil, cocoa powder, and salt. Place on medium-low heat until it just starts to simmer, whisking every now and again to get rid of any lumps of cocoa powder. Remove from the heat, add the chocolate, then let it sit for 1 minute before whisking to melt and combine. Add the powdered sugar and mix to combine—it will be quite lumpy and will look like it's splitting. Whisk in the remaining 3 tablespoons of soy milk and the mixture will re-emulsify to form a smooth and glossy icing.

As soon as the cake comes out of the oven, pour the icing all over, spreading it out to cover the corners. Sprinkle with the flaked sea salt and set aside to cool before serving.

Kaiserschmarrn

Pancake
¼ cup/25g raisins
2 tbsp rum or brandy
3 tbsp unsalted butter, softened
½ cup/100g granulated sugar
4 eggs, yolks and whites separated
  (you need 3 yolks and all of the
  whites)
½ cup/100g sour cream
scraped seeds of ½ a vanilla pod
  (pod reserved for another use)
⅔ cup/85g all-purpose flour
¼ tsp salt
½ tsp ground cinnamon
½ tsp ground star anise

To serve
powdered sugar, for dusting
plum compote (see page 296)

These were apparently created for the Austrian emperor Franz Joseph (hence the *Kaiser* before the *schmarrn*) but Helen first came across these torn pancakes in a resort in the Alps with our colleague and friend Cornelia Staeubli. Noticing that every single table at a coffee house on the mountain had ordered the same dish, Helen and her boys took their cue to follow. Serve it with compote for breakfast or chocolate sauce for dessert.

Serves 4–6

Place the raisins in a small jar and add the rum or brandy. Let soak for at least 1 hour (or overnight) to macerate.

Smear 1 tablespoon of the butter liberally over the bottom and sides of a roughly 9½-inch/24cm ovenproof frying pan. Sprinkle with 1 tablespoon of the sugar, shaking the pan and tapping all over to coat evenly. Shake off any excess and place in the fridge until ready to use.

Preheat the oven to 375°F.

Put the 3 egg yolks into a medium bowl. Add 2 tablespoons of sugar and, using a whisk, mix to combine until smooth. Add the sour cream, vanilla seeds, and the brandy (from soaking the raisins) and whisk again to combine. Sift the flour over the top, fold in with a spatula, and set aside.

Place the egg whites in the very clean bowl of a stand mixer. Whisk on medium speed for 1 minute, until foamy. Add the salt and beat for about 2 minutes, until the egg white just begins to hold its shape, then gradually stream in 40g—just under 3 tablespoons—of sugar. Once this sugar has been added, increase the speed to high and whisk until stiff peaks form. Using a spatula, scoop a third of the egg white mixture into the egg yolk batter. Fold to loosen, then continue with all the remaining egg white, combining and folding it into the batter.

Scrape the batter into the prepared chilled pan and scatter the drained raisins on top. Place immediately in the oven and bake for about 20 minutes, or until a skewer inserted into the middle comes out clean.

Mix the remaining 1 tablespoon of sugar with the cinnamon and star anise and set aside.

Remove the pan from the oven and, using two spoons, tear the pancake into irregular pieces—roughly 2 inches/5cm—and set aside on a plate. Melt half the remaining butter in the frying pan and place on medium-high heat. Drop in half the pancake pieces so that they form a single layer and sprinkle with half of the sugar mixture. Cook for 3–4 minutes, tossing gently, until starting to caramelize at the edges. Transfer to a serving dish while you repeat with the remaining butter, pancake pieces, and sugar. Pile onto the serving dish, dust lightly with powdered sugar, and serve warm, with the plum compote alongside.

Brownie cookies with tahini cream and halva

¾ cup/100g all-purpose flour
6 tbsp/35g cocoa powder
¾ tsp baking powder
¼ tsp baking soda
½ tsp salt
packed ⅔ cup/150g dark brown
    sugar
6 tbsp/75g granulated sugar
2 eggs
1 tbsp malted milk powder
    (we like Horlicks)
3½ oz/100g good-quality milk
    chocolate (37–40% cocoa solids),
    roughly chopped
5¼ oz/150g dark chocolate
    (70% cocoa solids), roughly
    chopped
7 tbsp/100g unsalted butter, cubed
1 tbsp sesame seeds (a mix of
    black and white, if possible),
    for sprinkling
½ tsp flaked sea salt, for sprinkling

Tahini cream
¾ cup plus 2 tbsp/200ml heavy
    cream
¾ cup/175g mascarpone
¼ cup/75g tahini
1 tsp vanilla extract
6 tbsp/50g powdered sugar
2⅓ oz/65g halva

These take everything that is great about brownies—chocolatey gooeyness—and everything that is great about cookies—soft, round perfection—and sandwich them together with a tahini-halva cream.

Storing notes: Once assembled, these are best eaten on the day. If you want to get ahead, make the cookies and the tahini cream—they both keep for a couple of days, the cream in the fridge—and assemble as you want to eat them.

Makes 15 sandwich cookies

Preheat the oven to 400°F and line 2–3 rimmed baking sheets with parchment paper. Have ready a piping bag or freezer bag.

Sift together the first five ingredients and set aside in a small bowl.

Put both sugars into the bowl of a stand mixer. Add the eggs and malted milk powder and whisk on high speed for 7 minutes, until creamy and tripled in volume.

Meanwhile, place both chocolates and the butter in a heatproof bowl and sit it on top of a pot of simmering water, taking care that the bottom of the pan is not touching the water. Stir until melted and then keep warm. Remove the bowl from the mixer and, with a rubber spatula, fold in the melted chocolate mixture, until it's just combined. Fold in the dry ingredients, until just combined and no streaks of flour are visible.

Transfer the mixture to the piping bag (or freezer bag); sitting it inside a tall-sided bowl will help it stay upright while you spoon in the mixture. Snip off the end, or a corner, and pipe out 30 cookies between the sheets, each cookie about 2 inches/5cm wide and spaced apart. Sprinkle the tops of half of the cookies evenly with the sesame seeds and salt, and immediately bake for 8 minutes, until puffed up and cracked. Move the sheets to a wire rack to cool completely—the cookies will deflate. If you're baking in batches, don't pipe out all the cookies until they are ready to go into the oven.

Meanwhile, combine all the ingredients for the tahini cream, except for the halva, and whisk by hand into medium peaks. Keep in the fridge.

Once the cookies are completely cool, spread a little of the cream all over the flat side of the cookies. Press a good pinch of halva into the middle and sandwich together with one of the cookies with sesame seeds on top.

Malty figgy pudding

1 cup plus 3 tbsp/150g all-purpose
 flour
2 tbsp cocoa powder
½ tsp salt
2 tsp baking powder
2 tbsp malted milk powder
 (we like Horlicks)
packed ¼ cup/50g dark brown
 sugar
½ cup/50g almond flour
½ cup plus 2 tbsp/130g unsalted
 butter, melted, plus 2 tsp extra
 for greasing the dish
7 tbsp/100ml milk
⅓ cup/75g crème fraîche
3 tbsp maple syrup
1 egg, lightly beaten
5¼ oz/150g dried soft figs,
 roughly chopped
1¾ oz/50g dark chocolate
 (70% cocoa solids), roughly
 chopped

Topping
packed ½ cup/100g dark brown
 sugar
1 tbsp malted milk powder
⅛ tsp salt
1½ tbsp unsalted butter, cut into
 small cubes
¾ cup plus 2 tbsp/200ml water
½ cup plus 2 tbsp/150ml
 heavy cream

To serve
6 tbsp/100g crème fraîche
 (or whipped cream or vanilla
 ice cream)
3 tbsp sliced almonds, toasted
2 tbsp maple syrup

If comfort means "warm and gooey" on the cake front and "low-key and easy" on the making front, then this is comfort dessert 101. It's super easy to put together—just 15 minutes—and then half an hour in the oven, ready to delight whoever is set to dive in. *Also pictured on page 306.*

Serves 6–8

Preheat the oven to 400°F. Butter a 10¼-inch/26cm baking dish with at least 2-inch/5cm sides and set aside.

Sift the flour, cocoa powder, salt, baking powder, and malted milk powder into a medium bowl. Add the sugar and almond flour, then mix well.

In a liquid measuring cup or bowl, whisk together the melted butter, milk, crème fraîche, maple syrup, and egg. Add to the dry ingredients, along with the figs and chocolate, and mix gently to combine. Transfer the mixture to the prepared baking dish.

Make the topping by mixing together the sugar, malted milk powder, and salt. Sprinkle evenly over the cake batter and scatter the butter. Combine the water and cream in a small saucepan and place on medium-high heat. Bring to a simmer, then carefully pour over the cake batter, starting from the outside and working your way into the middle, and then transfer to the oven. Bake for 30 minutes, until the pudding has formed a crust and the sauce is bubbling up around the sides.

Let cool for 5 minutes before spooning some of the crème fraîche over the top. Sprinkle with some of the toasted almonds and drizzle the maple syrup. Serve warm, with the rest of the crème fraîche and almonds alongside.

311

Index

Unless otherwise stated: all eggs are large and all milk is whole. Yogurt, sour cream, coconut milk, coconut cream, and crème fraîche are all full fat. Herbs, curry leaves, and ginger are fresh, and parsley is flat leaf. Onions, shallots, and garlic are peeled, and green onions are trimmed. Where a specific type of chile flakes is used, these can be substituted with regular chile flakes. Anchovies and capers are not the kind packed in salt; they are in oil/brine and drained. Olive oil is extra virgin, salt is fine sea salt, and black pepper is freshly cracked.

A

affogato, baked custard 277
aïoli: egg and cress 25
aligot potato: garlicky aligot potato with leeks and thyme 231
almond milk: cinnamon baked oatmeal with bananas and strawberries 273
almonds: curry leaf dukkah 106
Dutch apple cake 290–1
anchovies: cheesy bread soup with Savoy cabbage 61
creamy eggplant Caesar dip 87
rigatoni al ragù bianco 206
tomato anchovy oil 153
apples: apple, blackberry, and ginger crumble cake 289
Dutch apple cake 290–1
artichokes, vegan creamed spinach and 97
arugula: silky zucchini and salmon salad 91
asparagus: fresh turmeric and peppercorn curry with shrimp and asparagus 169
spinach and asparagus loaf 263
Auntie Pauline's marinade 121
avocados: green tea noodles with avocado and radish 184

B

bacon: Dutch baby with oven-roasted tomatoes 22
baharat spice mix: beef, black garlic, and baharat pie 252–3
spiced yogurt 78
bake, potato, fennel, and smoked salmon 232
baked potatoes with eggplant and green tahini 234
bananas: cinnamon baked oatmeal with bananas and strawberries 273
basil: pesto pasta with charred beans and potatoes 201
beansprouts: chicken and lime leaf curry with noodles 174
poached chicken congee 194
beef: beef, black garlic, and baharat pie 252–3
rigatoni al ragù bianco 206
stroganoff meatballs 210–11

beetroot: roasted beets with tarragon and walnut tarator 115
black-eyed peas: braised fennel and cod with black-eyed peas and 'nduja butter 148
blackberries: apple, blackberry, and ginger crumble cake 289
blueberries: lemon and blueberry meringue kataifi mess 280
Bohemian fish pie 260
bok choy: lemongrass and galangal tuna curry 170
Bolognese, Helen's 207
bottomless cheesecake with plum compote 296
boureka: breakfast boureka with spinach 238–9
bread: bread rolls 266–7
carrot and vadouvan quick-bread 264
cheesy bread soup with Savoy cabbage 61
cumin and coriander flatbreads 165
green beans on toast 102
maple mustard croutons 87
spiced chicken sando 78
spinach and asparagus loaf 263
summer chicken cacciatore with herb sauce 132
walnut tarator 115
breakfast boureka with spinach 238–9
brownie cookies with tahini cream and halva 302
Brussels sprouts: charred sprouts with olive oil and lemon 110
bulgur: shawarma meatloaf with caramelized onions 139
burrata: caponata with celery and 86
butter: cheeseball lemon rice with chile butter 133
lemon butter sauce 232
linguine with miso butter, shiitake, and spinach 205
'nduja butter 148
roasted hispi cabbage with miso butter 140
butter beans: braised lamb with butter beans and yogurt 179
butter beans with roasted cherry tomatoes 101

butter-braised kohlrabi with olive chimichurri 109
cheesy curry crêpes 42
buteries, cheese and onion 242–3
butternut squash: butternut, tamarind, and coconut stew 164
cauliflower and butternut pakoras 72

C

cabbage: cheesy bread soup with Savoy cabbage 61
mung bean and kimchee "falafel" 69
quick-pickled red cabbage 234
roasted hispi cabbage with miso butter 140
spiced chicken sando 78
white-poached chicken with Chinese cabbage and peanut rayu 136
cacciatore, summer chicken 132
Caesar dip, creamy eggplant 87
cakes: apple, blackberry, and ginger crumble cake 289
Dutch apple cake 290–1
Verena's back-to-childhood marble cake 295
cannellini beans: celery root and cannellini mash 260
capers: olive chimichurri 109
sauce 153
vegan creamed spinach and artichokes 97
zucchini and fennel lasagne 214
caponata with celery and burrata 86
caramel: caramelized onion orecchiette 202
chocolate mousse with orange caramel 286
carrots: carrot and vadouvan quick-bread 264
mulligatawny 54
pea and ham soup 55
roasted carrots with curry leaf dukkah 106
cashews: curry leaf dukkah 106, 128
cauliflower: cauliflower and butternut pakoras 72
hawaij-roasted cauliflower with gribiche sauce 144
cavolo nero: cheesy bread soup 61
celery: caponata with celery and burrata 86

celery root: all-purpose mushroom ragù 98
celery root and cannellini mash 260
slow-roasted celery root with Gorgonzola cream 105

cheese: baked polenta with zucchini and green harissa 223
breakfast boureka with spinach 238–9
caponata with celery and burrata 86
cheese and onion butteries 242–3
cheeseball lemon rice with chile butter 133
cheesy baked rice with okra and tomato 146
cheesy bread soup with Savoy cabbage 61
cheesy curry crêpes 42
creamy eggplant Caesar dip 87
Dutch baby with oven-roasted tomatoes 22
easy, cheesy rice cakes 68
garlicky aligot potato with leeks and thyme 231
green beans on toast 102
leek, cheese, and za'atar rugelach 254
parmesan and black pepper roasted parsnips 116
pesto pasta with charred beans and potatoes 201
potato, cheese, and chermoula hand pies 249
sausage ragù lasagne for one 215
slow-roasted celery root with Gorgonzola cream 105
spinach and asparagus loaf 263
tomato galette with cheese and Marmite 256–7
zucchini and fennel lasagne 214
see also mascarpone; ricotta

cheesecake: bottomless cheesecake with plum compote 296

chermoula: potato, cheese, and chermoula hand pies 249
salmon fishcakes with chermoula remoulade 80

chicken: cheesy curry crêpes 42
chicken and lime leaf curry with noodles 174
chicken meatballs, potatoes, and lemon 176
chicken stock 58
chicken with Steph's spice 122
mulligatawny 54
one-pot chicken with orzo and porcini 213
oyakodon 158
poached chicken congee 194
roasted chicken with Auntie Pauline's marinade 121
roasted chicken with curry leaf dukkah 128
sambal spiced chicken 125
spiced chicken sando with harissa mayonnaise 78
summer chicken cacciatore with herb sauce 132
white-poached chicken with Chinese cabbage and peanut rayu 136

chickpeas: chickpea and fennel purée 63
hummus 62

chiles: cheeseball lemon rice with chile butter 133
chicken with Steph's spice 122
chile dipping sauce 76
chile ginger sauce 191
fresh turmeric and peppercorn curry with shrimp and asparagus 169
hummus 62
Indonesian "home fries" 227
nasi goreng with shrimp and green beans 187
nuoc cham 83, 92
one-pot chicken with orzo and porcini 213
quick sweet chile sauce 68
rice vermicelli with turmeric fish, dill, and green onion 92
vegan creamed spinach and artichokes 97
white-poached chicken with Chinese cabbage and peanut rayu 136
zhoug 29

chimichurri, olive 109

Chinese cabbage: white-poached chicken with Chinese cabbage and peanut rayu 136

chives: herb sauce 132
steamed eggs with shrimp and chives 34

chocolate: brownie cookies with tahini cream and halva 302
chocolate mousse with orange caramel 286
chocolate ripple fridge cake 282–3
GF caramelized white chocolate and macadamia cookies 274
malty figgy pudding 305
sesame and hazelnut chocolate praline spread 40
vegan Texas sheet cake 298
Verena's back-to-childhood marble cake 295

cinnamon baked oatmeal with bananas and strawberries 273

coconut: baked custard affogato 277

coconut cream: mulligatawny 54

coconut milk: butternut, tamarind and coconut stew 164
chicken and lime leaf curry with noodles 174
coconut rice with peanut sauce and cucumber relish 124–5
fresh turmeric and peppercorn curry with shrimp and asparagus 169
lemongrass and galangal tuna curry 170

red lentil dal with potato and fennel 157
roasted chicken with Auntie Pauline's marinade 121

cod: braised fennel and cod with black-eyed peas and 'nduja butter 148

coffee: baked custard affogato 277

compote, plum 296

congee, poached chicken 194

cookies: brownie cookies with tahini cream and halva 302
chocolate ripple fridge cake 282–3
GF caramelized white chocolate and macadamia cookies 274

coriander: cumin and coriander flatbreads 165

corn: spiced corn salad 46

cream: baked custard affogato 277
bottomless cheesecake 296
chocolate mousse with orange caramel 286
garlicky aligot potato with leeks and thyme 231
potato, fennel, and smoked salmon bake 232
tahini cream 302
yogurt cream 280

cream cheese: cream cheese pastry 254
tomato galette with cheese and Marmite 256–7

cream cheese pastry 254
leek, cheese, and za'atar rugelach 254
potato, cheese, and chermoula hand pies 249

creamy eggplant Caesar dip 87

crème fraîche, mustard 181

crêpes: cheesy curry crêpes 42
lemon, mascarpone, and thyme 44
sesame and hazelnut chocolate praline spread 40
see also pancakes

crispy roasted potatoes with rosemary and za'atar 228

croutons, maple mustard 87

crumble cake, apple, blackberry, and ginger 289

cucumber: cucumber relishes 124–5, 169
dressed cucumber 207
meatballs with nuoc cham, cucumber, and mint 83
Verena's potato salad 224

cucur udang 76

cumin and coriander flatbreads 165

curry: cheesy curry crêpes 42
chicken and lime leaf curry with noodles 174
fresh turmeric and peppercorn curry with shrimp and asparagus 169
lemongrass and galangal tuna curry 170

curry leaf dukkah 106, 128

custard affogato, baked 277

D

dal: red lentil dal with potato and fennel 157
dill: rice vermicelli with turmeric fish, dill, and green onion 92
dips and dipping sauces: chile dipping sauce 76
  creamy eggplant Caesar dip 87
  honey mustard dipping sauce 246
  kimchi 69
dressings: lemon soy dressing 184
  spiced sesame dressing 192
  tarragon dressing 115
dukkah, curry leaf 106, 128
Dutch apple cake 290–1
Dutch baby with oven-roasted tomatoes 22

E

easy, cheesy rice cakes 68
eggplant: baked potatoes with eggplant and green tahini 234
  caponata with celery and burrata 86
  creamy eggplant Caesar dip 87
  roasted eggplant, pepper, and tomato soup 53
  silky steamed eggplant 93
  tomato and eggplant one-pot baked pasta 218
  tortang talong 30–1
eggs: baked custard affogato 277
  chocolate mousse with orange caramel 286
  crêpes 3 ways 39–45
  Dutch baby with oven-roasted tomatoes 22
  egg and watercress 25
  egg sambal "shakshuka" 26
  gribiche sauce 144
  leek, tomato, and turmeric frittata 29
  matza balls 58
  nasi goreng with shrimp and green beans 187
  oyakodon 158
  soy-braised pork belly with eggs and tofu 162
  steamed eggs with shrimp and chives 34
  tortang talong 30–1

F

"falafel," mung bean and kimchee 69
fennel: Bohemian fish pie 260
  braised fennel and cod with black-eyed peas and 'nduja butter 148
  chickpea and fennel purée 63
  potato, fennel, and smoked salmon bake 232
  red lentil dal with potato and fennel 157
  zucchini and fennel lasagne 214
figgy pudding, malty 305

filo pastry: breakfast boureka with spinach 238–9
fish: Bohemian fish pie 260
  braised fennel and cod with black-eyed peas and 'nduja butter 148
  cheesy bread soup with Savoy cabbage 61
  creamy eggplant Caesar dip 87
  gingery fish and rice 191
  lemongrass and galangal tuna curry 170
  potato, fennel, and smoked salmon bake 232
  puttanesca-style sheet pan salmon 153
  rice vermicelli with turmeric fish, dill and green onion 92
  rigatoni al ragù bianco 206
  salmon fishcakes with chermoula remoulade 80
  silky zucchini and salmon salad 91
flatbreads, cumin and coriander 165
French beans: green beans on toast 102
fridge cake, chocolate ripple 282–3
fries," Indonesian "home 227
frittata, leek, tomato, and turmeric 29
fritters, shrimp spoon 76

G

galangal: lemongrass and galangal tuna curry 170
galette: tomato galette with cheese and Marmite 256–7
garlic: beef, black garlic, and baharat pie 252–3
  braised fennel and cod with black-eyed peas and 'nduja butter 148
  braised lamb with butter beans and yogurt 179
  butternut, tamarind, and coconut stew 164
  charred sprouts with olive oil and lemon 110
  chicken meatballs, potatoes, and lemon 176
  creamy eggplant Caesar dip 87
  egg sambal "shakshuka" 26
  garlicky aligot potato with leeks and thyme 231
  Indonesian "home fries" 227
  one-pot chicken with orzo and porcini 213
  roasted chicken with curry leaf dukkah 128
  roasted eggplant, red bell pepper, and tomato soup 53
  slow-roasted celery root with Gorgonzola cream 105
  soy-braised pork belly with eggs and tofu 162
  tomato anchovy oil 153
  tomato and eggplant one-pot baked pasta 218

tomato galette with cheese and Marmite 256–7
German-style sausage rolls with honey mustard 246
GF caramelized white chocolate and macadamia cookies 274
ginger: apple, blackberry, and ginger crumble cake 289
  chile ginger sauce 191
  cucumber and ginger relish 169
  gingery fish and rice 191
  oyakodon 158
  poached chicken congee 194
green beans: chicken and lime leaf curry with noodles 174
  green beans on toast 102
  nasi goreng with shrimp and green beans 187
  pesto pasta with charred beans and potatoes 201
  puttanesca-style sheet pan salmon 153
green harissa 223
green onions: garlicky aligot potato with leeks and thyme 231
  gingery fish and rice 191
  mushroom and kimchi mapo tofu 196
  rice vermicelli with turmeric fish, dill, and green onion 92
  green onion oil 188
  zucchini and fennel lasagne 214
green split peas: pea and ham soup 55
green tahini sauce 234
green tea noodles with avocado and radish 184
gribiche sauce 144

H

halva, brownie cookies with tahini cream and 302
ham: cheesy curry crêpes 42
  pea and ham soup 55
hand pies, potato, cheese, and chermoula 249
harissa: green harissa 223
  harissa mayonnaise 78
  tomato and harissa sauce 238–9
  tortang talong 30–1
hawaji spice mix 58
  hawaij-roasted cauliflower with gribiche sauce 144
hazelnuts: caramelized onion orecchiette with hazelnuts and crispy sage 202
  sesame and hazelnut chocolate praline spread 40
Helen's Bolognese 207
herb sauce 132
honey mustard dipping sauce 246
hummus 62
  hummus by way of southern France 63

I

Indonesian "home fries" 227

K

Kaiserschmarrn 300–1
kataifi pastry: lemon and blueberry meringue kataifi mess 280
kicap 187
kimchee: mung bean and kimchee "falafel" 69
kimchi: kimchi dipping sauce 69
    mushroom and kimchi mapo tofu 196
kohlrabi: butter-braised kohlrabi with olive chimichurri 109

L

lamb: braised lamb with butter beans and yogurt 179
    shawarma meatloaf with caramelized onions 139
    tortang talong 30–1
lasagne: sausage ragù lasagne for one 215
    zucchini and fennel lasagne 214
leeks: garlicky aligot potato with leeks and thyme 231
    leek, cheese, and za'atar rugelach 254
    leek, tomato, and turmeric frittata 29
lemon curd: lemon, mascarpone, and thyme 44
lemongrass and galangal tuna curry 170
lemons: charred sprouts with olive oil and lemon 110
    cheeseball lemon rice with chile butter 133
    chicken meatballs, potatoes, and lemon 176
    hummus 62
    lemon and blueberry meringue kataifi mess 280
    lemon butter sauce 232
    lemon soy dressing 184
    lemon syrup 280
    quick-pickled shallots 91
    slow-roasted celery root with Gorgonzola cream 105
lentils: mulligatawny 54
    red lentil dal with potato and fennel 157
    sausage and lentils with mustard crème fraîche 181
lettuce: creamy eggplant Caesar dip 87
lime leaves: chicken and lime leaf curry 174
limes: nuoc cham 92
    roasted chicken with Auntie Pauline's marinade 121
linguine: linguine with miso butter, shiitake, and spinach 205
    stroganoff meatballs 210–11

M

macadamia nuts: GF caramelized white chocolate and macadamia cookies 274
malty figgy pudding 305
maple mustard croutons 87
mapo tofu, mushroom, and kimchi 196
marinade, Auntie Pauline's 121
Marmite, tomato galette with cheese and 256–7
mascarpone: green beans on toast 102
    lemon, mascarpone, and thyme 44
    tahini cream 302
mash, celery root and cannellini 260
matza ball soup 58
mayonnaise: chermoula remoulade 80
    harissa mayonnaise 78
    Indonesian "home fries" 227
meatballs: chicken meatballs, potatoes, and lemon 176
    meatballs with nuoc cham, cucumber, and mint 83
    stroganoff meatballs 210–11
meatloaf, shawarma 139
meringues: baked custard affogato 277
    lemon and blueberry meringue kataifi mess 280
mint: green tahini sauce 234
    herb sauce 132
    meatballs with nuoc cham, cucumber, and mint 83
    pea and mint sauce 55
miso: linguine with miso butter, shiitake, and spinach 205
    roasted hispi cabbage with miso butter 140
mother and child 158
mousse: chocolate mousse with orange caramel 286
mulligatawny 54
mung bean and kimchee "falafel" 69
mushrooms: all-purpose mushroom ragù 98
    linguine with miso butter, shiitake, and spinach 205
    mushroom and kimchi mapo tofu 196
    one-pot chicken with orzo and porcini 213
    quick ramen noodles with mushrooms 188
    stroganoff meatballs 210–11
mustard: honey mustard dipping sauce 246
    maple mustard croutons 87
    mustard crème fraîche 181

N

nasi goreng with shrimp and green beans 187
'nduja butter 148
noodles: chicken and lime leaf curry with noodles 174
    green tea noodles with avocado and radish 184
    quick ramen noodles with mushrooms 188
    rice vermicelli with turmeric fish, dill, and green onion 92
nuoc cham 92
    meatballs with nuoc cham, cucumber, and mint 83

O

oats: cinnamon baked oatmeal with bananas and strawberries 273
    GF caramelized white chocolate and macadamia cookies 274
oils: green onion oil 188
    tomato anchovy oil 153
okra: cheesy baked rice with okra and tomato 146
olive oil: charred sprouts with olive oil and lemon 110
olives: beef, black garlic, and baharat pie 252–3
    caponata with celery and burrata 86
    cheeseball lemon rice with chile butter 133
    herb sauce 132
    olive chimichurri 109
    potato, cheese, and chermoula hand pies 249
    sauce 153
    tomato, olive, and bell pepper topping 63
omelette: tortang talong 30–1
one-pot chicken with orzo and porcini 213
onions: caramelized onion orecchiette 202
    cheese and onion butteries 242–3
    poached chicken congee 194
    shawarma meatloaf with caramelized onions 139
orange caramel, chocolate mousse with 286
orecchiette, caramelized onion 202
orzo: one-pot chicken with orzo and porcini 213
oyakodon 158

P

Padrón peppers: creamy eggplant Caesar dip 87
pakoras, cauliflower and butternut 72
pancakes: Kaiserschmarrn 300–1
    polenta pancakes with spiced corn salad 46
    "thousand" hole pancakes 49
    see also crêpes
pancetta: Verena's potato salad 224
pappardelle: Helen's Bolognese 207
    stroganoff meatballs 210–11
parsnips, parmesan and black pepper roasted 116
pasta: caramelized onion orecchiette 202
    Helen's Bolognese 207

pasta, *continued*
linguine with miso butter, shiitake, and spinach 205
one-pot chicken with orzo and porcini 213
pesto pasta with charred beans and potatoes 201
rigatoni al ragù bianco 206
sausage ragù lasagne for one 215
stroganoff meatballs 210–11
tomato and eggplant one-pot baked pasta 218
zucchini and fennel lasagne 214
peanuts: coconut rice with peanut sauce and cucumber relish 124–5
curry leaf dukkah 106, 128
rice vermicelli with turmeric fish, dill, and green onion 92
spiced corn salad 46
white-poached chicken with Chinese cabbage and peanut rayu 136
peas: easy, cheesy rice cakes 68
pea and ham soup 55
pea and mint sauce 55
pecans: "thousand" hole pancakes 49
peppers: creamy eggplant Caesar dip 87
green harissa 223
mulligatawny 54
roasted eggplant, red bell pepper, and tomato soup 53
sausage and lentils with mustard crème fraîche 181
slow-roasted celery root with Gorgonzola cream 105
tomato, olive, and bell pepper topping 63
pesto: egg and watercress 25
pesto pasta with charred beans and potatoes 201
pickles: quick-pickled red cabbage 234
quick-pickled shallots 91
pies: Bohemian fish pie 260
potato, cheese, and chermoula hand pies 249
pine nuts: breakfast boureka with spinach 238–9
pesto pasta with charred beans and potatoes 201
silky zucchini and salmon salad 91
pistachios: pesto 25
plum compote: 296
bottomless cheesecake with 296
Kaiserschmarrn 300–1
polenta: baked polenta with zucchini and green harissa 223
polenta pancakes with spiced corn salad 46
turkey rags-to-riches 220
pomegranate yogurt 139
porcini, one-pot chicken with orzo and 213

pork: Helen's Bolognese 207
meatballs with nuoc cham, cucumber, and mint 83
pea and ham soup 55
rigatoni al ragù bianco 206
soy-braised pork belly with eggs and tofu 162
stroganoff meatballs 210–11
potatoes: baked potatoes with eggplant and green tahini 234
beef, black garlic, and baharat pie 252–3
chicken meatballs, potatoes, and lemon 176
crispy roasted potatoes with rosemary and za'atar 228
garlicky aligot potato with leeks and thyme 231
Indonesian "home fries" 227
pesto pasta with charred beans and potatoes 201
potato, cheese, and chermoula hand pies 249
potato, fennel, and smoked salmon bake 232
red lentil dal with potato and fennel 157
rigatoni al ragù bianco 206
salmon fishcakes with chermoula remoulade 80
Verena's potato salad 224
praline: sesame and hazelnut chocolate praline spread 40
puff pastry: beef, black garlic, and baharat pie 252–3
German-style sausage rolls with honey mustard 246
potato, cheese, and chermoula hand pies 249
puttanesca-style sheet pan salmon 153

R
radishes: creamy eggplant Caesar dip 87
sake-pickled radish 184
ragù: all-purpose mushroom ragù 98
rigatoni al ragù bianco 206
sausage ragù lasagne for one 215
ramen: quick ramen noodles with mushrooms 188
rayu, white-poached chicken with Chinese cabbage and peanut 136
red lentil dal with potato and fennel 157
relishes, cucumber 124–5, 169
remoulade, salmon fishcakes with chermoula 80
rice: cheeseball lemon rice with chile butter 133
cheesy baked rice with okra and tomato 146
coconut rice with peanut sauce and cucumber relish 124–5

easy, cheesy rice cakes 68
gingery fish and rice 191
meatballs with nuoc cham, cucumber, and mint 83
mulligatawny 54
nasi goreng with shrimp and green beans 187
oyakodon 158
poached chicken congee 194
rice cakes, easy, cheesy 68
ricotta: breakfast boureka with spinach 238–9
cheeseball lemon rice with chile butter 133
zucchini and fennel lasagne 214
rigatoni al ragù bianco 206
rosemary: crispy roasted potatoes with rosemary and za'atar 228
rugelach, leek, cheese, and za'atar 254
runner beans: green beans on toast 102

S
sake-pickled radish 184
salads: silky zucchini and salmon salad 91
spiced corn salad 46
Verena's potato salad 224
salmon: potato, fennel, and smoked salmon bake 232
puttanesca-style sheet pan salmon 153
salmon fishcakes with chermoula remoulade 80
silky zucchini and salmon salad 91
sambal: egg sambal "shakshuka" 26
sambal spiced chicken 125
sando, spiced chicken 78
sauces 153
herb sauce 132
pea and mint sauce 55
sausages: German-style sausage rolls 246
sausage and lentils with mustard crème fraîche 181
sausage ragù lasagne for one 215
seafood: Bohemian fish pie 260
semolina: "thousand" hole pancakes 49
sesame seeds: sesame and hazelnut chocolate praline spread 40
spiced sesame dressing 192
"shakshuka," egg sambal 26
shallots, quick-pickled 91
shawarma meatloaf with caramelized onions 139
sheet pan dishes: puttanesca-style sheet pan salmon 153
vegan Texas sheet cake 298
shiitake: linguine with miso butter, shiitake, and spinach 205
shrimp: fresh turmeric and peppercorn curry with shrimp and asparagus 169

nasi goreng with shrimp and green beans 187

shrimp spoon fritters 76

steamed eggs with shrimp and chives 34

silky zucchini and salmon salad 91

silky steamed eggplant 93

smoked salmon, potato, fennel, and smoked salmon bake 232

soups: cheesy bread soup with Savoy cabbage 61

matza ball soup 58

mulligatawny 54

pea and ham soup 55

roasted eggplant, red bell pepper, and tomato soup 53

sourdough: cheesy bread soup 61

green beans on toast 102

summer chicken cacciatore 132

soy sauce: lemon soy dressing 184

soy-braised pork belly with eggs and tofu 162

spice mixes: chicken with Steph's spice 122

hawaji spice mix 58, 144

spiced chicken sando with harissa mayonnaise 78

spiced corn salad 46

spiced yogurt 78

spinach: breakfast boureka with spinach 238–9

linguine with miso butter, shiitake, and spinach 205

spinach and asparagus loaf 263

vegan creamed spinach and artichokes 97

split mung beans: red lentil dal with potato and fennel 157

spread, sesame and hazelnut chocolate praline 40

sprouts: charred sprouts with olive oil and lemon 110

squash: butternut, tamarind, and coconut stew 164

cauliflower and butternut pakoras 72

stew, butternut, tamarind, coconut 164

stock, chicken 58

strawberries: chocolate ripple fridge cake 282–3

cinnamon baked oatmeal with bananas and strawberries 273

stroganoff meatballs 210–11

summer chicken cacciatore with herb sauce 132

sweet potatoes: salmon fishcakes with chermoula remoulade 80

Swiss chard: sausage and lentils with mustard crème fraîche 181

T

tadka 54

tahini: green tahini 234

hummus 62

silky steamed eggplant 93

tahini cream 302

tahini sauce 30–1, 238–9

tamarind: butternut, tamarind, and coconut stew 164

tamarind sauce 72

tarator, walnut 115

tarragon dressing 115

"thousand" hole pancakes 49

thyme: garlicky aligot potato with leeks and thyme 231

lemon, mascarpone, and thyme 44

tofu: chilled tofu with spiced sesame dressing 192

mushroom and kimchi mapo tofu 196

soy-braised pork belly with eggs and tofu 162

vegan creamed spinach and artichokes 97

tomatoes: beef, black garlic, and baharat pie 252–3

Bohemian fish pie 260

braised lamb with butter beans and yogurt 179

butter beans with roasted cherry tomatoes 101

caponata with celery and burrata 86

cheesy baked rice with okra and tomato 146

Dutch baby with oven-roasted tomatoes 22

egg sambal "shakshuka" 26

green beans on toast 102

leek, tomato, and turmeric frittata 29

mulligatawny 54

pea and ham soup 55

puttanesca-style sheet pan salmon 153

red lentil dal with potato and fennel 157

roasted eggplant, red bell pepper, and tomato soup 53

sausage ragù lasagne for one 215

summer chicken cacciatore with herb sauce 132

tomato anchovy oil 153

tomato and eggplant one-pot baked pasta 218

tomato and harissa sauce 238–9

tomato galette with cheese and Marmite 256–7

tomato, olive, and bell pepper topping 63

tortang talong 30–1

tuna: lemongrass and galangal tuna curry 170

turkey rags-to-riches 220

turmeric: fresh turmeric and peppercorn curry with shrimp and asparagus 169

leek, tomato, and turmeric frittata 29

rice vermicelli with turmeric fish, dill, and green onion 92

turnips: beef, black garlic, and baharat pie 252–3

V

vadouvan: carrot and vadouvan quick-bread 264

vegan creamed spinach and artichokes 97

vegan Texas sheet cake 298

Verena's back-to-childhood marble cake 295

Verena's potato salad 224

W

walnut tarator 115

watercress: egg and watercress 25

pesto 25

spinach and asparagus loaf 263

white-poached chicken with Chinese cabbage and peanut rayu 136

Y

yogurt: bottomless cheesecake with plum compote 296

braised lamb with butter beans and yogurt 179

butter beans with roasted cherry tomatoes 101

carrot and vadouvan quick-bread 264

creamy eggplant Caesar dip 87

pomegranate yogurt 139

roasted carrots with curry leaf dukkah 106

spiced yogurt 78

tahini sauce 30–1

yogurt cream 280

yogurt sauce 176

Z

za'atar: crispy roasted potatoes with rosemary and za'atar 228

leek, cheese, and za'atar rugelach 254

zhoug 29

zucchini: baked polenta with zucchini and green harissa 223

zucchini and fennel lasagne 214

shawarma meatloaf 139

silky zucchini and salmon salad 91

Acknowledgments

Yotam Ottolenghi
Big thanks to my creative collaborators on this journey of comfort and joy: Helen Goh, Verena Lochmuller, and Tara Wigley. It's been bumpy, on occasion, but always delicious.

Thank you also to our wonderful creative team: Jonathan Lovekin, Caz Hildebrand, and Wei Tang.

Huge gratitude to my fellow Ottolenghi co-founders: Noam Bar, Cornelia Staeubli, and Sami Tamimi.

As always, I am totally grateful to Felicity Rubinstein and to Team Ebury: Lizzy Gray and Emily Brickell, our editors, and Joel Rickett, Sarah Bennie, Stephenie Reynolds, Lara McLeod, Catherine Ngwong, Anjali Nathani, and Joanna Whitehead. Thanks also to Kim Witherspoon and to the team in North America: Aaron Wehner, Katherine Tyler, Molly Birnbaum, Maria Zizka, and Robert McCullough.

I'd also like to mention with gratitude: Mark Hutchinson, Malinda Reich, Chaya Maya, Jens Klotz, Jake Norman, Katja Tausig, Michal Nowak, and Milli Taylor.

Helen Goh
Thanks firstly to Yotam, for many wonderful years of fruitful (and fun!) collaboration. This book is the cherry on the cake. Immense love and gratitude to a host of people who supported me through the process, most notably David Kausman for reasons as he knows, too numerous to list; Sam and Jude for their life-affirming exuberance; Cornelia, Sami, and Noam for their friendship and wise counsel. Heartfelt thanks also to a galaxy of gals for the constant support and cheer: Kathy, Sherry, Melly, Caroline, Lisa, Alice, Nicole, Betsy, Goli, Shehnaz, Ramona, Irada, Samira, Tanzila, Julia, Yassira, and Lulu. Finally, to my mother and siblings for their enduring love.

Verena Lochmuller
To my husband Simon and daughter Olivia for constant comfort and love. To my late mum, for showing me what it means to be a true home cook. And to my sisters Christiane and Daniela for always championing me.

Tara Wigley
Thank you to my family. To Mum and Dad: thank you for having my back (quite literally, quite often). And to my peeps: turning the kitchen upside down with Scarlett and Casper on the weekend, while Theo or Chris play piano nearby, is my idea of heaven and home. Huge thanks also to my girlfriends—my comfort blanket, my safety net—in particular, with *COMFORT*, to Annie and Neache, Katherine, Katie, and Nessa. You've really been there for me.

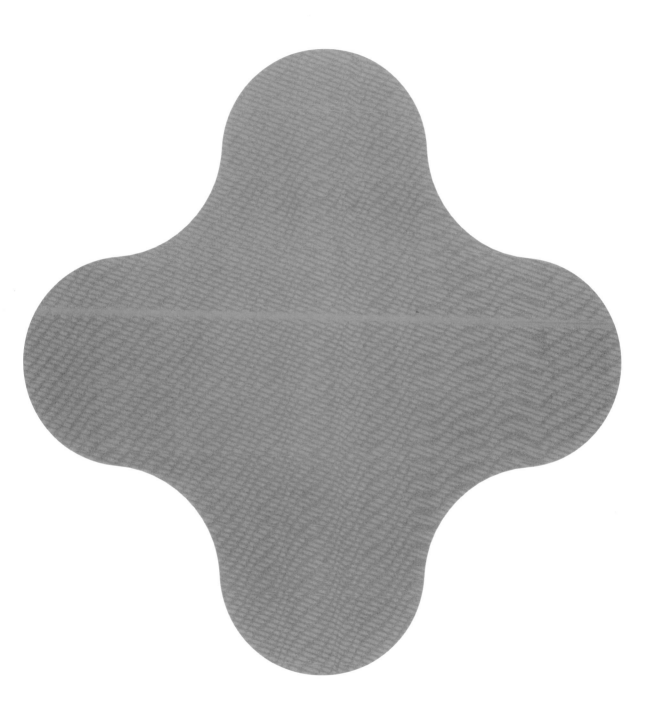

Originally published in the United Kingdom by Ebury Press, an imprint of Ebury Publishing, a division of Penguin Random House UK, in 2024.

Typefaces: Radomir Tinkov's Gilroy and Sofia Mohr's Mohr Rounded

Library of Congress Cataloging-in-Publication LCCCN is 2024936866.

Hardcover ISBN: 978-0-399-58177-9
eBook ISBN: 978-0-399-58178-6
Special Edition ISBN: 978-0-593-83694-1

Printed in China

Acquiring editor: Molly Birnbaum | Production editor: Joyce Wong
Editorial assistant: Gabriela Ureña Matos
Designer: Caz Hildebrand | Design manager: Kelly Booth
Production designers: Mari Gill and Mara Gendell
Production manager: Jane Chinn
Photographer: Jonathan Lovekin
Prop stylist: Wei Tang
Americanizer: Maria Zizka
Publicist: Jana Branson | Marketer: Monica Stanton

10 9 8 7 6 5 4 3 2 1

First American Edition